Thoughts
of Home

Thoughts of Home

Reflections on
Families, Houses, and Homelands
from the Pages
of *House Beautiful* Magazine
Edited by Elaine Greene

Hearst Books
New York

It is the policy of William Morrow and Company, Inc., and its imprints and affiliates,
recognizing the importance of preserving what has been written, to print the books
we publish on acid-free paper, and we exert our best efforts to that end.

Library of Congress Cataloging-in-Publication Data

Thoughts of home : reflections on families, houses, and homelands from the pages
of House Beautiful magazine / edited by Elaine Greene.
p. cm.
Essays originally published in House Beautiful, 1991–1994.
ISBN 0–688–14383–0
1. Home—United States.   2. United States—Social life and
customs.   I. Greene, Elaine.   II. House Beautiful.
HQ536.T46   1995
304.2'3—dc20   95–14551
CIP

Printed in the United States of America

2   3   4   5   6   7   8   9   10

BOOK DESIGN BY ANDRZEJ JANERKA

Preface

When Louis Oliver Gropp became editor in chief of *House Beautiful* in January 1991, he asked me to produce a monthly column that would bring our magazine "another dimension of home." He wanted something more literary and more emotional than our illustrated articles on decorating, architecture, and gardening—something that would explore the essence of shelter and family and homeland.

So began "Thoughts of Home," our most talked-about feature, the one tens of thousands of readers turn to first. We know this from survey findings and from random comments at dinner parties and business gatherings. Now and then, we receive an appreciative letter or phone call.

A letter from a *House Beautiful* subscriber in Georgia told us that she read "The Love Nest" aloud to her husband but could hardly get through her favorite passages for the tears.

Responses to "The Palazzo Years," an account of an American family's life in Rome, included a letter saying that an American women's writing workshop in Milan had read the piece aloud and found it helpful in dealing with homesickness.

One reader's husband wrote to say that he had never opened a decorating magazine until an attack of flu confined him to bed and the reading material at hand. He discovered "Thoughts of Home," located every back issue in the house, and became a loyal fan, one who told us he had "not expected to find fine writing in such a place."

A month after "The Grandma Who Could Do Anything" was published, the author sent us news of a "fat brown envelope" sent her by former Senator Eugene J. McCarthy. His scribbled note said, "Dear Claudia Limbert—Just read your Thoughts of Home in HB. Thought you might like Poem Page 32 and others. Gene McCarthy." *Ground Fog and Night* is the name of the book he sent, and the poem on page thirty-two is "The Death of the Old Plymouth Rock Hen," which closely echoes Limbert's own memories.

"Worldly Goods," an Arkansas remembrance by Diann Sutherlin, elicited a note of appreciation from Hillary Rodham Clinton. At the bottom of the typewritten letter on White House stationery the First Lady wrote in her own hand, and clearly from her heart, "Your article portrayed the real Arkansans I know, love and remember but who are too often, apparently, hard for some to appreciate."

In its early days, "Thoughts of Home" was written on assignment, but after a few months, the unsolicited manuscripts began to come in. We now receive from five to ten a week, and of the forty-four essays in this book, twenty-four came in over the transom. The unsolicited material gives the column great variety. One month our readers are immersed in the life of a Brahmin in her twenties, torn between her homeland and the United States; next month a son guides the reader through the austere rooms of a 1690 Cape Cod house presided over by his unforgettable mother—the work of two writers previously unknown to me.

The single most popular topic of the volunteer writers is probably grandmothers, but they, too, vary greatly. Among them we have met the stern, bonneted grandmother of the Plain People sect who inflamed her grandson with a passion for gardening; the grandmother in an oceanside summer house run by servants who was too vain to admit she had a grand-daughter; and the grandmother who retreated from her daughter-in-law's hostility but still managed to enrich a child's life.

For prospective writers, I prepared a set of guidelines. It explains that we look for "complex pieces that are universal yet unique, that have a strong theme or narrative threaded all the way through, that reveal at least one person clearly . . . and that have a vivid sense of time and place." We explain that we are "not interested in superficial anecdotes or lyricism that does not develop. Instead, we look for depth, subtexts to the main action. . . . We look for an essentially celebratory spirit, but this is not to be confused with sentimentality."

What we are really after is the form and texture and effect of fiction. Luckily, we find what we want at least twelve times a year—if not in the first version, then in the revise, or, in some cases, in the third revise. Some of our writers are working newspaper, book, or magazine people, or published novelists, or teachers of writing. A few have never appeared in a national magazine before. Often, it seems that the new writers give us something more dense and deeply felt than the better-known writers, who have less unpublished material to pour into the funnel.

In producing this feature, I regularly rely on the critical judgment of my colleagues Elizabeth Hunter and Jane Margolies, and, as always, on my book-editor husband, Lawrence Weisburg, to whom I bring each manuscript for its ultimate polish. I thank these three as well as Lou Gropp, who, in addition to having started "Thoughts of Home," has an instinct for appropriateness that is always right on target and always there when we need it.

Elaine Greene
Features Editor, *House Beautiful*

Contents

Contents

Thoughts
of Home

A Passion
for Place

Innocents at Home

1

ike many old New England
houses—I mean two-hundred-fifty-something—ours is structurally sound.
"Good bones," I told friends who were amazed we bought a house at all,
"but a few bad teeth." Not that we were as knowledgeable as this sounds;
no couple was less prepared to become home owners.

Rootless by temperament and profession, we took this step after
thirty years in the Foreign Service, bouncing in and out of European town
houses, tropical bungalows, and Mediterranean villas whose maintenance was
not even remotely our responsibility. Now we have acquired our first mortgage, our first commitment to place and continuity—a novel concept for a
family more interested in where it was going than where it came from.

An invitation to my husband to teach in Boston settled the question
of location, at least for me, who had borne the brunt of frequent moving
and was ready to make a nest. My husband had been born in Cambridge

3

and we had once spent a happy sabbatical year at Harvard. On these slender ties I decided that henceforth we would come from Massachusetts.

Our children concurred. Spoiled by spacious quarters abroad, they were anxious to know when they could park excess baggage and significant others in a proper homestead.

My husband was imbued with the diplomat's instinct to keep all options open, and stalled for time by sending me on reconnaissance missions to Boston. "Don't get locked into anything; just have a look." I paid no attention. Fed up with living in transient rentals in Washington, D.C., I began a serious search. Every weekend I inspected cookie-cutter houses differentiated only by the tension spring on their aluminum screen doors, or dilapidated firetraps touted by agents as wanting just a little paint and perhaps a sump pump in the basement.

It was a revelation when I finally stumbled on our house, the last on the list for the day. The white clapboard brick-ended farmhouse stood somewhat aloof from the ramblers and split levels that had sprouted on its original pasturage, transforming a rural copse into a suburban scene of sidewalks and driveways. Basketball hoops hung over garage doors that opened on workbenches well stocked with power tools. Each house sat on a rectangular patch of lawn, but not this one. Four very tall chimneys and a hip roof rose above an untidy growth of lilacs and forsythia. To the side and rear, the property had been laid out, long ago, on the lines of an English country garden, its upper and lower levels marked by boxwood, yews, and rough stone steps. The house had once faced this private sanctuary. At some point— perhaps when the street went in—the back door became the front door, into which I stepped with a pounding heart.

Our house. I fell instantly in love with its character: simple in concept and design but elegant in its detail; tested by time and found sturdy; and—so like ourselves—a little out of place, but determined to persevere in alien surroundings.

"Only five families have lived in this house," the owner explained. "The road is named after one of them." She sighed before adding, "I always hoped my daughter would be married under the larch tree in the lower garden." She pronounced it *latch*.

The real estate agent flashed warning glances at me. Why does this woman with her pretty collection of antique furniture want to sell? But I didn't care, didn't want to know. I was already walking through the sunny rooms with a sense of recognition, arranging our own haphazardly accumulated possessions as I went, placing a favorite Buddha on a broad windowsill, laying our woven Greek rug on the diagonal in the living room (originally two parlors), and pulling our reading chairs up to the fire.

Four bedrooms and an attic loft were wallpapered too restlessly for the prints we liked to hang over our beds, but no matter. As on the ground floor there were fireplaces in every room, wide-plank pine floors, and blessed light streaming through delicate small-pane windows.

"Forty-two of them," the owner said. "So pretty. I could never bear to hide them behind storm windows. . . ." Her voice trailed off. "A few might need replacing."

"Perhaps so," I replied vaguely. I had no idea what replacing windows entailed.

The real estate agent was poking around in the basement. "Better check out the furnace and the heating bills," she whispered as she emerged panting from the precipitous steps. "If you're thinking about a rec room, forget it. It's a root cellar." She turned to the owner. "What's behind the heavy bolted door down there?"

"An escape tunnel, from Indians and brigands," the owner replied. "It leads to the lower garden. The children used to play in it. Now, it's full of rusty lawn chairs awaiting a decent burial." She brought out a stack of historical notes and curling photographs previous owners had collected. Over apple pie at the kitchen table, she showed me how the building had evolved over the years, when the Victorian porch had been added and two maple trees on the street side had gone down in a storm. She showed me more recent pictures of the house at Christmas, a wreath in every window, her children hanging stockings by the hearth.

"Is that your husband?" I asked, pointing to an adult male beside them.

"Was," she said wryly. "He's somebody else's husband now." Was that why she was moving? "Don't bet on it," the agent cautioned as we drove away. "She may be pulling out because the house is too much for her. She's gussied it up with paint, but I still wonder. Did you hear those floors creak?"

"Loved them! And those windows—too beautiful."

"Suit yourself. . . . You may be in for a lot of upkeep. Speaking of which, how's your husband with a wrench and a hammer?"

"Oh, fine," I said, trying to remember if I had ever seen him with either. "As good as I am."

I clutched the borrowed photographs and flew back to my husband.

5

His mind was not on buying a house but on the more immediate needs of our four still-dependent children and his widowed mother, for whose sakes we had made the decision to return to the United States. To take leave of a secure international career—even by choice—was a difficult step, embarking on an uncertain domestic one even more so. He worried that it was not an embarkment but a walk off the plank.

I poured wine into our landlord's plastic cups while my husband studied the pictures in silence.

"There it is, our first, last, and only home!" I leaned over and pointed at the windows. "We sleep here, your mother in this corner room, Emily gets the adorable attic, and the three boys can fight over the remaining two bedrooms—correction, one bedroom. I promised you a study."

He looked at the photos again. "Where's the garage?"

"Um, I'm not sure." I took a gulp of wine. "Come to think of it, there isn't one."

He reached for a map of metropolitan Boston and searched in vain for the town. "Just how far out is this house with no garage?"

"How should I know? I was driving in circles all day. It's no farther than anything else in our price range. Besides, we can always build a garage." I didn't like being on the defensive. "The point is," I persisted, "this house has our name on it—trust me."

We discussed it for days. "Let's not leap into this," he advised. "We can easily rent something first and see if we want to stay in the area." I wept and railed against the prospect of a nomadic old age, rolling down the interstate in wheelchairs, still telling each other that one of these days we really ought to think about putting down roots.

But the house, when he agreed to see it, proved more persuasive than my pleas. He loved the built-in desk and shelves in the bedroom that would become his study, the Adirondack feel of the screened porch, the seven fireplaces, even the root cellar, such a good temperature for storing wine.

We made an offer and entered the lupine thicket of real estate. Title searches, points, closing costs, and mortgage rates attacked us from every side. All we really understood about the process was that it existed to the detriment of the buyer, but once committed, we had nowhere to go but forward. Like childbirth, it would be worth it in the end.

We revisited the house with an inspector who, like us but undoubtedly for different reasons, made a perfunctory check on its inner workings.

We pretended to be experienced, patting the furnace and peering dutifully at the pipes which ran like octopus tentacles across the basement ceiling.

"Ah yes. Oil," we repeated after him, wondering where such fuel might be stored. "And this tall cylinder over here would be . . ."

"The hot water heater."

"Of course, the hot water heater. Make a note of it, darling." In a few months, when the furnace exploded, we would be relieved to learn the water was heated by electricity, which had something to do with the fuse box on the wall that was so hard to find in the dark without a flashlight.

Foolish innocents at home! We were about to discover that a house, particularly an old one, is not a backdrop to life but a project to occupy it. The first year was filled with disasters lightened only by their absurdity. We were engulfed by soot when the furnace failed, then by water when faucets came off in our helpless hands. In winter, rodents scurried noisily within the walls; in summer, a musty odor emanated from the attic, where a colony of bats had been waiting to swoop down the stairs, usually when we were entertaining. My fingers ran through the Yellow Pages as bills and tempers mounted. The garage was postponed until we had taken care of internal emergencies, which seemed to come around as regularly as the trash collectors.

"It's called maintenance," my mother-in-law liked to remind us, although I resisted putting bats into that category, "and we simply have to budget time and money for it, like everybody else." She was a staunch pragmatist. Over ninety, severely handicapped by total deafness and encroaching blindness, she had come to live with us on her terms: not as a dependent but as a contributor, a participant, and—although she would be the last to admit it—as a mentor.

Much as she admired her son's public-spirited profession, she took a dim view of the decadence lying just below its surface, especially in the Third World where servants worked in luxurious surroundings but lived in squalor. On her visits to us, she had always resisted being waited on; self-reliance was the hallmark of her Scottish character. But she was no Calvinist. Optimism and generosity, bred on the western frontier, were among her many virtues, along with a redemptive spirit. Tainted though we were by too much of the good life, we had come home at last, and could still be saved.

My mother-in-law led by example, setting out to repair the street side of our garden, or at least what she could see and reach of it. She pruned the lilacs with a vengeance, planted the bare oval in front of the curved driveway with bulbs, shrubs, and two maple saplings to replace the ones that had gone down so many years before. With a tool bucket hung from her walker and a hose draped over her shoulder, she worked under sun and rain, unaware of the greetings and cries of admiration extended to her by the neighbors. When they realized she could neither hear nor see them, they marveled all the more, and kept a solicitous eye on her as she worked, or tottered around the block for additional exercise.

Several years passed. Inexorably, the boundaries of my mother-in-law's world shrank to her bedroom and the kitchen, where she still insisted on washing the dishes. Her interest in maintenance was now limited to her sense of touch: the sticky drawer, the loose handle, the wobbly newel post on the stair.

My husband and I were finally learning to clean filters and chimneys on schedule, service the lawn mower before spring, and insulate the windows before winter. In fits and starts our competence increased, from assembling mail-order bookshelves to papering tilted walls. We were getting there at last. A new furnace hummed efficiently beneath our feet; the walls were silent, thanks to the arrival of our last and cheapest exterminator, the cat. The cracks around the attic were sealed against bats. A few still tried to get into their old home but when they did, Felix was ready. We looked forward to a hiatus from repairs and toward—dared we say it—a garage.

We shouldn't have dared. The harshest winter of the century took its toll on the outside of our house, and paint chips the size of manuscript pages fell from the clapboards along with the snow. It was time to bring in the painters. An educated consumer by now, I called lots of them. Like doctors breaking bad news, they gently explained that they were the last link in the recuperative chain. First, specialists were needed to repair and replace loose boards and soffits (*soffits?*) and windowsills that yielded like bad molars to probing screwdrivers. On closer inspection of house and garden, the list of repairs grew longer, from loose flashings to ominous cracks in the larch tree. Here we go again.

But we are without our intrepid companion and mentor, whose last months were eased by the satisfaction of two grandchildren's weddings and the prospect of more generations to come. She was certain her room had once been a nursery and talked cheerfully of it becoming one again. When she died, it was on her terms, which meant at home. Home, where the maple trees she planted reach her bedroom windows, where the walker and tool bucket still stand in tribute by the kitchen door.

As the winter wreaked havoc on the East Coast, my husband carried her ashes to the west, scattering them over the temperate soil of the California garden she had left behind. For many months her new garden, her legacy to us, lay buried under a crushing weight of snow. I feared for its survival. She would have laughed and told me not to worry, that snow is nature's best fertilizer. And indeed, this year our view is blocked by a jungle of overgrown and overcrowded greenery she would have been the first to attack with pruning shears and saws, with shredders and bulldozers if necessary. "It's just maintenance, my dears. Go ahead and clean it out. Be sure to budget for it!"

We will, as soon as the painters have gone and we have studied the gardening guide, now next to the household encyclopedia and *The Awful Handyman's Book*. Sooner or later, we'll have to prune the lilacs again. If we don't, there won't be enough room for that garage.

The Trying-to-Leave-New-Orleans Blues

n the French Quarter of New Orleans, there's a crumbling pink Creole cottage on St. Ann Street that leans a little, as if it's tired. My paternal grandmother was born in that house before the turn of the century and grew up walking on those dense and narrow streets long before they were plastered with T-shirt shops and dubious jazz clubs. Sometimes, when I'm wandering around the French Quarter, I think about how pure and fabulous the area must have been in those days, and I wonder at the peculiar magic of this town which has held all of my grandmother's children and most of her children's children, including me, tight in its grip.

New Orleans is a powerful force field, and for those born here, it is all but impossible to achieve escape velocity. And yet I have tried to get away from New Orleans since I was old enough to drive a car—so many times that it's something of a joke to certain more settled friends. When I was

fifteen, without the slightest family encouragement, I took it upon myself to
transfer to a high school in Boston. The next year I did the same thing, only
this time, I shipped out to a school in San Francisco, with money I had made
working at a hamburger joint. By now, my parents were starting to worry
about my unusual restlessness and harebrained independence, but I was the
type of child who appeared to know just what she was doing, even when I
didn't have the faintest idea.

For the next fifteen years, it was back and forth, to New Orleans
and then far away. For college, I moved to Providence, Rhode Island, and
refused to come home in the summers—New Orleans was just too hot and
backward a place for a girl who had tasted the more intellectual pleasures of
the East Coast. Tropical torpor and thick, close family ties were things I
badly wanted to be rid of.

I longed to pass for a Yankee woman, and so I wore secondhand
men's tweed jackets and black boots. Although I lived in a series of grim
student apartments in Providence, my fantasy house had low Connecticut
ceilings, Shaker cupboards, and wild blueberries in the garden. I craved thin,
stern air. I wanted four crisply etched seasons as opposed to one long hellish
blur of summer. I didn't want to sit in winter in an overgrown garden full
of wisteria and palm trees, laughing and sipping café au lait and feeling as if
I were sinking, body and soul, into the swampy ground, as people do in New
Orleans. No, I wanted to gaze across an endless, open snow-white field punctuated by a solitary trail of boot prints. I wished to have star-stained thoughts,
not earthbound feelings.

But after college, in a spectacular knot of ambivalence, I moved back
to New Orleans. I suppose I was caving in to my fear of entering the work
force; I was trained for nothing in particular and knew only how to read
stacks of novels. Eventually, I got a general-assignment reporting job with
the local newspaper, made great friends there, and got to know New Orleans
in a new way by hanging around its archaic, tragicomic courthouses and
sprawling blue-collar neighborhoods lined with rows of tiny, careworn Greek
Revival cottages. I got to know it by interviewing its unfamous, unglamorous
people, the ones who fry oysters in rewelded iron pots in the closet-sized
kitchens of soul food restaurants, or who sit all day in St. Charles Avenue
beauty parlors, watching the streetcars rumble past while giving manicures
to dowagers with wispy white pompadours. But as entertaining and interesting as this was, it didn't cure my leaving problem.

After three years, I moved to rural New Hampshire to take a teaching job at the state college in Durham, a hegira that stands out in my mind as the one that made me the most flamboyantly homesick.

I didn't know a soul there, but once in town, I met a woman who had an apartment to sublet inside an old barn. A barn! This was even beyond my Yankee fantasies. Naturally, I moved in. I learned to chop wood with a black ax nearly as tall as I am. The barn had a beautiful wood stove with its name scripted across the breast, and at night, I would sit feeding it badly split logs and cultivating my loneliness. One day, I began putting wild New Orleans music on the phonograph—piano men like James Booker and Professor Longhair and accordion wizard Clifton Chenier—and this music seemed all the lustier against a backdrop of frigid Yankee air. I lasted about a year before tumbling back down into the green map of Louisiana. All my friends were just where I had left them, in their same gingerbread cottages, holding their same dinner parties. That's the blessing of New Orleans: It always welcomes you home and is kind enough not to ask too many questions. Even the newspaper took me back.

My next flight was a different story. It was two years later and I was twenty-eight. An old moving man who told me he had never left the city limits of New Orleans stood in my airy French Quarter apartment and packed up my belongings. As he balled up some white Wedgwood teacups in sheets of *The Times-Picayune*, he told me I would regret leaving because "it's so beautiful here." But that year I wasn't interested in beauty; I was interested in stimulation.

So I moved to New York City to write about architecture for *New York Newsday*. From the start, I adored the city and felt that I had finally found a place as heady and quirky and emotionally consuming as New Orleans. Sometimes, I would imagine that it was the same city—only bigger, denser, colder, more vertical and playing at fast-forward speed. I still believe that New York bears an uncanny resemblance to New Orleans. In both cities, eccentric people are not only tolerated but cherished as they are in few other places in America. Marching to a different drummer is almost the norm in New York, which in my experience was like an out-of-control symphony of different drummers, and as a New Orleanian, I felt completely at ease there. But two years passed and I began to have days when I wanted to find the master switch that would turn off New York, or at least slow it down. I began missing the lollygagging pace of New Orleans. I decided to try moving back.

I have been here two and a half years now, working as a free-lance writer. I seem to have abandoned my strenuous, overzealous search for the perfect town, the place where I would finally feel like myself and meet up with my destiny, in the guise of a graduate school, a great job, or the right man. After so much fighting and fussing with my hometown, I'm content in New Orleans after all.

I'm living in a nondescript apartment building surrounded by huge, twisting oak trees. On Mondays, I stand in my kitchen and make red beans and rice exactly the way my mother does, the way thousands of other local women and men still do every Monday. I live around the corner from the old, gentle-looking Sacred Heart convent where I went to grammar school and part of high school. I ride my bike through aisles of oak trees in the same park where I used to feed the ducks as a baby. As someone who never dreamed of making a life here, I can think of nothing stranger than all of this.

How did it happen? Maybe they put something addictive in coffee. Maybe it's the fried soft-shell crabs or the sweet olive trees. Or maybe it's the music of screen doors slapping. All I know is that I'm here and that it's amusing and lovely. Even if this is a one-note town, it's a precious note, a poignant note that has to do with joy and death and the urge to celebrate every possible occasion with as much crackpot enthusiasm, fanfare, and splendor as possible. It's a note worth hearing. I'm not saying I won't leave town again. But if I do, it will not be a search for home. I think I've laid that question to rest: New Orleans is my home. It's like growing up Catholic, or having brown eyes or a port-wine birthmark. I can't change it and it's pointless to try.

Most of the natives who leave New Orleans again and again keep gravitating back. Part of the reason is that this really *is* the Big Easy; it's a warm nest of old haunts where the same cast of dear and legendary characters keeps reconvening, telling the same stories with new embellishments each year. But the main reason people like me cannot truly leave New Orleans is that in growing up here, we absorb such a potent and irrefutable sense of place that the rest of America will always seem insipid by comparison. We can't leave. Where would we go?

I recently took an office downtown, on Canal Street, in a Beaux-Arts building with human beings operating the elevators. At lunchtime, I often walk down to the Napoleon House bar and café, one of the most wistfully beautiful interiors in America, and always get a table looking out onto Chartres Street. In the Napoleon House, the old still life paintings of lemons and bottles are always hung a bit crookedly, and the crumbling plaster archways seem like Roman ruins. Opera music plays perpetually. The waiters are languid, understanding men in white button-down shirts with old-fashioned ribbed undershirts showing through. For about $4, I eat lunch: iced tea or a long-neck Dixie beer and a muffeletta sandwich—a huge round Italian loaf of bread stuffed with meats and cheeses and pungent olive salad. These are the moments we live for in New Orleans—the small sensory pleasures that seem so abundantly available here.

I have also come to know my family again, and to like that feeling of being gusseted and cosseted in complicated, consanguineous affections that stretch across the generations and span the city. I have gotten quite close to a sister I grew up fighting. I take walks with my mother. And I could sit all day listening to my father tell stories about his mother, the handsome, cultured, gently spoiled French lady who liked to don white gloves and pearls and take the streetcar downtown to D. H. Holmes (ladies didn't drive), where she and her friends would have prolonged coffee parties in the old department store's ladies' lounge.

My parents live on a quiet, magnolia-scented block in the genteel Uptown section of the city. They are still in the 1909 house where I grew up—a big, forthright stucco affair that was built to last, a structure more reassuring than graceful. It is furnished with family antiques, some of which sailed across the ocean from France more than a hundred years ago. It is my personal time capsule of fluted silver cigarette lighters, painted candy dishes, and nuggets of Newcomb pottery that I have been fondling forever. My parents further the illusion of timelessness by having an exceptionally low redecorating drive. I don't think they have moved so much as a candlestick in ten years.

The walls of my father's bedroom and den are crowded with family pictures, and sometimes I go up there, stare at them, and fall into a deep trance. Lately, I've been gazing into one of my father's mother. She died when I was seven. In the picture she looks pampered and young, wearing a dark tailored coat, a lace jabot, and a preposterous furry hat garnished with bird-of-paradise feathers. I can easily put her face together with all the stories about her that are compressed in memory.

I suppose that one reason I have been able to move around so much is that I always knew there was this solid, rooted house for me in New Orleans, an unchanging place I could keep returning to, its walls lined with a gallery of faces that, unlike all the other faces in the world, have something to do with me.

A Haunted Place

ach of us has a true personal landscape, it seems to me, but some people never find it. I was lucky to find mine when I was a child, and never to lose it.

It is a haunted place where the bloodred waters of the Mullica River rise in the bogs of a New Jersey town once known as Long-a-Coming. The cedars that line the riverbanks stain the waters their deep color. Stunted pitch pines stand motionless, their shallow roots anchored precariously in gleaming white sand. Silence reigns.

Yet there are wild spirits in the Pine Barrens, and even my old, familiar house has its ghosts.

The legend of the Jersey Devil is widely known, not only here but throughout the state. Of course, there are skeptics, but those who live near the swamp hear odd noises and walk carefully after dark. On cold winter nights when the wind howls in the chimney, old-timers tell tales of a misshapen creature with the face of a horse, wings, horns, hooves, a tail, and red eyes that appears before wars and other disasters. When the setting sun touches the river with fire and the woods begin to darken, it's easy to picture devilish eyes glowing in the underbrush.

Another legendary creature of the Pine Barrens is the White Stag. Like the sighting of the Jersey Devil, a glimpse of this magnificent animal is also a warning of danger, but of danger that can be averted. They say that one stormy night, a white stag appeared in the middle of the road and prevented a speeding stagecoach from hurtling into the Mullica River. The coach was heading for Quaker Bridge, which moments before had washed out. The ghost stag has been seen as recently as 1953 in the vicinity of Chatsworth, and earlier, at Indian Mills.

In the year of the last sighting of the White Stag, when I was thirteen, my parents bought a tall, awkward house a few miles from the river on the western edge of the Pine Barrens. I saw the house for the first time on a raw February day, and there was nothing welcoming about the neglected property. On one side of the land stood the bare black trees of a peach orchard, and on the other, a forest of pine, cedar, and scrub oak. Far behind the house, railroad tracks and a pond glistened as the sunlight reflected off bright metal and dark water.

As the summers passed, my parents repaired the house and worked the sandy soil, planting flowers and vegetables, while I swam in the Mullica, my body taking on a reddish hue from the sun and the cedar-stained waters. I explored not only the river but the old house, which I quickly grew to love. In the attic, I found an old brass headboard and some rusty spoons. The cellar was much more interesting; it contained pieces of a stone foundation that spoke of another house on this hill, teaching me for the first time the thrill of history. The present house, dating to the turn of the century, is shaded by huge silver maples that must have shaded the tantalizing early building.

At seventeen, with a brand-new driver's license, I indulged my craving for exploration. Driving the family Studebaker on narrow roads that shoot as straight as arrows through field and forest, I would occasionally notice the ruins of a house similar to ours. I would follow sandy roads that lead to ghost towns like Crowleytown, Hampton Furnace, and Atsion, where a lone crumbling chimney or a clump of lilacs is evidence of a vanished dwelling. Some roads are merely long driveways to unpainted cabins deep in the woods. Others are Indian trails made by the Lenni Lenape, who lived here in the not-so-distant past. Holding an arrowhead found in the sand, I could see the tepees and the swift canoes on the calm water.

There are also old coach roads. The stagecoach once thundered through here, stopping at the inns and taverns in the forest. Our house stands on such a road.

Each weekend from early spring to late fall, we came here from Philadelphia, and I was allowed to invite my best friend to spend the summers. The romance of living on an old stagecoach road fired my imagination. I devoured books and pamphlets on the history of the Barrens. I found that the peaceful Lenni Lenape came down the rivers every autumn to feast on the plentiful clams and oysters. Later, after white settlers drove the Indians north, the Pine Barrens became a bustling place with iron foundries, glass works, and cotton and paper mills. Then coal was discovered in the Pennsylvania hills and the railroad overtook the river as the main source of transport.

On one of my ramblings, I went looking for the grave of Joe Mulliner, who, I had read, would come into the tavern for a pint and a dance with the prettiest girl after a hard week's work robbing stagecoaches. When the good citizens of the Barrens had enough of him, he was brought to justice. His marker, THE GRAVE OF JOE MULLINER HUNG 1781, stands on the crossroads near the town of Pleasant Mills. No monument stands to General Benedict Arnold, commander of this town before his acts of treason.

•　　•　　•　　•　　•　　•　　•　　•

My mother and I came early the summer she died. She was pale and drawn after months of hospitals, radiation, and chemotherapy treatments. It was late May; the lilacs had finished blooming.

Others were there on weekends to help: my father, my older brother, and his wife. We younger family members would steal away to the river and leave our parents alone. The cool waters of the Mullica were a balm and a salvation for me, making bearable the rest of the week when I was responsible for my mother's care. Each morning, I would help her down the stone steps and seat her on the sunny lawn or in the shade of the silver maples, then I would pull a chair beside her. We watched the hawks circling high in the sky. She talked about her childhood in the country and her youth in a far-off city.

Then, as fresh June gave way to sultry July, she stopped talking entirely. To break the painful silence, I started telling her the history and legends of this region. I somehow believed that as long as she could hear me, she would not leave, but she died in late August, a few months short of her fifty-sixth birthday. We buried her in the old cemetery in town under two spreading pine trees. On Labor Day, I returned to my sophomore year in college.

The heart seemed to go out of my father. Nine years my mother's senior, he outlived her by sixteen, and as soon as he retired, he lived alone at our summer place full-time. "How does he stand it?" my brother asked over and over, and invited him to be with his family in California. Father visited during the cold, hard winters but was always eager to return to the solitude of the Pine Barrens. I was married by this time to an Air Force officer and we led a peripatetic life on bases in the United States, Europe, and Asia.

My father seemed content among his books and flowers and he had some old friends down the road. An educator to the end (he was once a college professor), he was happy to teach one day a week in the church school. Ceaseless work in the garden firmed up his scholar's body, the outdoors gave him a perpetual tan. My husband, Edward, was stationed in Washington, D.C., and we came whenever we could, with children now, to drink my father's raspberry wine and eat the tomatoes and watermelons that grow so well in the sandy soil.

Too soon came orders to the Far East. The last time I saw my father was on a hot August day on his seventy-fifth birthday. My girls and I kept waving to him as he stood on the lawn until the trees hid him. He died well, literally with his boots on, skiing at Tahoe with my brother's family. I got the call in my sunny kitchen in Hawaii as I was grading compositions (I was teaching now). I remember sliding down the kitchen cabinets unmindful of the brass handles digging into my spine.

We brought him back and put him in the cold ground next to Mother. My brother and I agreed not to sell the house right away. We closed it up and returned to our homes. In the summer, we would come back and decide what to do.

When we arrived in June, the familiar earthy smells of bog, wild blueberry, cedar, and, above all, pine, welcomed us home. Indoors, we were soothed by the soft fragrance of newly mowed grass, which was present even in winter.

My brother, Edward, and I worked all day boxing Father's books and cleaning out the cellar and attic. Eleven-year-old Kathy and five-year-old Valerie played outdoors, climbed in the attic, looked at yellowed photographs. That night the children, tired from the sun and fresh air, slept downstairs on sofas. Edward and I were in my parents' large bedroom and my brother was in the small room next to us.

I woke up suddenly, chilled to the bone in a darkness and silence as complete as at the bottom of a well. Lying motionless in my parents' bed, I imagined, as vividly as if I had seen them from my window, two figures on the lawn. They danced to a tune I could not hear and shimmered in the moonlight under the silvery maples. Then I heard footsteps on the creaking stairs, footsteps that stopped on the small landing outside the bedroom doors. The coldness in the room was palpable as time stood still.

Then Valerie started screaming in the room below. My paralysis was gone. I rushed down. There was no one on the landing or the steep narrow staircase. Switching on the light, I saw Valerie tossing in her sleep as though in the throes of a nightmare. I put my arms around her and she calmed down. I stepped through an open door to check on Kathy in the next room, but she was sleeping peacefully.

At breakfast, when I tried to joke about the events of the night, my brother said that he too heard footsteps on the stair. "I knew it was Father," he said, "and I wanted to ask him to come in, but I couldn't move either." Kathy said she had awakened briefly and felt the presence of someone in her room. "Were you afraid?" I asked. "No," she said, "the feeling was friendly." Interestingly, my husband was the only one who was not disturbed by the strange nocturnal happenings.

We felt we couldn't let go of a place that was so much a part of our family it received our ghosts. We decided not to sell. As it turned out, Edward was assigned to the Washington area for the next twelve years. We spent as much time as possible at the old house but never again did I hear footsteps on the stair. Still, the experience affected us deeply, giving my brother, Kathy, and me a special bond. We often relive it when we are together, and we finally decided that our parents had come back one time to reassure us that death was not the end.

· · · · · · · ·

The Pine Barrens had become Edward's personal landscape, too. A full colonel now, he spent his free time planning the renovation of the old house. Drawings of the building and the property littered his desk. He wrote away for booklets on brickwork and turn-of-the-century hardware and wood-work. He had stationery made up with "The Maples" as the letterhead. Having lived in many places for more than twenty years, we knew only one real home, and when Edward left the military, we were going to live there at last.

It was not to be. Edward died of cancer, like my mother, ten years younger at his death than she.

Immobilized by grief, I did not go to the old house for almost a year. When I finally drove up one summer evening, I saw that one of the bedroom windows was broken, the tendrils of vines insinuating themselves into the house. The garden was gone: The roses had died in the cold winter and, of course, there were no annuals. Tall grass grew on the lawn. The Pine Barrens had already begun to reclaim its own.

I knew what happened to untended buildings. We loved the house so much we had to let it go. My brother and I sold it soon after. With my half of the proceeds, I paid for Valerie's law school. Her professor grandfather would have approved.

But each year I return to the Pine Barrens. I always visit the cemetery and drive by the house that I still think of as mine. It is being kept up nicely: New window sash has been put in, fresh paint applied. The garden is not like it was in my father's day, but then he worked on it full-time. I still can't bring myself to knock on the door and ask the new owners to show me what other improvements they have made. Maybe someday.

I have gone on with my life. Lately, I have been to the Pine Barrens with my new husband. He, too, has ties to the region; his late wife's parents live here. Though the mother is in her eighties, she still gardens, with help from her grandsons and, occasionally, my husband.

Our lives are busy. We have four grown children and two careers between us, so we don't get to the Pine Barrens as much as we would like. In my thoughts, though, I often revisit my haunted river. I picture the white sand, the stunted pines, the bloodred water, and I listen to the silence.

The Love Nest

nyone who has ever been involved in going from a large, unwieldy ménage to something more in keeping with a diminished household knows there is a surfeit of opinion on the subject and little consensus. Then, once the move is actually made, there is ongoing commentary. Last week, I received a letter from a distant classmate who had caught up with our news through the grapevine. "I do hope, Jean," the letter concluded, "that you have made a wise move." Who knows? Who ever really knows?

Layng and I had retired from our advertising business, long snugly housed on our vast second floor, and our great old house was sold. Gone the beautiful white rooms with windows looking out to deep lawns and those incredible tall trees. Gone the white-fenced back gardens and the little well house whose hidden spring had seen us through one long parched August. The big, cool cellar, whose thick stone walls had absorbed the sounds of unnumbered nights of teenage band practice; the wide garage, home to doll carriages and bikes and later to motorcycles and open-jawed cars in various stages of intensive care—all someone else's spaces now.

It had been a long good-bye. Beginning with Layng's almost offhand "Now that we're unemployed, we really should look into less extravagant housing," it proceeded at a snail's pace until a letter from the tax assessor's office shocked us into action. Our taxes were about to go to the moon, leaving us no option but to move—and quickly! The foot-dragging was over and we went instantly into fast forward.

The task was Herculean—no other word comes close to doing it justice—beginning with the winnowing. Our five children were in on that. A lot.

"You certainly aren't giving away Person's crib! (Our first grand-child's pet name, short for *Persona Grata* tended to surface at emotional moments.) Didn't you promise him you'd save it for *his* kids?"

Total recall was rampant. "But you actually said I could leave Aunt Eileen's furniture with you more or less forever!" "I distinctly remember that my football helmet was to be gold-plated as a fiftieth birthday present."

Winnow we did, nonetheless. We rented a Dumpster and got rid of decades of squirreling: kindergarten report cards, thousands of faded pho-tographs I had inherited from my parents (who *were* all those people?), maybe two or three hundred broken things we never got around to fixing, boxes and boxes of letters too wonderful to throw away until we arrived at our everything-must-go mode. The Salvation Army and Goodwill relieved us of rugs and lamps, old dog bowls and leashes, ancient skis and sleds, playpens and crutches. No one wanted our elderly record albums, and I eventually gave them to a reluctant consignee over the protests of our young-est son, the family's self-appointed prophet, who foresaw their ever-increasing value. "Ma, they'll be a gold mine for you in a few years. They'll be worth a fortune, mark my words."

Somehow, we thinned it all out. The house was down to its bare bones, relatively speaking. We had it painted and refurbished and it looked absolutely marvelous. We put it on the market, and to our astonishment, it was sold almost overnight.

The real good-bye came then, and it was gut-wrenching, to put it mildly. It wasn't just that fierce streak of possessiveness that rose up in me totally without warning: the sudden pain at the thought of someone else sleeping in our room, of other people finding all our secret places—the skylight in the attic that opened to the roof and gave us that spectacular view all the way to Long Island Sound, the cluster of bushes just big enough to hide two small chairs and us with our drinks at summer dusk. No, this was something else, something primal—a choking, sobbing, tear-drenched good-bye to all those babies, all that sweet closeness, all that fun.

By moving day, the feelings had spent themselves, and as Our Van was taking things away to storage and Their Van was bringing things in, I felt light of head and heart. I felt footloose and emancipated and about twenty-five years old; something in me had shifted into another gear. It has been this way from that hour. Miraculously, for both of us the letting-go was swift and complete, accompanied by a huge surge of energy propelling us toward the new, the uncluttered, the small.

"Let's look in Old Greenwich," said Layng, as we settled into the no-man's-land of temporary digs. "Why not try for a glimpse of salt water in our old age?" It was a long-ago dream of ours, so far back in my memory I had almost forgotten it. "Yes!" said I, picturing it already—spare, Shakerish, redolent of the Sound.

Mac, our real estate broker and old friend, told us firmly at the start of our search that we would have to go "way upcountry" to find anything near the water in our price range, but of course, we didn't *want* up-country. We wanted here, nourished by family ties, by people and places dearer to us than all the waters of the earth. We wanted what we wanted, we told Mac, practically stamping our septuagenarian feet.

Saintly Mac kept showing us pretty houses in pretty neighborhoods not too far from Greenwich Point, certain that one of these days, we'd find a little landlocked treasure with at least a whiff of salt that appealed to us both. Weekend after weekend I kept combing the newspapers looking, ever looking, for something promising a glimpse of sea. It seemed a vain search as the weeks passed, akin to my adolescent quest for the dream job in the real-world help wanteds in *The New York Times*. Then one Sunday—one magical Indian summer Sunday—I chanced upon an ad!

It was a very low-key little ad tucked away in the Connecticut column of the real estate section, where hyperbole is the mother tongue, and it struck a wondrously peaceful note. SMALL HOUSE ON THE WATER read the headline above a dim photo of a rather scruffy bit of lawn and an indistinct stretch of water. OPEN HOUSE THIS WEEKEND. The description of the house was modest almost to the point of self-effacement, so the price at the very end was a shocker—much more than we had been advised to spend if we wanted a secure retirement.

It was absolutely insane for me to continue peering at that picture. Hadn't we been told by people whose counsel we respected that the quality of the remains of our day was contingent on the wise investment of the money we had made from the sale of our house? What in the world could I possibly be thinking of, eyes glued to the page and putting on my reading glasses to get a better look. SMALL HOUSE ON THE WATER it still said, but this time, the words sang like poetry, like something from Yeats, alive with misty images that resonated in my heart.

I was possessed. I dropped every plan I had for the day to get to this open house. I called our daughter Anne to see if she was up for an adventure, which she was, and scarcely an hour after I first spied the ad, we were part of a sizable group walking past the balloons to sweet little Number 27.

It was more fisherman's cottage than Shaker, but totally irresistible. We entered a small foyer and squeezed past a monumental piece of furniture into a darkish living room dominated by a Franklin stove. My brain busied itself with buckets of white paint and floor sanders as we kept walking, through some odd sliding doors into the dining room. "Considerable carpentry here," said the besotted mind, undaunted.

Then beyond the masses of boxes packed and ready for the movers, past the piles of books and magazines and through the glass doors—at the very same moment—Anne and I saw the picture in the ad, liberated from the newsprint fuzziness. There was the lawn, not scruffy at all, just a stretch of pale green September grass sloping down to the water, and the water itself, bright blue and studded with white sails. The whole scene was framed by a curve of windswept grasses, overhung with sunshine and gulls and smelling of salt.

Several young couples clustered around the host broker, asking questions about the heating system and the roof while their small children shrieked up the stairs to stake out their rooms. Other people wandered about, mired in concerns about the dark kitchen floor, the septic system, and the overbearing Franklin stove. A few meandered around outdoors, examining the condition of the deck and the brick barbecue. Anne and I walked down to the water's edge and sniffed the air. We looked back at the house in all its unpretentious adorableness, an ancient lilac bush bending close to what looked like an old potting shed, a clothesline bright with bathing suits in assorted sizes and colors, a ragged flower patch.

"This is our house." I'm not sure I really spoke the words or just felt them deep inside.

I heard Anne saying over and over, "I *love* this place. I *love* it."

"I can't believe it," I murmured in her ear. "We've been out of four-sixty less than a month, and here I am just plain loony over this funny little house—a total stranger. It's almost indecent."

"It's the way it should be," Anne spoke softly, but with much conviction. "Four-sixty was a perfectly marvelous house, a glorious house. We adored it. But it was the whole family's house. This is a love nest, sweetie."

Within an hour, we were back at the water's edge with Layng, having pulled him from the tennis on TV. "It smells like summer in Spring Lake," he said, squinting into the sun. Spring Lake: Layng's Narnia. The magical childhood place against which all subsequent places were to be measured. "I like the untamed look of it," he said. "I like the crooked little dock." That night he said, "I think we should buy it."

We called Mac and told him our story. He knew the property, of course, and it was plain that he thought, *Well, the marbles are finally gone.* "It's way out of our ballpark, kids," he reasoned gently. "What about the 'secure retirement' numbers? Weren't they pretty well carved in stone?" He said, "Maybe we'd better sleep on it." We did, and the next morning he made an offer for us. Within two months we had moved in, and now here we are, living happily ever after.

The painters have come and gone, with their thermoses and boom boxes, their off-key whistling and unfailing good humor. The dust from the masked floor-sanders has settled and been vacuumed away. Our world, quiet again after all the noise, glows with white walls and polished floors, with bowls of Queen Anne's lace from the backyard, with the comforting familiarity of our belongings. We seem to be engaged in a love affair of a most mysterious kind.

For me, it's not just loving the house itself, it's more like falling in love with my life all over again. So much of the excess is gone from our surroundings that there seems to be time and inclination to savor. To browse through the days rather than to hurtle. To gaze deeply. Now, inexplicably, there are tears of gratitude at the clear cry of a phoebe piercing the morning quiet, a sharp intake of breath at the way the light strikes the water at a certain moment.

Today, we carried our lunch out to the little tree perched on the bank overlooking the water. Me with the bread and cheese, tomatoes and basil from our garden, the plates; Layng with the Pinot Grigio and the olive oil. A tidy meal it was not, but lingering there in the shade with a small breeze ruffling the water around us, we knew the measure of our incredible good fortune.

"The mundane," I read once, "is the edge of glory." I think I've known that for a long time in a cerebral way, but these days, it is heartfelt. Ordinary things are no longer ordinary: A comfortable bed with clean sheets and soft night sounds and night smells all around. The morning coffee, black against the white cup, dark and hot in my mouth. Village streets to walk along, with kids on skateboards whizzing by, grinning their hellos or deep in their own dreams. And wonder of wonders, a friendly man to live with who knows me through and through and lets me be the way I am with only an occasional protest.

Is it the newness of this house that is opening my heart to these blessings that have been mine for a long, long time? It's partly that, of course; partly a recent birthday that took me quite by surprise; partly some sort of alchemy I don't pretend to understand. Our deepest feelings seem to resist the intrusion of the prying mind. All I really know is that suddenly, all is gold.

Of course, it puts into question the whole notion of what constitutes "a wise move." If either one of us were to have a bad fall or begin to ail, would we rue this choice? I can't be sure, but I honestly don't think so. It feels as if in choosing this small sanctuary with its slanting floors and offbeat charms we have committed ourselves to love in some profound way, and maybe in our brief, amazing sojourn on this earth, that is the best any of us can ever do.

Pointing East

It was a jewel-bright day in spring two years ago when my wife and I moved from Massachusetts to Oregon, leaving the small village where we had lived for seven years. A job had opened up for me in the West. Advice was sought and considered, a mature decision was made. My professional self, the reasonable man with a pen in his pocket, carefully drew up a list of pros and cons, drew it up on a sheet of yellow legal paper, with a line down the middle and items numbered on either side. There were twelve reasons to go and ten reasons to stay. Five of the reasons to stay were all the same odd word: *Nahant*.

I still have that sheet of yellow paper. It is pinned to my office wall and I often stare at it in the long glow of a late Oregon afternoon. From my window, I can see the vast green muscle of the Northwest forest, and a spindly heron hanging over the river, and the enormous open arms of the Willamette Valley stretching away, lush and inviting, toward the Pacific. But in my heart

27

I see Nahant, the seaside town we had to leave; and sometimes when my memory is especially clear, I remember the very last thing I saw there: a long line of cormorants slicing across the Atlantic. They were flying west.

Nahant, pronounced Nah-HAUNT, is a windswept rock, a defiant fist thrust into the maw of the sea, a relentless memory, a paradox. Attached to the land, it sticks two miles into the ocean. Nahant is a peninsula, but its inhabitants, almost completely surrounded by water, call it an island and call themselves islanders.

In the mid-nineteenth century, Nahant was a popular resort on the East Coast, yet today it is virtually unknown. It is a clean, quiet, reserved, dignified old village exactly one square mile in size, dotted with the rambling homes of some of New England's most ancient aristocratic families, but to reach it, you must drive through Revere and Lynn, two of the seedier cities in the Commonwealth.

Nahant is entwined with the sea, its history teeming with sailors and ships and fish, although today its fishing fleet is reduced to a handful of boats skippered by aging men. Its waters are tainted by the proximity to the soup of Boston Harbor, and a bit of the pungency of its sea-swept past slips away each year. But I found much left to love in Nahant: the rich salt air, thick as wool; the muted silver clang of the buoy bell at midnight when all else was still; the intricately folded faces of my elderly neighbors; the laughter of my younger neighbors' children, their crystal voices wind-splintered and flung across the island like benedictions.

We are reminded of what we have lost by photographs, shells, stones, songs, smells. Sometimes people are the keys to memory. This is so with me; when I think of my friend Ted, who stayed behind, I am reminded of my lost village.

He and I met in college back in the seventies and we both ended up in Boston, where I became an editor and he became a banker. I met Mary, she found Nahant, and the three of us moved into a lovely old shingled Colonial house where the lawn ran into the sea and ducks slept on the porch. In time, Mary and I married and moved around the corner to be caretakers of a place where Oliver Wendell Holmes once lived. Built in 1840, it was an enormous house with thirteen bedrooms, four fireplaces, and hallways lined with books beyond counting. Ted got married too, and bought a dog, and fathered twins, and stayed in the house we had shared.

•　　•　　•　　•　　•　　•　　•　　•

You can smell history in Nahant. It smells like tidal flats and codfish guts and woodsmoke. There are ruins in the woods and wrecks in the water; the skeletons of drowned boats loom up at low tide. When I walked the narrow streets of the town, I thought I could hear the voices of the dead. When I rummaged in the woods for kindling, I found the edges and corners of the past. Some are marks of vanished walls: houses, barns, two inns, a boathouse, a carousel. Near my house, fence planks remained from a garden wall, the garden long gone. The fence is overgrown with thorn bushes and tamarack but there are stains in the wood. I like to think the stains are from pears and apples and cherries that lashed against the fence in storms and bled juice on the oaken planks. The fruit trees are still there, overgrown and unpruned. When the wind was particularly robust, I often walked over to watch the tips of the branches sweep the ground.

Long ago in Nahant, there was a hotel on a hill. Late in the last century, when it had grown old and empty, the hotel was uprooted and rolled away on logs drawn by mules. Where it stood you can still see log marks cut like letters in the dirt. In that century, there was a fish house near the beach. Where it stood you can still find piles of pale, thin bones.

In the woods behind my house, a line of beech and oak trees marked the property line. The trees were planted by a teacher who died long ago— the father of our landlady, the heir to the house. His picture hung on the wall of the study. I read a hundred of his books when I lived in his house. In one, I found a photograph of him in the study. He was sitting in my chair, hunched over a book, beaming. His daughter, who has come up to the house from Maryland every summer since she was a child, told me that he could always be found in one of two places: in his study reading, or sitting on the back porch under the exploding wisteria, staring at the woods and hedges. In either place, he would say, he was getting an education.

Among the lessons he learned, I am sure, was that Captain John Smith was among the first white men to see Nahant. Captain Smith noted in his diary in 1614 that Nahant was "a league in the main," and was notable for "some rocks, that appear a great height above the water, like the Pieramides of Egypt." An Indian chief eventually sold Nahant to a white man named Thomas Dexter. The price was a full suit—a jacket and two pairs of pants—and a jug of whiskey. This transaction is commemorated in the town seal, which shows two men and a suit but not the whiskey. The Indian's name was Poquantum. White people called him Black Will for his picturesque habit of impaling freshly cut wolves'

29

heads on his fence. Later, he sold Nahant three more times, once for a mortar and pestle.

When I lived there, I wrote a play about the first sale for Ted and Mary to perform at the Nahant Arts & Crafts Day, at which poetry was read and houseplants were sold on the town wharf. The play consisted of four lines:

Dexter: Hello.
Poquantum: Hello.
Dexter: Here's your suit.
Poquantum: Here's Nahant.

There is a Summer Street and a Winter Street in Nahant. There is a Pleasant Street. Unlike those of Boston, in which Winter Street leads to Summer Street, Milk to Water, and Joy to the Burial Ground, the street names of Nahant are not educational. Most of them are named after Nahant people. Tudor Road is named for Frederic Tudor, the ice king, a millionaire who made his money sending frozen pieces of New England to India. He shipped ice to Calcutta and brought back muslin, which he sold at a great profit. His ships were not clean. It is said that when Tudor's ships docked in Boston, the town dogs would flee up State Street pursued by cockroaches as big as cats.

In Nahant, the ocean waits at the end of every street, alive and huge. Around the town nearly a hundred ships have died. One was wrecked in the last century on Shag Rocks on Christmas Day. Its men were all rescued and taken in, clothed and fed; its goods were all stolen by the villagers before sunset. The captain stood shouting in the surf, shaking his fist at the people who had saved his life and made him penniless.

One wreck means a great deal to me: the *Anne & Elizabeth*, which went down off our beach a century ago. It was loaded with Canton ware. Pieces of china the size of dimes still wash up on the sand after storms. Children and historians collect them. After we were in Oregon a few months, a package came one day, the size of a beer can. In it was a thin glass jar filled with seawater and twenty-one pieces of blue-veined Canton china. There was a scrawled note from our neighbor, Prescott Kettell, who was seventy-eight years old. "The contents in this box are jewels," he wrote. "All were harvested when we were young. I have included a small hearing device to cure home-sickness; you stick it in your ear and point east." It was a shell from our beach.

Two years after leaving, I can close my eyes and see the odd corners of the island where the herons and pheasants and goldfinches nest. I know where the opossums and rabbits live. I remember the exact hours that Mr. Kettell went to get the mail: 8:00 in the morning and 3:00 in the afternoon. He hungered for mail and never got enough of it. I wrote him a long letter when I heard he was dying, but it arrived too late.

Sometimes even now I lie in bed remembering the hinged accents of the Kettells and the pleased snuffle of their dog when he smelled my wife, who walked him. Such memories crowd in on me when I sleep, and I hold them in my heart as gently as I cup my daughter's face in my hand. Lily is almost two now and has never known Nahant. I tell her stories about it at night, after we finish reading our books about elves and whales and cats. She stares at me and smiles, my little flower of the West, as I tell her about the music of the buoys, and about Mr. Kettell's accent, and about my friend Ted.

In our last months on the island, Ted would leave his wife and the twins still drowsing and walk his dog at dawn. Spring made dog and man eager to be out and about. Their route on those amber mornings took them past our house just after sunrise. They would cross our east lawn, clamber up on the porch, and peek in the kitchen window. If he saw us, Ted would tap on the glass and mime a desperate prayer for coffee. Often we were up and the three of us would sit in the kitchen, sipping the deep black brew and making each other laugh until Robert Emmett, a golden retriever the size of Rhode Island, whined his boredom. Then Ted would pull his gloves on and they would resume their walk.

But there were many mornings when my tiny wife and I stayed in bed, curled like spoons in the warm hollow of the blankets. I loved that stolen sleep for the spice of sheer laziness, but came to hate the runes I read in the lawn when we finally shambled downstairs. I would see gleaming wakes in the deep dewy grass: Ted's huge boot prints, marching straight toward good coffee, and Emmett's tracks running circles around the trail of his master. Then I would sit in the window in my beloved house, in my beloved little town, and stare at the vanishing trails of friends I would leave behind.

With time, I have come to love the West—the long smile of it, its honesty, its enormous emptiness. But although I live here, I do not live here. I wonder if I ever will. Real homes are built of stories, and the stories I love most are of a little wooden town cupped in the vast hand of the sea.

KIM WALLER

A Family, an Island

here was a blackberry bush here when I was a child." My grown son and I are lugging gas cans up the path from the cove to the generator house. Our sneakers are covered with cove mud, the mud with spruce needles. We are almost at the center of our family's island in Maine, at the place where the forest opens to a ferny field, when for the first time in years, I miss the blackberry patch. Suddenly, I remember the perilous feeling of reaching up for blackberries through a thicket of brambles. *I am six, mosquito-bitten and happy. My grandmother's face appears, shadowed under a white brimmed hat: "You've eaten more than you've saved!" She laughs.* My son and I go on down the path.

On the island, the heart of our family's summer life for five generations, that sort of memory ambush is just part of the landscape.

I'm not sure if my grandfather had any idea what he was starting when, early in the century, he bought an uninhabited thirty-acre island in the middle of a fine Maine harbor to save it from a logging company. He and my grandmother just let it be. They rented a village house on the mainland every summer and rowed to the island for festive lobster cookouts on the beach. But my father certainly knew what *he* was up to when he designed and built a practical two-bedroom camp on the island in 1959.

Dad's plan includes everything a family camp needs, and not a whit extra. There's a screened porch (which barely deters the mosquitoes), a Franklin stove instead of a fireplace, and for meals, a big, picnic-style table pulled up to a picture window overlooking Penobscot Bay and its scattering of islands. My dad loved this spot more than any other on earth. He lived to see his first great-grandson, Daniel, come to love it too as he practiced rowing off the dock and ran barefoot up the path to the camp, his hands cupped around some treasure from the beach—a sea urchin shell the gulls had dropped, a battered lobster buoy tossed up by the tide. And that, precisely, is what my foresighted father had intended.

By now, the favorite stones and driftwood finds of several generations threaten to overwhelm the windowsill, and I'd happily throw half of them back in the sea, but of course, no one wants his special treasures tossed out. I can just hear my younger son: "But, Mom, the snake stick is the one I found on Crow Island the summer I got to run the speedboat! It belongs on that windowsill. Don't move it!" And I don't, and we haven't moved much else for thirty years. My husband notes dryly that the *National Geographic*s beside the sofa are about countries whose names have changed. Last summer, I counted five containers of thoroughly cemented garlic powder (but threw out only three). Some of the wicker picnic baskets must date from the twenties; one has a nifty little pop-up tent of muslin meant to cover your blueberry pie. We never use it and wouldn't dream of throwing it out because it reminds us of long-skirted picnics held on this very beach. Would I toss out the varnished transom of my brother's beloved first boat, hung like an icon over the sideboard? Would he take down my kids' childhood drawings of a certain baby witch whose escapades eased many a bedtime? Of course not.

Now that some twelve souls call the island their own (ranging in age from my octogenarian mom through my nephew's new baby, Chris), it must be admitted that a certain amount of intergenerational clutter has its value. One doesn't bring wet-weather gear; it's there, in all sizes. On cold nights, when a northwest wind polishes the stars and sends the waves smashing, one is sure to find extra sweaters in the bottom of the blanket box. The loft over the bedrooms holds jelly jars, sails for the dinghy, sugar stored three years ago in an antproof can and forgotten, and a few deeply brown bedrolls that still smell of Boy Scout camp. Before long, baby Chris will be into the toy drawer: a tumble of puzzles and games plus three sturdy wooden boats carved by an old man who lived long ago on a nearby island. Was it my brother who first pushed them through make-believe harbors along the sea-weedy ledges? Or my sons? I no longer remember.

Not only the family has grown over the years; so have the trees. The yachts that slip by the island keep getting lost in the branches. But Granny, my mother and current matriarch, is protective of any tree (as she is of any child) that she saw grow up. "Certainly not *that* one," she says when we point to some bushy view blocker we're dying to topple. My nephews fret; their chainsaw fingers itch. Finally, defiantly, they attack the offending growth anyway, slashing their brawny way to the sea as the sun floods in. "Oh, now that's much better, isn't it?" says Granny.

Somehow, so far, decision making for the island has worked by such more-or-less consensus. Since the families vacationing here have branched from one to five, the sharing of the island and its small but elastic camp (it takes eight in a squeeze) has evolved along these lines: My husband and I and our issue are July people, as they say locally; my brother and wife and their issue are August people. (This is flexible.) June and September, often frigid but always splendid, are up for grabs. The elders split the bills; the youngers split the wood. Between such required rituals as skipping stones, clamming, having guests, or sailing, we all try to repair something.

Because the pine walls of the camp are sensibly stained inside and out, there's nothing much to paint—just window trim, two porches, the Adirondack deck chairs, the dock landing, and four boats. Mostly it's gray. although it seems that no store within fifty miles carries the same shade of gray paint two years in a row. Under the heading of repair, include not only cracked thwarts but essential systems that break down on the third day of your two-week vacation. When the toilet or the generator quits, you have to go to the mainland and call for professional help—which is sure to arrive the very day before the two weeks are over.

Sometimes, I admit it, the island seems nothing but work. Trouble, bills, and work. I'd rather go to Paris and be waited on, I mutter, once more by flashlight washing the dishes in salt water because both the lights and the freshwater pump work off the generator, which is out of order. ("What, and not go to *Maine*?" they'd all cry.) Instead, on Memorial Day weekend, my sister-in-law and I plant a vegetable garden, which is more work. ("What's that stuff in the bottom of the boat?" my husband asks incredulously every July—"Manure?")

But all is forgiven on those rinsed mornings straight from the birth of time when the islands beyond our island seem to float between sea and sky. As we pull the muffins from the oven, cruising boats and windjammers put out of the harbor and raise sail right in front of our window. The day's schedule depends on the weather, and the weather depends on the wind. If the flag on the flagpole starts flapping west, meaning wind from the east, you don't paint the porch because it will surely rain. If the wind's offshore, turning the bay so fierce a blue that the islands appear black, you sail but don't swim: water's too cold. If the breeze settles into a gentle onshore south-westerly, it's a good day for most anything—depending on the tide. And if you wake to nothing but soft fog wadded from here to an invisible eternity, it's a day for popcorn and puzzles. The fire crackles. People nap. Someone gets cabin fever and goes off to bail the rowboats or just sit on a rock.

A Maine island, like no other chunk of land, tends to wrap its inhabitants in sweet smells and long, private thoughts. In many ways, I think our time-out-of-time here has made us who we are. My dad, a pilot and airplane designer, sat on these rocks as a boy, studying the gulls as they coasted updrafts from the warm ledges—and determined to learn to fly. Wanting to be a writer, I hid out in a mossy glade and scrawled vivid (well, purple) adolescent journal entries about my island insights. At the proving age of fourteen, one of my nephews fished alone with almost frightening persistence and no luck every morning from five to nine for a week, then landed the only bluefish anyone in these parts had ever caught. And just last Memorial Day, my elder son back from far Tucson with his delightful girl-friend, chose our reunion time on the island to create a memory with a capital *M*. After a morning of helping cut and haul brush, he and she slipped off alone and came back beaming and engaged. (Of course, he'd first made sure she liked the place; we don't marry people who don't.)

Is a family like an island? I wonder, as I hang the sea-green curtains my mother chose thirty years ago, and which still seem fresh. No, a family keeps on growing, touching new points of land and experience, stretching out to lives no one—even one who can read the weather from a flagpole—could ever predict. And yet a family is like an island: a sustaining place of return nestled in the wide blue world, where one is at home with what one knows and celebrates.

Nature
Lovers

Almost Like Hibernation

We live in the woods. We're about as remote as you can get in the Lower Forty-Eight. There's no telephone or electricity throughout much of this part of the Yaak Valley in northwestern Montana. Much of it has been logged savagely—almost exclusively with large clear-cuts—but there are still some dark forests left.

That's where we like to spend our time—my wife, Elizabeth, and I, and our daughter, Mary Katherine. She was born three springs ago: We drove down to the nearest real town—Libby—an hour and a half away; and on the summit leading out of the valley, we stopped and took a picture of Elizabeth with the snowy top of Flatiron Mountain behind her. It would be the last day we would be able to take such a picture: that profile. Then we got back in the truck and drove slowly, carefully, to Libby.

It's different up here. It's at the U.S.–Canada border, and the Idaho-Montana border as well. Creatures from both the Pacific Northwest and the

39

Northern Rockies live together in this valley: wolves, grizzlies, woodland caribou, sturgeon, and giant owls and eagles. Trees from both regions grow here—cedar, hemlock, and spruce from the Northwest; aspen, ash, and alder from the mountains. I spend huge amounts of time mailing out cards and letters to Congress asking them to save this valley, which is almost all federal land without a single acre protected in perpetuity. Some days I'll mail out thirty or forty letters.

We live in a tiny log cabin by the side of a pond. The pond is actually the oxbow of a river, formed by a beaver dam. There's just a single wood stove to heat our drafty one-bedroom house, the oldest in the valley. It was built in 1903, when whites first drifted up here looking for gold. They didn't find any and drifted back south, out of this strange snowy valley of giant trees. The cabin has a large plate-glass window put in by an earlier owner that looks out at the pond twenty feet away.

There's always something to see out that window. In the winter, otters play on the ice. When they dive through a hole, they disappear for a minute, then come back up with a fish, which they share with their whole family right there on the ice, not seeming to mind the twenty-below weather. Bald eagles fly low across the pond—an extraordinarily beautiful sight through falling snow. One winter, a deer fell through the ice and I had to creep out and lasso her to help her out.

The cow moose and her calf like to stand out there on hot days. Blue herons stalk along the cattails, spearing frogs and small trout. I'll take my canoe out on the pond and fish for a trout or two for supper once in a great while; other times, I'll catch them for fun and throw them back. Bats swarm the pond in long summer twilight, dipping insects from the water's surface.

The mother beaver brings her babies to the pond every spring. In March, when the geese and ducks come sailing in, their wings spread and feet dropped for landing, set on a long glide, it seems they are going to come sailing right on in through that big window.

It's a window on the world—or on the one we know and love. We used to live in cities, where we felt clumsy, rushed, prone to mistakes. Then we moved to small towns, but now, finally, I think we have found our level, somewhere way down near the bottom of things. Perhaps a hundred people live in this valley. I write, Elizabeth paints. A hundred people probably doesn't sound like a lot to someone who lives in a city of five or six million, but it seems like a lot of people to me. Think how it would be if you had them all over for dinner together. One man up here has a pig roast every Fourth of July and everybody comes, but he's got a big yard.

There are two churches, two bars, and a general store, the Yaak Mercantile, in the center of the valley, which is as close to a town as you can get without going to Libby. We play cards in the winter—pinochle—with whoever wants to join in when the loneliness gets bad. But it hardly ever does.

We're ecstatic where we are. The solitude is the thing we crave. Out here we fit the cycles better, with less wear and tear, fewer adrenaline surges. Except for the struggle to help protect the valley, to keep the last few uncut mountains up here uncut, I hardly ever get upset. I practice going slow, at a pace that can be sustained. I practice looking around at things.

Out here you can see cycles in almost everything. We're learning things we never dreamed we'd learn, noticing things we never dreamed we'd notice: the way snow covering a rotting log is the last to melt, which means it's well insulated, a good place for creatures to hibernate or stay warm; the way deer drop their fawns around the second week of June when the grass is lush and at its absolute highest, giving them maximum concealment.

It feels like some weight of humanity has been lightened, if not actually jettisoned. No—definitely not jettisoned. Just put at arm's length. We don't get any radio stations—the mountain walls ringing the valley are too high—and there's no television reception, either. A few people, the bars included, have satellite dishes that they run off gas generators, but we choose not to have one. If there's a football game we want to see, once or twice a year—the playoffs, the Super Bowl—we'll drive the seven miles to a bar.

There's no telephone in most homes in the valley. The two pay phones outside the mercantile, also seven miles away, are the world's coldest pay phones, with stumps for seats. The only thing that really keeps us connected to the world we left—the thread thinner than spider's silk—is the mail.

I've made our valley sound pretty, and it *is* pretty—it's breathtaking, with a new sight every day. But in winter, even for those of us who love solitude, we're glad to see the mail. It's how we shop, how we speak, and how we listen to the outside world. In the winter, something we usually turn our backs on becomes appealing, even vital: *human contact*. We have this

December-January-February hunger for it: not a lot, but definitely some, and every day, like a pinch of spice. Not a lot, but without it, the rest of the day would grow darker and colder.

The mail run comes only five days a week, Monday through Friday, around 1:00 in the afternoon, and in the winter, especially near the middle and end of it, that weekend stretch gets kind of long.

In the winter, you can hear the mail lady coming long before you can see her. There's something different in the stillness of the air. Elizabeth stands on one side of the fireplace warming her hands and I stand on the other side. Even the dogs sit up, sensing the mail lady's approach, although they stay close to the fireplace. We look out the window, across the great field of white. Mary Katherine may be looking at a book. She'll come to the window, too, and watch the woman take our personal letters and our letters to Congress out of the snow-covered mailbox and slide new ones in. Some days, we can barely see her, down there on the road through all the thick falling snow.

"Do you want to go get it, or shall I?" Elizabeth asks. We've got a set of binoculars by the window, and we'll try to see what is being put in the box. If it's a fat mail day, we'll be anxious to go check it out. If it looks like just a few thin circulars, I'll say "Let it rot," though we never do. There could be some small letter or postcard—from Arizona, perhaps, or the Caribbean—tucked in among the flyers that advertise snow chains. We'll trudge down to the mailbox, wading through all that snow, pulling a bundled-up Mary Katherine on the sled behind us.

One day is like the next. It's wonderful. Although even for hermits there are limits, we try to push those limits. We try to see how long we can last without having to go into the real town—into Libby.

When we do go, the chores are mundane: laundry, grocery store, gas station. A cup of coffee from the Hav-A-Java. Always something from the hardware store. Sometimes a haircut. Once in a while, a visit to the chiropractor. Elizabeth might swim at the indoor pool. I'll take Mary Katherine to the park. We'll ski and sled and knock the ice from the swings and take turns on them, in that cold air.

You can get just about anything from a catalog now, and in the winter, that's how we do a lot of our shopping. It's luxurious, letting the goods come to us. Skis, snowshoes, boot oil, gloves, sock liners, food, books, a child's snowsuit—anything, everything. We've got a whole bookshelf of nothing but mail-order catalogs, like the reference books in a mechanic's garage.

When we need something, we sit on the couch and thumb through those well-worn catalogs, noticing how the same models appear in many of them. After a winter's worth of long study, we know them by the nicknames we have given them: The Smiler, Mr. Heavy, The Winker, The Bull, Little Joe, The Marlboro Man. We compare prices and try to gauge from the photographs just how durable the goods they advertise really are.

There are three ways to get the merchandise delivered once a choice is made. The first is by the mail lady. She drives a small red Subaru. She is petite, and carries neither chain saw nor ax. If a tree splits from the cold or the wind and falls across the road, blocking her way from town to the valley, then no mail arrives that day, and the outside world is silent. Occasionally, on days when she has not arrived by her usual time, I'll clear my throat and say, "I believe I'm going to run up to the mercantile for a cup of coffee"— and I'll check to make sure my saw's in the back of the truck, just in case I happen to come upon the mail lady, and just in case she needs my help.

Even more sporting than wondering if the mail will come that day is awaiting the arrival of the UPS man. His deliveries are less frequent. He usually brings books, which we open ravenously. He's got a 250-mile route, and our cabin is the last stop. Sometimes he'll stand around in the falling snow and chat, in no great rush to start that long drive back across the snowy pass at dusk.

"I saw a mountain lion today," he might say, or, back when Mr. McIntire was still alive, "Today I delivered a package to the wagonmaster." (Most of the movie people live over in other valleys, but we have always had the McIntires, since they came here more than sixty years ago, just married. Mr. McIntire was the wagonmaster on the sixties television series *Wagon Train*.)

We stand there and talk, the UPS man and I, as if to ward off the dusk, as if to hasten spring—and then he drives away, his big brown high-topped van swaying and slipping down the snow-rutted driveway, and disappearing into the falling snow.

The Federal Express man is the rarest of all sightings, but reliable— he carries a chain saw. He's a big strapping young man, with arms like some kind of melons; if his van gets stuck in a drift or a ditch, he simply wades out into the snow and lifts it free. He's got the kind of build that old fogies like to believe they used to have, back in their glory days. The Federal Express guy is often overly cheerful, refusing to match the gloom and silence of the landscape. He drives up in a rush, sliding to a fishtailing stop much too close to our parked trucks. He hops out as if he's got a bomb, or a live animal, in his envelope, and rushes across the snow like a commando. But he's always welcome, especially in winter.

There's something in us that loves the winter, and something in us that is a bit discomforted by it. We like those edges. We sit and watch and wait for glimpses—just glimpses—of the rest of the world's strange fury and speed. The mail is the proper arm's length. We move slowly, at our own pace, and at winter's. It's not quite like hibernation, but almost. Voices come to us like whispers, in the mail, or like echoes. There's time to think about what's being said, and what to say back. There's time for everything—no rush—all the time in the world. It's a little frightening, and a little reassuring, both. It's why we're here.

Flower Child

flower bulbs are to me what the seed pods of the *Papaver somniferum* are to opium addicts. They make me forget my cares. I can never have enough.

I come by this addiction naturally. I grew up on the coast of Ocean County, New Jersey, in the forties and fifties, when it was still possible to call it the Garden State without rolling your eyes. Both my parents loved flowers, and because we frequently went on vacation during the summer, spring-flowering bulbs were their plants of choice. My father did the work and my mother did the picking. He referred to her with both affection and consternation as The Grim Reaper. But what the garden lost, the house gained.

In the spring, my mother saw to it that every room had at least one bouquet. Some visitors complained that the heady scent of the hyacinths (followed in due course by the narcissus, then the lilies) gave them headaches, that it was funereal. But as a child, I had different associations. One of my earliest memories is of falling asleep on the soft blue carpet, a slice of sun warming my shoulders, the fragrance of my mother's harvest wafting over me.

The planting of those bulbs was a fall ritual as exciting to me as carving a jack-o'-lantern. When the weather was right—cool blue-sky days with colored leaves still on the trees—my father and I hauled burlap bags, bushel baskets, and old nylon stockings full of bulbs out of the cellar and into the garden. It delighted me to think that these brown, flaky balls would turn into flowers. Why my father didn't wear a proper hat while gardening I couldn't tell you. Instead, he donned a handkerchief, knotted at all four corners to fit his head. The only special gardening paraphernalia I had were my own small-sized gloves, and when my father pulled his on too, I felt we were as important as a team about to perform life-saving surgery.

My father, generally a flexible, congenial sort, had an undeviating procedure for planting bulbs. First, he dug a hole, the depth checked by notches on the trowel—five inches for tulips, two inches for crocus, and so on. Next, he put in a handful of dead leaves for root nourishment, and a mothball or two to repel rodents. Finally, I was allowed to press the bulb into its leafy nest, pointed end up, and cover it with dirt. Unlike our burials of dead canaries, cats, and goldfish, this was a beginning.

Halloween was our usual cutoff date for planting bulbs. After that, the roots might not have time to develop before winter set in. But one Thanksgiving vacation, I arrived home from college in the early afternoon, expecting to find my father taking his customary nap. When I couldn't find him in the house, I went outdoors and spotted him at the far end of the garden. He stood still, handkerchief on head, leaning on some sort of pole, as obviously sapped of strength as Millet's *Man With a Hoe*. He didn't notice me, and began to struggle with what turned out to be a posthole digger. When the hole was deep enough, he reached into a wheelbarrow and dropped dead leaves, mothballs, and a flower bulb from on high. I watched, appalled. It was my first inkling of my father's heart condition—one that not only made bending forward painful, but was also life-threatening. I was shaken by this glimpse into my father's new fragility, but he was jubilant as he walked up the path to greet me. It had taken longer this year, he said, but the bulbs were finally in.

Ten years before, my first attempt at planting on my own had made me jubilant, too, although my wanting to add a bulb was like trying to add another key to a piano. My father was born in our house, and his mother, who lived with us, had planted her fair share. There was hardly a space left that wasn't covered with cold frames, clay pots, paths, and the plants themselves. I did find one patch of unoccupied dirt near the cellar steps, and there I planted my bulb. Like many first loves, this effort ended in disappointment.

It was a gladiolus bulb. The minister had given one to me and to all the other children at Easter (along with a solemn message about resurrection and eternal life). That first summer, the plant was glorious—tall green spikes with stalks of blooms so tomato red they appeared to throb. Partway through the next summer, though, I realized that my gladiolus had failed to reappear. I poked in the dirt where it had been but found only a crumbly brown mass of fibers. I was stricken. No one had told me the gladiolus had to be lifted out of the ground for the winter.

The only bulb planting I did in college was compulsory. When I was a first-year student at a women's college in Philadelphia, the graduates from the previous spring, the class of '62, had left our class a malevolent legacy. They had bought thousands of daffodil bulbs for the campus with the stipulation that our class plant them. And plant them we did, one wretchedly cold October afternoon, carefully digging holes, and just as carefully replacing the plugs of sod. We left no sign that a conspiracy was at work. Winter passed, we survived our first set of final exams, and in April, we were delighted to see daffodils emerge in swaths two feet wide spelling out Class of '66, complete with apostrophe. Passing by every day, we reveled in our triumph and revenge.

It was only a few years later, in our junior and senior years, that we were again protesting, but this time, it was on a different level. We had sit-ins after the Tonkin Gulf incident, and we went south to help black citizens register to vote. In the early sixties, we did not yet know that we were part of a larger movement, that by the end of the decade, the Vietnam War would be raging, and that some of us would be pushing blossoms down the barrels of soldiers' M16 rifles.

I fell in love with another flower child, and just after my graduation, we married. The wedding presents were the usual gift-registry silver and china, with two notable exceptions. One of my aunts, fearing starvation for unemployed me and my meagerly paid bridegroom, gave us a boxful of canned goods—the first month's groceries. My grandmother gave us a pear tree and three bushels of bulbs.

We found an apartment over a barn in an upstate New York apple orchard and our farmer landlord was more than happy to plow up a large garden plot for me. October found me getting out my grandmother's wedding present bulbs, stored in old nylon stockings in the barn. I grabbed a box of mothballs, pulled on my gloves, notched my trowel, and began to dig.

By late winter, the garden began to come alive. Each bulb's debut gave me a rush of pleasure. The hope of seeing a newly unfolded crocus was enough to get me out of bed on a weekday morning, and the surprise of the Red Emperor tulips popped open was my favorite welcome home after a disappointing day at work. And that second fall, when my husband began from time to time to stay away all night, the soporific smell of the Oriental lilies underneath my bedroom window dulled my humiliation and helped me as effectively as any pill to escape into a torpid sleep. During the day, when I pulled weeds or marveled at my garden's richness, my grandmother's message came through: A love of gardening is a precious inheritance to sustain me and someday pass along.

The roots put down by my bulbs turned out to be stronger than the roots put down by my husband and me. Although the marriage regenerated itself for several years, it eventually withered and died.

Armenian-American friends tell the story of a woman leaving her homeland pursued by the Turks; she stopped only long enough to dip the tip of her head scarf into yogurt. By carrying the yogurt culture in the cloth, she hoped to preserve what was for her a basic necessity. And when I finally left our apartment in the orchard, it was not only with my half of our goods and chattels; tucked in every crevice of my trunks, packed carefully in excelsior and burlap, was a sampling of *my* necessities—King Alfred daffodils, Pink Taffeta iris, Red Emperor tulips, Better Times peonies.

When I fell in love again, I was naturally cautious—not another weed-filled marriage for me. We had been seeing each other for a few months when I felt the urge to plant some tulips, just a few, in a corner of his backyard. He, cautious too, was against it. He said if I wasn't there in the spring when the tulips came up, he would stomp on them. But I was there, and so was he, and that spring we were married in my father's garden—like my aunts before me—when the peonies were at their peak.

For the first forty years of my life, I had been content to live in the eastern United States or western Europe. When it became clear that for better jobs we would have to be sensible and move from Philadelphia to Ohio, I cried for a week. That summer, weighed down with resignation, we looked for a house, consoling ourselves that it was surely a nice place to raise children.

I was not prepared for what greeted us: lilies, thousands of them. As we drove into town, lilies lined both sides of the road, making me feel like arriving royalty. They spilled over every piece of land that wasn't already claimed by corn or soybeans. Clearly, I could be happy here. A few months later, when we moved into our American four-square, neighbors appeared from every direction to get acquainted and invite us over—for breakfast, even. When they heard that my passion was flower bulbs, they returned with rhizomes, corms, tubers, and bulbs of every description. Tact and gratitude prevented me from telling them that many of those cartons sitting around waiting to be unpacked contained bulbs freshly uprooted in the East.

We live now in a house I hope never to have to leave, surrounded by flower bulbs I hope never to have to dig up. The pink narcissus from my godchild's garden in France appears around the base of the linden tree and reminds me to send her a birthday card. The wood hyacinths by my doorstep, which never fail to surprise me each May, make me pause to wonder what their donor, a close friend in Germany, is doing that very moment. The lily of the valley planted at the beginning of our lane is a memento of Indonesia, where we adopted our first daughter.

There is hardly a bulb in my garden that came directly from a store or a catalog. The irises I can see from my study window were a present from a friend who asked me to be with her when her baby was born. I can count on another addition to my collection on Mother's Day every year: My daughters favor amaryllis, in particular the African reds that have the same vibrant tomato color as the gladiolus of my childhood, but in Brunhildic proportions.

When my mother had a heart attack, she didn't complain about her exercise regimen or the hospital food. Her only lament was, Why did it have to be now, in April, when she would have to miss the daffodils? I potted some up from her yard and took them to her room, but by then, she had slipped into unconsciousness. I sat holding her burning, unresponsive hand, listened to the relentless thunk of her breathing machine, and hoped that some part of her brain was absorbing the fragrance of my harvest.

Those daffodils are in my yard now. They are a part of the bounty that I have accumulated and nurtured for almost five decades. Some, like their givers, have died, the victims of disease or old age. But most survive and go on to multiply.

Recently, my two daughters came running in from the school bus all agog: "Mom, Mom, there's a new pink flower by the mailbox." They took my hands and pulled me out into the sunshine and down the rock steps to the road. And there, sure enough, was a new pale pink scilla, certainly not of my planting. I speculated it was the work of birds. That this gossamer bit of good fortune could be the result of bird droppings fascinated my daughters. Adopted, transplants themselves, they stared at the flower a while, and then the younger shrugged. "Well," she said, "welcome to the family."

On Feeling Small

We bought this house on a bleak day a couple of Aprils ago. We were in a mood to indulge ourselves, to celebrate an intermittently turbulent twenty-five-year-old marriage that had settled into an exuberant stability. We wanted something special, something unexpected, maybe a little crazy. Then we drove up a steep winding road and there was this enormous yellow dinosaur of a house. A week later we owned it and the fifty-two acres it sits on.

On a hot July morning soon after we moved in, I was out in the backyard while a pair of hawks—probably redtails—swooped in the sky high above me. I lay on my back in the stiff, sparse grass and watched them. It seemed that they were also watching me—as prey, perhaps? I know their eyesight is formidable, that even from the heights they reached they could spot me, a speck on the earth. They rose and fell in a choreography that, if diagrammed, would be a complex but coherent series of intertwined helixes, but always with me as their center.

I should have realized that hawks have more sense, and better things to do, than to endlessly check out an alien, motionless being spread on the grass behind a house. They were stalking something else entirely or, more likely, simply flying for the sake of flying, riding the air currents on a breezy summer afternoon because flying is what they do and presumably they do it with pleasure. There are the humans, with their Peterson's guides and their field glasses and their foolish speculations, and there are the hawks, living their lives. In the world of the hawks, I didn't exist.

It sounds misleadingly grand to say so, but this is our country residence. I live here from May to October, and spend the other half of the year in a modest 1923 Tudor Revival house on a severely domesticated quarter-acre lot outside one of southern Connecticut's troubled cities. A writer's work is portable, and my husband's teaching job gives him long weekends free and summers off. We had been thinking vaguely that we'd like a place in the country, and the house was a great bargain, even if it is covered in tacky asbestos siding.

The three-hour drive from one house to another, from our flat, congested shoreline city to the isolated grandeur of gentle green hills in upstate New York, is like a journey into an alternate universe. The two places are as different as a bouquet of pansies and a field of rampaging pokeweed.

The country place, for one thing, is enormous, much too big for an empty nest—more like an empty barn, an empty airplane hangar. The architecture is classic Greek Revival farmhouse, circa 1840, with a large, badly planned and unfinished addition tacked on one side like a lumbering rhino grafted to the sleek flank of a leopard. We have nearly 3,000 square feet spread over only five rooms: bedroom, living room and kitchen downstairs, and upstairs another bedroom plus a 30-by-30-foot unfinished space over the addition that we have simply closed the door on and don't think about; for now, we leave it to the mice. The rooms downstairs are so big that if we call to each other from bedroom to kitchen across the cavernous wastes of the living room and hall, we can barely be heard. It's easy to feel alone in all those square feet. Finding privacy and solitude is not a problem; sometimes simply locating one another is. When guests retire upstairs to the spare bedroom, it's as if they have dropped off the edge of the earth.

The living room goes up a step at one end to a windowless raised area resembling a stage. It was boxed in with a square proscenium arch and track lighting. We have rounded off the arch, removed the cheap paneling, and opened up the space with a pair of French doors that lead to the back lawn, a crumbling remnant of terraced rock garden, and a concrete slab where we have set up a wobbly picnic table and some folding chairs from a yard sale. The stage intrigues us. Not so long ago it must have been used for some kind of performing, though no one around here can tell us what. The room is big enough for a concert or even a small square dance. Or was the place a whorehouse that included entertainment? (No: not enough bedrooms.) Or did it belong to doting parents who invited the neighbors in while their kids tap-danced or played the accordion or did interminable magic tricks?

We will never know the whole story. The pretty little original house has been so hacked at over the years, so tortured with jerry-built sheds, and lately so unloved and untended, that its real history is impenetrable. When we moved in, the place seemed to have no tangible past beyond the thirty bags of trash we hauled to the dump our first week here, the remains of the family that had been renting it and was finally forced out after controversies about the rent—leaving behind, as revenge, every possession they had ever owned that was worthless and scuzzy. All that really remained of the heart of the old house were the massive supporting beams and the stone foundation, the curving maple banister in the hall, the elegant pilasters flanking the front door, and the gable with its characteristic diamond window in the peak.

Gradually, we managed to learn a little background. An old-timer I talked to told me about the farmer who got mixed up with the wrong woman, took to drink, and drowned in the creek at the bottom of the property. Someone else said our place was once a thriving hill farm, with cows grazing on the back slopes and the best butter for miles around. The state trooper who lives up the road came to the door one day and told us that the place was last farmed by a great-uncle of his. The trooper and his wife have one acre in the middle of what, for miles up and down our road, used to be his family's land. They lost the farm when he was a boy, he doesn't know why. The subject seems understandably painful to him. We let him hunt deer on our property; I don't see that we have a right to say no. Last year, he brought down a huge buck out by the base of the ridge, a place where I surprised a delicate, terrified fawn at dusk one day. It took one look at me and ran up that steepness so fast I almost thought it had been a trick of the light.

Without the deer's agility, we struggle up the ridge ourselves and look down at our house through the trees, the old apple orchard, the ruined barns and chicken coop, the vast sunny meadows full of daisy fleabane and wild thyme. From that deer's-eye view, our house looks small and lost, abandoned, unloved. For the hawks in the air above us, it's merely something to fly over.

We resolve to love the place, and we do—the way we might adopt an orphan and set out to compensate for a sad history of neglect. We plan improvements, but there is so much to do and things go very slowly. The landfills in our county are overloaded and dumping is restricted, so we hired a man with a bulldozer to bury the litter of abandoned refrigerators and rusted farm machinery where the vegetable garden will be. We hacked brush out of the yard, reseeded the lawn, and planted the beginnings of a glorious perennial bed. We sanded floors and ripped off wallpaper. We stripped the maple banister of its layers of paint and polished the beautiful amber wood until it gleamed. Next year, we'll build a trellis over the side door, with clematis or climbing roses, and a small screened porch. The year after that, maybe we can get to work on the unfinished room—divide it up into a study and another guest room. Some day we want to dig a pond, rip off the asbestos siding, build a garage and barn. . . .

As we add our own chapter to the history of the house, we are careful to document our improvements. We pencil dates on the molding above doorways, sign our names inside the window seat we built in the upstairs hall, tuck a package of news clippings and photographs into the wall we opened up. Our house is proof that the long history of a place can be erased in a generation, swallowed up by bad luck and neglect. It seems important to me that we not pass through here without leaving a trail: tracks through this old space that can be followed by anyone who wants to go hunting for them.

When we bought the house, our only child was a blasé nineteen-year-old, a city girl who loves black tights and dangling earrings, whose idea of a good time is sitting in a café with a cappuccino and an argument. "You'd better get up here and see this place," I told her on the phone. "You're going to inherit it someday."

"The first thing I'll do is call the developers," she said—always joking, my daughter. When she did come to visit, she realized what a joke it was. No developer in his right mind would want this choppy acreage in the middle of nowhere. And, of course, she was enchanted. She forgot to bring her sneakers so we couldn't show her much of the property, but she stood on the porch and looked out the windows and pronounced the views magnificent. "I could come up here and write," she said—high praise. She proposed inviting friends to visit—higher yet.

She swears she'll never have children. A lot of her friends also swear to this. It's not a world to bring children into, they say. People have always said that, and children continue to be born. And she's barely twenty-two. Some day, she'll change her mind. She'll find a mate who talks her out of it. She'll make a mistake and decide, what the hell. I tell myself all of this on days when I imagine taking my grandchildren for a walk to the orchard to pick the small, perfect, sweet golden apples—thinking of the trooper's family, all that's left of them a mean little trailer up the road and a mailbox with the family name on it. I don't have valuables of any kind to pass on, just this house. It's huge, I know, and ugly, and unwieldy, maybe not a legacy to welcome. It's not like money in the bank, or jewelry you can toss into a box. Maybe it's wrong of us to lay it on her. But here it is.

For city people, fifty-two acres is the state of Montana. Once, we were actually lost on our property, although not for long, and not seriously. It isn't possible to get truly lost on these acres: If you strain your ears, you can hear the occasional hum of traffic on our two-bit state highway. In a pinch, you can walk toward that and follow it to the bottom of our road. But in high summer, if you are hiking in a hollow between two hills and surrounded by thousands of muffling trees in leaf, the noise is hard to make out. We had friends staying for the weekend; none of us had a compass, and the day was overcast. By the time we lost our bearings, we had been hiking all afternoon and were getting tired.

We trudged on for a while and scrambled down a small hill and found ourselves in a grove of tall evergreens planted in straight lines, row upon row of them—a timber grove that never got harvested. Parked in their midst, between the rows, was a stripped 1947 Buick: a large, black, ponderous beetle of a car, its windows broken, seat covers crumbled away to reveal rusted springs, hood ornament gone, the carcass riddled by hunters with bullet holes that gave it an eerie *Bonnie and Clyde* feeling. A little farther on was a muddy creek bed—hard as pottery in that summer's drought—and then our orchard and barns, the east meadow where the deer sleep, the backyard with the rusty clothes poles and the burn barrel and the old picnic table. We had been lost fifteen minutes from the house, in a part of the property that, for all our exploring, we had never stumbled on before.

The size of our holdings struck me then, really, for the first time, and also the reason why people want this immensity—why they exclaim enviously at our fifty-two acres, get a far-away look in their eyes when they contemplate the idea of it. Why we bought this decrepit farm in the first place. It's because we want to feel small—to see ourselves as mere dots on a topographical map, dwarfed by the vastness of nature, scorned by hawks.

It must mean something that when we are actually confronted with our insignificance, we are not depressed but exhilarated. Feeling small must fill an important human need. A Mohawk chief, pausing at the top of our ridge to look out over his domain—what three hundred years later would be our steep mountain road—would see, in addition to the trees and hills and sky and circling hawks (thicker trees, greener hills, bluer sky, many more hawks), his own death and the deaths of those he loved, and feel not afraid, but uplifted.

What is staggering is that he would experience this constantly. The feeling of smallness which was once a part of daily life is much more elusive now, especially for those of us who live in cities. We go to the Grand Canyon for it, we climb to the peaks of the Adirondacks, we hike the dry brown hills of southern California, we gape at the fjords or peer out the window of an airplane at the limitless, fathomless ocean. I consider myself lucky that I could stand in an old forest marveling at the still-shiny chrome on a car that was new when I was, and feel it more strongly than I ever had before: the joy of insignificance, the large and blessed feeling of being small and, as it turned out, not lost at all.

We ambled back through the old orchard; the Golden Russets were far from ripe. We were starving, thirsty. The day was beginning to darken. We returned to the house, opened a bottle of wine, ate some spaghetti, found comfort and warmth in the old kitchen and in being together around the table.

I retrieved the one beautiful chrome hubcap the Buick had been left with—heavy, barely dented, shiny as a mirror—and I hung it on the living room wall. We often look into it. Our faces in its convex surface are goggle-eyed, slightly crazed, stunned by happiness.

WILLIAM BRYANT LOGAN

Confessions of a
Dendrophile

was raised in the West; I live in
the East. To me a house is just a house and I can take it or leave it. To feel
at home I must have trees.

What I really want from trees is to touch them, to hold them, and
as my hands creep up them, to feel for the branch that I'll swing up on,
leaving the ground for the world of the sun. I have been known to haunt
Christmas tree lots, plunging my face into their branches to catch the smell,
rubbing the pine tar between my fingers.

Since I first came East two decades ago, I have loved the yellow
rooms that the northern maples make in autumn when the low sun lights
them, but the pines are the trees that actually sweat viscous drops of sun.
This is not a metaphor: Sunlight makes the sugars in maple sap, but in pines
it binds the sugar so tightly that, touched by fire, the stuff explodes in flames.

Once in the Sierras in early June, when I was sixteen, a late snowstorm at twelve thousand feet caught two friends and me flat-footed on the trail. By the time we camped, everything was sodden and cold. Not a twig would catch fire. So we walked from tree to tree, scraping congealed drops of pine resin from the wrinkles of the bark until each of us had a little handful. We wrapped all three lumps in one twist of paper and placed it beneath the wet twigs. The first match caught, and it blazed continuously until at last the wood burned. Now I am very fond of maple syrup, but if I had to choose, I'd take pine tar every time.

I was born in Boston, Massachusetts, right beside Harvard Yard. Six months later, during the Korean War, my father was taken in the doctors' draft. He bundled us into a black Ford station wagon and we started west for an Air Force base in the Mojave Desert. They tell me my nursing bottle exploded at an elevation of eight thousand feet, as we were crossing the Great Divide at Berthoud Pass. It must have been this shock that triggered my first memory—trees. With absolute clarity I can still see the logs laid across a mountain parking lot and the huge trees crowding right up to the edge. And I can smell the lovely acid dust that hangs in the forest air, yellowing the light.

The Mojave in southern California did not entirely lack trees. There were willows by the river, but they didn't really count. There's something wrong with a tree if you can't stand under it without getting your feet wet. To my three-year-old eyes, my father's tomato vines took the place of trees. Trained up thick stakes and smelling of that sharp tomato musk, they were as much greenness and verticality as the desert could produce. I loved watching my father hand ripe tomatoes through the kitchen window to my mother; it seemed to make her cheeks turn pink.

About that time, my father decided that although he'd been trained for surgery, he did not have a surgeon's hands. So that he could be retrained, we migrated to Millbrae, a newly planted suburb south of San Francisco. Once there might have been trees in Millbrae, but if so, the developers had gotten rid of them, replacing them with sod and low juniper on a landscape from which they'd scraped the topsoil to make level plots. Since my parents were no longer living in an official desert, however, they determined to plant trees. They brought home a brace of paper birches, plugging them into the hardpan just beyond the edge of the concrete patio in the backyard. Their height was terrific, their exfoliating bark mysterious, but they were as skinny as broomsticks.

My parents had a tender regard for them—born of the pain it had cost to plant and nurture them in the stiff clay—but I had discovered other trees. Way up the hill, where the street ended abruptly, there was a fat grove of eucalyptus. The tracks of bulldozers zigzagging in the mud all around it suggested the frenzy of a wish to destroy them and push the street all the way to the sea. But this had not happened yet.

These days, a lot of people are not sorry to see a eucalyptus go: It's an exotic from Australia and a mess. But the eucalyptus represents a definite advance over the eastern tree in the matter of deciduousness. It doesn't just lose its leaves in autumn; it drops leaves, pods, flowers, and great chunks of bark as tall as a man, all year long. So much falls from it that it is hard to see how anything is left. When a winter storm blew in, to stand among the eucalyptus trees was like having a house come down on your head. It was wonderful.

Someone had long ago planted these shedding behemoths up and down El Camino Real, so it was through a double file of eucalyptus that our parents drove my baby brother, Jeff, and me to the third and final family home. Hillsborough was a privileged town, as they made certain to let us know, where the schools were better than private schools, and where by law there were neither shops nor sidewalks. We left the eucalyptus behind. Instead, there were live oaks and redwoods, and cedars, firs, and pines. Ever since Hillsborough, I have been sure that the finest privilege of the privileged is to live among trees.

From the moment we reached the driveway—we couldn't even see the house!—I knew that we had moved to paradise. Three decades later my father, now widowed, lives there alone. When I visit, the rooms seem as small as my parents had often complained they were. The poplar tree has been toppled, three of our favorite pines and deodars are gone, but the place remains thickly cloaked in immense trees. Still today, the trees put me in my place, show me my true scale. Atop the highest pinnacle of the Atlas cedar in front—whose trunk is as broad as the 49ers' huddle—a swaying red-tailed hawk looks no bigger than a sparrow.

But when we were kids, we were not pious about trees. We just lived in them. They were our allies, our adversaries, our summer homes, our theaters. One fifty-foot pine bowed out over the rough-paved road, right at the corner where the occasional passing car would have to slow. At first, my brother and I were content to spy on the unsuspecting travelers. From our hidden perch directly above the windshields we saw every movement of lips and eyes. Later, we began to drop pinecones. Inevitably, we decided to experiment with a water balloon. The direct hit, the surprise, the squealing of brakes made the shouts, the capture, and the day spent in our rooms almost worth it.

Robert Frost wrote that home is the place where they have to take you in, but our home could only take so much of my brother and me before the foundations shook and our mother trembled, shouting, "Out!" Then the trees would take us in. The trees always sheltered our dreams. We could design elaborate battle scenes among the lower branches, suspending a toy Stuka bomber stuffed full of firecrackers, dawdling an hour before lighting the fuse. Higher up were the branches that we knew like we knew our mother's arms; we would swing there by our knees at a great height. Above that was the frontier of the air. There in the country at the top, the branches were wrist-thick and the trunk itself dwindled to the width of our chests. This was my first inkling of a sexual embrace, swaying in the wind at the top of a pine, terrified and exhilarated, with the sense that at each end of the pendulum arc, the trunk would break. I felt there the trembling of something I did not understand, of a wilder world.

There was one tree that defeated us, yet we loved it more than the others. I don't know why. Only one of its branches was low enough to climb, as though the thing had deigned to let us sit on its knee. More baseball games than I care to remember ended when the tree swallowed a pop fly. It is a Monterey cypress that was there when the house was built in the 1930s and will doubtless be there when the house is gone. Since I first saw that tree, two generations of neighborhood children have grown up and moved away, earthquakes have cracked the neighbor's walls, the lemon tree and the pittosporum have died in a freeze, the proud, brittle poplar—once the tallest tree for miles around—has lost its top. But the cypress keeps quietly adding to its girth and its impenetrable ranks of dark-green branches. Now its cantilevers have almost reached as far as the house. Under this tree if anywhere is our family home.

Here we came to regard shade as the natural condition of the earth. That our father should increase it by means of planting still more trees did not seem odd. With one old spade and three pairs of shoulders, we planted apples, maytens, and the avocado that my brother, Jeff, had grown from seed. I remember so clearly wedging the earth from the hole, watching my father's pleasure in measuring the right depth, placing the tree, covering the roots, tamping the earth. I also remember his comical consternation on planting an abutilon when he hit a sprinkler pipe and found his hole turning into a little pond.

Let other people admire the coiffed arrangement of their perennials. Gardening for us was the shepherding of trees; it was work shared among us for no other reason than my parents' whims. Though I frequently complained about it, I swear that much of what I know of tenderness comes from planting with my father. Then I learned something about care and grace.

Recently, I was out west on a business trip and visited him briefly. He has a pink-tiled bathroom on the second floor where once my head scarcely reached the sink. In the morning of my last day there, I had just shaved when I began to notice a beaded drop in the pink sink, fixed on a needle of a shadow.

"What if he sells this house?" I thought. "Well, I guess I have outgrown it anyway." The shadow moved. It was made by the tip of a cedar branch, now grown all the way to the verge of the window. "But what will I do for trees?"

Later that afternoon, he asked me to climb up one of the deodars to change a light bulb that is supposed to shine down on the driveway. When my feet left the ground, I felt that old tingling of fear and excitement running from the nape of the neck to the groin. But something was wrong. My arms were longer, it was easier to reach from branch to branch, yet I felt as though I was dragging some weight behind me. I was. It was my body.

My father stood below. I remembered when I was a boy and his body had the girth, the solidity, and the incipient softness that mine has now, and when mine was as light and taut as my eight-year-old son's. My son's body is the instrument of his wishes. Sometime between the ages of thirty-five and forty, it seems, wish and body come unglued. My tree-climbing days are over.

So now, in New York, in a vacant lot famous for its rats, I tend the trash trees. That's what horticulturists call them. Silver maple and ailanthus. Woody weeds, they are short-lived and weak in the branch. They are ecologically incorrect, I realize, but I love to prune them and to help them grow. I may not be much of a gardener, but I am a shameless dendrophile.

My son and I visit a nature sanctuary in New Jersey where once, after a heavy storm, we found a big carp trapped in a pool and unable to return to the pond. Herding it through a gap between rocks, Sam found a way to save it. Proudly, we told a ranger what we'd done. "A trash fish, you should have let it die," he said, and it was all I could do to keep from strangling him on the spot.

When a creature is struggling to live, you help it if you can. When I was eight, I went out to the bus stop early one morning. The Monterey cypress towered over my head. And there on the ground was a robin, too drunk on the fermented pyracantha berries it had eaten to move. It pecked when we tried to pick it up, so we called my father. He appeared in his gray suit, the stethoscope sticking out of one pocket. He lifted the bird despite its biting him, and set it on a fence.

It might be that a cat got it, but I prefer to think it recovered and flew up into the safety of the impregnable cypress. Even the notorious weed, the mustard seed, deserves a chance to live, for, as it says in Matthew, though the smallest of seeds, when it is grown it becomes a tree and the birds of the air nest in its branches.

City
People

Tree of Dreams

he Christmases of my child-
hood were dazzling. I grew up in New York in the 1940s and 1950s, at a
time when you could live in something fairly palatial on Park Avenue for
about what it would cost to share a studio in a decent neighborhood today.
I remember cobblestones, double-decker buses, the tall mansard roofs of
Beaux-Arts mansions along Fifth Avenue, trees in Central Park glazed with
ice. I remember one snowy evening when there were no taxis outside F.A.O.
Schwarz and my mother flagged down a horse and carriage to take us home.
I remember that the best present I ever got—better even than Schwarz's
Moderne dollhouse with sun porch and garage—was one of those lavender
metal Louis Sherry candy boxes full of playing cards my father had collected
for me to trade with my friends. My sister and I didn't see a lot of our
parents; it seemed to me they were always waltzing out the door, mother
looking like a goddess in gold Fortuny pleats. But I imagined my father

65

interrupting card games all over town and asking if he could please have the joker or the card with writing on it. This made me feel wonderful.

My guess is that all of us Christmas compulsives have some vision of the perfect holiday season dancing ahead of us like Gatsby's green light—an illusion we put together from movies and books, department store windows and magazines, the Christmases of our childhoods and the more brilliant bits of other people's Christmases.

At my best friend, Cecile's apartment, the tree, which I had been invited to come admire, wasn't as nice as ours except for a flock of wax-faced, velvet-robed and, Cecile informed me, very expensive Nuremberg angels. But the guest bedroom, with its quilted-silk chaise longue, its peach satin comforters, and its glittering view across the East River, was a sea of boxes and shopping bags, reams of gleaming paper, and rolls of sumptuous ribbons, most of them, I later learned, saved from year to year. (Thrift holds no terrors for the rich.) A tea tray sat on a tufted ottoman, carols wafted from the radio. Cecile's mother was wielding a pair of silver-gilt, stork-handled scissors, and this graceful and ceremonial Wrapping of the Presents was an event I suddenly saw, in capital letters, as a celebration in itself—the epitome of comfort and joy.

My second-best friend, Emily, lived in a brownstone with Lautrec lithographs in the red-lacquered powder room, the kind of ancestor portraits that go all the way to the feet, and sleek blond paneling in the living room that I recognize in retrospect as Jean-Michel Frank. Emily's father, the sculptor, and her mother, the fashion editor, invited my whole family to a Christmas party one year. I remember peals of laughter and a tall tree shimmering with ancestral ornaments: huge, softly colored blown-glass shapes, swans and santas, cherubs with glass dolls' eyes, oversize parasols tangled in tarnished tinsel.

"Oho," said my father, impressed. "I wonder if they have the boy in the boat."

"The what?" I said.

"You don't know about the boy in the boat? Look!" And there, sailing overhead, was a somewhat football-shaped glass ornament that formed a hull with twisted gold-wire rigging and a paper boy in a sailor suit lashed to the mast. "The boy in the boat," said my father. "Now. Let's see if they have the boy in the balloon."

So dies are cast. A couple of Decembers later, slogging up Lexington Avenue one slushy evening after my tenth-grade typing class, I spotted them in the window of a small, dusty store: the boy in the boat, the boy in the balloon, a bluebird (of happiness, I thought) with spun-glass wings, a golden Cinderella coach, all wrapped in coils of twisty tinsel. I took my finds home (six weeks' allowance they cost me). Mother hung them on the perfect branches. Daddy didn't see them. He had changed partners by then and danced off into the night.

The first Christmases after a divorce, or any loss, I suppose, are thin ice. Joy turns poignant on you; memory curdles; the things you have managed to keep the same only remind you of the things you have not; and Santa Claus—even in the most metaphorical, yes-Virginia spirit—suffers a severe loss of credibility.

What my sister and I really wanted to do was wrap up a new husband—I had a distinct mental picture of Tom Kitten in *The Roly-Poly Pudding*—and put him under the tree. What we wanted to give our mother was her old life back. What we did instead was shower her with a 1950s teenager's idea of glamour. The next few Christmases were a cornucopia of mirrored lipstick cases, rhinestone compacts, silver perfume funnels, shiny paper cigarette holders in fashion colors, and celluloid boxes of translucent, jewel-toned bath-oil beads.

We sent away for *Harper's Bazaar*'s annual perfume sampler. Collected all our friends' broken costume jewelry and assembled a giddily baroque choker of mismatched pearls and amethyst glass beads. Took advantage of Bonwit Teller's special purchase on elbow-length velvet gloves ($2.99) and bought three pairs—the turquoise and lavender we slid into a shiny green box; the cherry-red gloves we stuffed with wire and tissue and arranged on top of the box, one glove languidly trailing its fingers over the edge, the other propped aloft, holding one of those trick brandy glasses full of unspillable liquid. *This*, we were saying, *this is how we still see you.* I can't say I recall my mother ever wearing any of those gloves, but for days afterward I could hear her on the phone saying, "*Guess* what the girls did."

It occurred to me then that it is absolutely more fun to give than to receive, that Santa holds the reins of Christmas.

And eventually, there were jollier Christmases, with a series of beaus in attendance and the kind of Yuletide bounty that put my mother in the position of having to explain—over our hoots—that she happened to like successful men, and that at a certain level of success, giving someone a mink coat or a television set or a solid-gold cigarette case studded with diamonds was really just the same as giving them a book or a toaster.

My sister moved to Paris, sent Mother a gold champagne stirrer from Cartier and me a box of tiny, tinsel-wrapped French ornaments.

I was married by then, living uptown in a neighborhood my mother wouldn't come to, on a block where sirens ululated every night and the winter wind off the Hudson River had been known to knock people down. And no, the apartment wasn't wonderful once you got inside. But we had our own tree. We had my treasures from Lexington Avenue and France; we had a dozen gold-foil roses—props fished out of the wastebasket in the art department of the magazine where I worked; we had a made-by-me Nuremberg angel, her wax face rather blodgily modeled from candle drippings, her robe a scrap of brocade from the magazine's fabric department, her wings parakeet feathers retrieved from the bottom of our bird's cage and painted gold. We also had a lifetime supply of gilded and jeweled walnuts. The tree was becoming a vision of opulence.

My father saw it once, in the mid-1960s, on one of his rare trips to town. "My stars! Would you look at that!" He stood in the doorway, his muffler half-unwrapped. "A 1910 Christmas tree! I wonder," he said, not missing a beat, "if you have the boy in the boat."

There was no stopping me after that. The tree grew into an extravaganza it now takes three days to trim. An auxiliary tree sprang up in the kitchen of our new, grown-up apartment—a folksy, 1970s tree meant for the egg-carton-and-pipe-cleaner bells our sons brought home from nursery school, and the things we all made together: bread-dough dinosaurs, clothespin soldiers, twig angels, acorn babies in horse-chestnut shells, rosy wax hearts molded in tart tins (up to my old tricks with candle ends), and the cranberries and kumquats that the boys—now grown—still think they must string or it won't be Christmas. The living room tree is glorious, but the kitchen tree, with its headdress of American flags, is the one that steals everyone's heart.

Every vision starts somewhere. A few years ago, somebody going through my father's effects came across an old sepia photograph of a very small, very astonished boy. He was surrounded by early-twentieth-century toys (I don't even want to think what they'd bring at auction today) and dwarfed by an enormous tree decorated in the lavish if oddly haphazard style of the time. Somebody—I forget who; it may have been my mother but she's not around to ask—told me that the picture was taken in a hotel (my grandparents, moving up in the world, moved around). The staff, feeling sorry for my father, had put up the tree just for him. Daddy seems to be about three in the picture, so it must have been around 1910. I keep looking for the boy in the boat. I can't find him, but he must be there.

Every year, with a certain amount of prompting from me, at least one person in our family makes something for someone else. When he was fourteen, my younger son painted us a fine and much-prized house portrait; when he was nine, my sister knitted him a ten-foot-long scarf. This year, my husband is carving fish decoys for the whole world and I am whipping up ruffled pillow shams for my niece's newly decorated bedroom, not letting the fact that I can't sew stand in my way. So I suspect I'm in for another Christmas Eve marathon.

To tell the truth, I'm looking forward to it. I'll have my tea tray on the ottoman, carols on the radio, and the company of ghosts who never did mind staying up all night.

Stardust

the other night, I dreamed I was driving down Marlboro Street with that lift of anticipation I always felt coming home. Suddenly, the sky went dark and I saw the house was gone. In its place there was a carnival—no people, just twirling lights and colors— and I never missed anything in any real moment as much as I missed that house in that dream.

Hollywood may seem like a carnival no matter how I describe it, but it was the only reality I knew, and when we moved away from the house I grew up in, I remember my father saying, "To be a survivor, you don't look back." My mother responded, "Women can always look back, women are stronger. Men are little boys." Nothing frightened my mother.

It was far more difficult for my father to give up the house, even though he was in New York rehearsing *Sunrise at Campobello* while my mother supervised the move. My father wrote the hit play about Franklin

Delano Roosevelt, and it brought him back to Broadway, where he had begun his career as a playwright and producer.

The house isn't really gone. Not long ago, I saw an ad for it in *The Hollywood Reporter*; the asking price was $3,950,000. My father, Dore Schary, who ran RKO in the forties and MGM in the fifties, and my mother, the painter M. Svet, bought this house for $25,000 in 1941, just after Pearl Harbor, from a man who believed California was going to be invaded the day after tomorrow.

My sister and brother and I would start to smile and our hearts would start to pound whenever the station wagon we were riding in accelerated up Marlboro Street. It never seemed like an ordinary return home. Even if we had only been at school (and I went there as little as possible), even if we had only biked down the street, we would come back to news: Spencer Tracy is here for a talk. Walter Plunkett is bringing over sketches of Elizabeth Taylor's outfits for *Raintree County*. Loretta Young is here with her daughter. Sinclair Lewis is in the library working on his script (Do not go in, he detests children). Young Senator Jack Kennedy is rehearsing his introduction to a film for the convention. Cary Grant is coming to catch Peter Ustinov doing his imitation of Senator Joe McCarthy after we see the rough cut of *Quo Vadis*. Johnny Green is playing the new score for *Easter Parade*, waiting for Judy Garland, who is late (she's the only one my father ever waits for). Who would not come home eagerly, who could go to school?

My attendance at school was very sketchy because I had asthma. Asthma was a far more difficult illness then, before Ventalin, and I spent many nights dealing with my difficulty breathing—sitting in bed drawing costumes for movie stars, making up stories that continued those my mother told me late at night in her room. Being with her worked better than any of the bitter powders I took or the kettles puffing fog through the night. I loved to hear my mother's silky negligee rustle through my sister's room to mine as she came to take me back to her pink-and-blue velvet Victorian room. Sometimes I sneaked out to the kennels to bury my face in dog fur so I could stay home from school.

The style of our house was country Tudor. A deep, thick-shingled roof gave it the rustic proportions and charm of a cottage. Heavy beams reached from wing to wing, and the upper walls were whitewashed and half-timbered in dark wood. The ground-floor walls were stone; the twelve-pane windows were painted ivy green. The main entrance was a Dutch door—we had our pictures taken sitting on the shelf with the leaded-glass top swung aside. The black doormat was huge, with SCHARY in big white letters. It came from our grandparents' catering place in Newark, New Jersey. And nailed to the doorpost was a brass mezuzah containing the traditional scroll of Mosaic law, which our father would kiss as he walked in.

The house was set high on a hill covered with ivy and dotted with incongruous palms, evergreens, pyracantha, and camellia bushes; honeysuckle vines hid us from the street. Over the years, rooms and studios and wings were added—more bedrooms, more bathrooms, a projection room, a pool house, a studio for my mother, a servant's cottage. Additions and changes were also made to the grounds: a swimming pool shaped like a small lake with a bay shallow enough for little children to stand up in, a glade planted with violets and in it a stone seat. Down from the pool was the rose garden.

The place looked relaxed and informal, with my parents' shaggy dogs running through the gardens, but it operated on a tight, organized schedule. In the projection room there were 35mm projectors and stereophonic sound. Every night, MGM's executive editor, Margaret Booth, came and worked. She and my father went over the dailies and rushes of each day's production. They watched every picture develop from screen test to rough cut to final cut, then through each preview.

Our first summer there, the projection room, my father's new bedroom, and the spiral staircase connecting the two had been finished. Like stylish European couples they knew, my parents had separate bedrooms. My father's room, his offices and the projection room were slate blue with dark-red leather chairs, oak furniture, and student lamps with red or emerald-green shades. He collected antique banks, brass toys and boxes, glass paperweights, Staffordshire dogs, toy soldiers, nutcrackers, toy cars, and silk mufflers and fine soft white shirts that he stored carefully in a dark oak-paneled dressing room.

My room was at the end of our house, over the laundry room and the five-car garage. My favorite view was the driveway. I would curl up on my window seat and take notes as I watched people arrive and depart, seeing my parents drive off, their heads turned toward each other in the back of a Chrysler limousine. When my parents were out, I drew pictures and wrote notes to leave in their bedrooms to welcome them home, then my brother and sister and I would fight with our governess, who thought we were too young to hear *The Green Hornet*. After lights out, the watchman came—I knew because the dogs always barked. We started having watchmen before the war, when the Ku Klux Klan burned a cross on our lawn.

Life in our house reflected my father's complex personality. He had a teacher's gregarious charm, a writer's perception and insight, and a tycoon's taste for total control. But tycoons place power first, and my father put his family and his liberal political causes ahead of his work—as long as the work was moving along well, that is. Like a lot of people in show business, my father thrived on the risk each project presented. He loved the big wins, but even a big loss was a kind of stimulus; you could get back in the game and go for the kick of the comeback.

My mother was a serious painter. She had studied at the Art Students League in New York and was therefore qualified to have people lie around nude on a platform in her studio. Some of my mother's most interesting paintings were of movie stars dressed as Shakespearean characters: Claudette Colbert as Cleopatra, Deborah Kerr as Portia, Louis Calhern as King Lear, James Mason as Brutus, and Marlon Brando as Marc Antony. They loved posing for her; she said portrait painting often had as much to do with listening as with looking, and she listened well.

On a typical day, Donovan Leighton, our houseman and one of the six or seven black people who lived with us, started by raising the American flag. Dorothy, my mother's personal maid, set out my parents' breakfast trays. They had side pockets for the *Los Angeles Times*. My father's place mat and napkin were embroidered with American eagles. My mother's were embroidered with flowers, hearts, and a name my father called her—Mary (everyone else called her by her real name, Miriam). Lois started the breakfast for the help and the children. Ethel, the cook, didn't make breakfast. Andrew came after church. He drove my father during the week.

My father was afraid we'd be spoiled. He heard us once yelling down the back stairs to Dotty for our laundry and he made us do the wash for a week. That was part of the paradox in this house, where there were all these servants but no one dressed up. My parents served plain American food and had their children at the table even when there were guests.

Every Sunday, my parents had buffet parties that began early in the morning with men gathering to play tennis. I'd be doing homework on my bed, and through the window overlooking the tennis court I'd hear the pop of tennis balls, the skid of tennis shoes. The smell of tangerine tree blossoms came through the window and I'd imagine the men licking their lips, tensing their thighs, then leaping up, their rackets high, and I'd hear the shout as they'd go for the ball.

When I'd come down for lunch, the tennis players would be there in the shadows of the wisteria arbor or out on the flagstone patio, hair curling over the white bands around their foreheads, sweat maps on their white shirts. I could tell which ones knew I wasn't looking at them the way a kid was supposed to. The directors just over from Europe saw right through me before they even learned English, and I could imagine them telling me in that hoarse whisper they use as the cameras begin to turn: "Just lie there, yes, sweetheart, just give me that look."

In the late forties, many of the new writers and directors were refugees, and they were astonished at the quantities of pastrami, bologna, salami, potato salad, coleslaw, and paprika-roasted chicken heaped on silver platters. After lunch, guests swam, played croquet, watched more tennis, and hung around the ice cream cart where Donovan in his dashing striped jacket made sodas and sundaes.

People were surprised that my father remained starstruck, but the quality he called "the motor" isn't there on the screen alone. Stars are not regular people. They have an extraordinary presence. They are always interesting, even when they are not smart, and many of them are not attractive, gracious, or radiant in person. Indeed, the ones who don't light up a room offscreen have a peculiar, almost sullen, magnetic intensity that you want to explore. This talent is something that shows all the time, and you want to understand the stars, take care of them, get closer to them. At the same time, you try to avoid giving any sign that you notice they are different.

Like ourselves as Jews, and like black people, movie stars could not cross into or out of their condition, which all of us were born to. None of us could go to most private schools, beach clubs, or golf courses, or live or shop in certain neighborhoods. And we always had to be on our best behavior because we were representing our entire community.

In our house, formal parties were scattered through the year the way musical numbers are scattered through a movie. My parents' twenty-seventh anniversary celebration in 1959 turned out to be the last big party. The movie business had begun to change. The studios were no longer like old theater companies. Low-budget television divisions were making bigger profits, and in the restructuring, the eastern board asked my father to resign.

The time had come to leave Hollywood. And even though no one mentioned it, there was an attentiveness to detail about my parents' anniversary party that made it particularly affecting, the way any ritual comes into high relief when you do it for the last time. My father's face was tender as he walked around checking everything. And although I was married by then and lived somewhere else, this was still my home. I was there watching.

I saw Donovan and Andrew roll back the red rug in the projection room and polish the broad oak floor so not one rhinestone on one star's Delman shoe would go unreflected. Around nine o'clock, fifteen musicians from the studio gathered in the den for drinks and sandwiches while dinner was still being served in the dining room and in the only Old English lanai in town.

After dinner, like proper Britons, the men remained at the table with cigars and the women retired to my mother's room. They gathered around, admiring a gift that Cedric Gibbons of the studio art department had made for her: a hand-painted, gilded miniature Victorian stage that was perched on her marble-topped dressing table. There was a mirror inside the proscenium, and day and night lighting so my mother could adjust her makeup. That night she observed, like a director, all those extraordinary faces taking turns sitting on her velvet Regency chair, preening, posing, gliding lipstick on with tiny brushes in gold cases, smoothing shadows, and powdering noses with tiny swansdown powder puffs. Others were adjusting gowns and stocking seams and jewels in front of the wall of mirrored wardrobes before they went downstairs.

At nine-thirty, the dancing began. The party seemed like a montage of all the years, all the parties, all the songs, and all the shows that friends put together for every special occasion. June Allyson and Dick Powell danced to "Thou Swell," Van and Evie Johnson did the new mambo, Janet Leigh spun by with Tony Curtis. My father exchanged a forearm clutch with Robert Ryan the way tough men do when they don't say good-bye.

Judy Garland and Tony Martin sang "Stardust," my parents' song, and as Martin danced off with his wife, Cyd Charisse, my father leaned forward to embrace my mother, his body away from hers as though the Hayes office censors were watching (the rule was that there must be light between the torsos). My mother's back was perfectly straight in the dress Helen Rose made for her of white embroidered net with tiny, starry silver sequins. She looked up at my father squarely, forgetting anyone else was there, as if she believed—for one evening—that this life in this house would last forever.

MARY E. MIHALY

View From the Inner City

n Saturday mornings, the aloneness feels like a gift. I sit in the kitchen, content to stare out the back window at the lavender border I planted along the driveway, letting the coffee wake me.

I do my best thinking in this room, where so many achievements surround me. Every surface here is my doing. I look at my kitchen walls and know that the ninety-year-old wainscoting wears a natural finish because I spent four months of weekends on my knees, stripping and scraping. Faux granite was my spray-paint solution to the problem of worn cabinetwork I could not afford to replace; adding a granite-look chair rail was a last-minute idea that pulls the room around me like a cozy shawl.

I know I will never take another house this seriously. This may be my maiden voyage in home ownership, but I am transforming my Cleveland, Ohio, inner-city wood-frame house into the personal statement of a lifetime.

I am committed to honoring the integrity of this building by obliterating all traces of the family who lived here before me—people who covered walls with contact paper, buried the original 1910 wainscoting (narrow, vertical boards of yellow pine they had first painted green, then pink) under cheap paneling, and carpeted the entire first floor with variegated brown-and-orange shag.

Most of my changes were made during the first year here. I was driven. Every evening and weekend I tore into this place, pulling down, nailing up, painting, making it mine. Every week brought more "firsts," each a bold stroke that I was sure everyone would applaud. The first time I changed the oil in my new lawn mower, I couldn't wait to phone my sisters with the details. When I finished the ceramic-tile backsplash in the kitchen, I hosted a dinner party just to show it off. For a solid year, my home-owning heroics were the best gossip I knew.

I cried only once in this house, over a botched kitchen floor. I had seen a fabric floor in a magazine and I wanted one. Nobody could convince me this was a stupid idea. After two tries, many calls to designer friends and an expenditure of about $400, my cotton ticking floor still bubbled and yellowed. I gave up, ripped it off, and painted the old linoleum white with black stenciled elephants around the edge to complement the faux-granite cabinets and chair rail. Since then, "fabric floor" has become a family metaphor for failed experiments (as in, "Uh-oh, looks like we've got another fabric floor here").

Taking on a house in the inner city, alone, had not been a personal dream. I am a single woman, and a writer for *Cleveland* magazine—gratifying work, occasionally even exciting, but not very lucrative. Buying a house on my own at that point would have been comically irresponsible. But then an editor friend in New York asked me to help her edit some manuscripts in my spare time; the project snowballed, and my bank account grew by $20,000 in five months.

I was renting a second-floor apartment in a sedate, largely white neighborhood near the edge of the city where quietude and tidiness prevailed. Property owners rarely spoke to each other. My landlord was an authoritarian sexist retiree whose every conversation was marked by slurs about a black family down the block. Living near him and his bigotry oppressed me and I wanted to move.

I was also about to turn forty, and something like dread had settled over me. I loved thinking of myself as a career woman in my thirties; forty seemed so drab and final, and I couldn't stop it from happening. I needed to do something positive and adventurous.

I had my $20,000, so I set out to buy a house. It had to be inside the city limits, partly because I need the stimulation of a city's bustle. Writing is solitary work; when a writer also lives alone, the isolation can be paralyzing, so the sounds of screen doors slamming and mothers yelling at their kids are welcome. It also makes economic sense to buy in the city. An urban pioneer can still find a fixer-upper for $15,000.

Mostly, though, I insist on city living because of the diversity and hospitality one finds in such neighborhoods. Homogeneous suburbs designed for escape do not interest me. I grew up in Akron, "the rubber capital of the world," about fifty miles south of Cleveland. Ours was a working-class neighborhood where everyone seemed connected. No one gave much thought to privacy; neighbors were people you talked to every day. They knew your business and sat on your front porch to tell you theirs. If you were at a friend's house at lunchtime, your friend's mom simply fixed an extra sandwich.

I looked for that sense of community in my new neighborhood, but it was just as important to me to fall in love with the house itself. Fortunately, I found both.

My sisters, Carol and Margie—one older, one younger, both married with families—knew my requirements and they drove the streets with me looking for the perfect combination. I wanted a big front porch with spindles and pillars, a backyard, a sit-in kitchen, and, even buying alone, four bedrooms (my bedroom, a home office, a spare bedroom, and that quintessential luxury, a room where I could keep the ironing board set up). And I could only spend $30,000.

The search took three months. The first time I walked into my vestibule—a vestibule!—I thought, this place feels solid, like the house I grew up in. And there was character here. Huge oak pocket doors in perfect condition separate the living and dining rooms and both these rooms have bay windows. A pantry off the kitchen has glass-front cupboard doors. A great oak ball tops the newel post, and the claw-foot bathtub runs almost the length of the bathroom.

What makes visitors gasp, though, is my mantelpiece of varnished oak, embellished with carved leaves and fruits. I have never seen wood so magnificently worked, even in picture books. Two oak shelves hang above and below a massive beveled mirror, drawing the eye to nine-foot-tall cove ceilings. Staring at the workmanship in that mantel for the first time, I stroked the rich wood, longing to scrub it clean with Murphy Oil Soap. That mantel symbolized what I knew my new home would mean to me: I would center myself here, spend solitary winter evenings by the hearth absorbed in a new Tom Robbins novel. Everyone in my life would see it as part of my identity.

Making that happen, I soon learned, would take a lot of my time and all of my savings. I stayed in my apartment for a month after buying the house; I wanted to paint all the rooms and put in new carpeting before the furniture came. Most of the sixty-odd items on my job list were cosmetic tasks I could handle myself ("Paint closets first!"), but a few—dedicated circuits for the microwave and computer, roof patch, extra phone jack—called for a contractor's skills.

I learned as I went, and along the way I reinvented my social life. When I lived in an apartment, I rarely invited friends over for an evening. We might have had a glass of wine there on the way to dinner, but my home wasn't truly mine and was almost never the destination. These days, I entertain every two weeks or so—informal affairs, usually. I'll cook up some pasta and make a Caesar salad and a few of us will watch *Murphy Brown* and *Northern Exposure*. Or on a summer night, we'll relax outside on my Adirondack chairs (my first new-house purchase) under the sweet gum tree I planted.

And I have begun special new traditions here. One of my favorite childhood memories is of picking my grandmother's black raspberries at her house in Akron. Ignoring the deep, painful scratches from the thorny vines that crisscrossed our arms, the four of us—my brother, sisters, and I—used to press on, blinking back tears, until every dark-purple jewel was picked and in Grandma's bucket. We were rewarded with all the berries we could eat, swimming in sugar and fresh cream. I was twelve when Grandma died, and my Uncle Joe rescued some of her bushes before the house was sold. For nearly thirty years it has been in my mind that when I finally owned a house I would grow some of Grandma's berries in my own yard.

I called Uncle Joe two years ago, the winter after I bought my house. That March, just before they emerged from dormancy, I transplanted the berries. For four months, I nurtured the bare canes, weeding, watering, and cultivating faithfully. I waited. The day they sprouted green buds, I ran for my camera and took photos to show Uncle Joe that I hadn't killed my share of the family treasure.

79

Pale pink clusters of fruit began appearing near the end of June. My family was coming for the July Fourth holiday, and I prayed for perfect timing. My prayers were answered. The morning of the Fourth, my bushes bore dozens of ruby-colored berries, and by noon the sun had ripened them to a deep purple. My mother ceremoniously picked the first berry and then my nieces and nephews pounced—the fourth generation of giggling, scratched-up Mihalys to reap the berry crop.

Most of my seven nephews and nieces spend at least one weekend with me every summer. Emily, the three-year-old, comes more often because she lives nearby. Emily and I have our rituals for these visits, memory-making activities that happen only in this house: picnic breakfasts on the window bench in the vestibule where we can wave at neighbors and stray animals as they pass; "work" sessions at my computer; a game she invented with my elephant collection.

My nephews prefer to visit when the Cleveland Indians are playing a home game at the lakefront stadium downtown—a seven-minute drive from my house. All the family visits me more than when I lived in an apartment. The whole clan spends the day after Christmas here, and from time to time my mother comes up from Akron for a weekend getaway; she says it does her good to sit in someone else's kitchen for a change.

And, just as I had hoped, my neighbors have become a part of my life. Nearly every summer night, there is a neighbor sitting on a porch, ready to share a beer and catch up on street news. Two months ago, a Lebanese family bought the house to the right of mine. The mother cooks more than her family can eat and she is forever at my door with another exotic plate of greens or soup, challenging me to guess the ingredients. Her oldest son mows my lawn, front and back, for $5, and her four-year-old named his kitten after me.

Sitting on my front porch, I, with my Czech and Yugoslav heritage, can see not only the home of the Lebanese family but also those of a Filipino couple, a Mexican family, an elderly Latvian woman, a Vietnamese family, a gay black couple and, because so many hill people migrated to northern cities from Kentucky and West Virginia to find work after World War II, six houses inhabited by families of Appalachian descent. All but two of the residents own their own houses—all, like mine, purchased for $30,000 or less.

When the elderly couple on my left sold their house last summer, neighbors met on porches and fretted, worrying about who the new, absentee landlord would rent to. I tried to distance myself from the anxiety but I should have worried. My new neighbors turned out to be an honest-to-goodness band of gypsies. They were an outgoing bunch, asking everyone on the street if they could borrow tools, a phone, a blanket, whatever they needed that day. And they were boisterous, singing and playing music several nights a week until dawn. ("We hold prayer services," one little girl told me. "We're Christian people.")

Their yard quickly filled with car engines, rusty fenders, and old tires. On laundry day, shirts and pants and towels were draped over the shrubbery in front. The street looked as though Sanford & Son had moved in, and no one had the nerve to confront them—least of all me, living alone on the property line. At *Cleveland* magazine co-workers, suburbanites all, relished this development. For five months, until the gypsies finally moved on, our Monday-morning planning meetings began with some tale of my weekend in the neighborhood. Occasionally, someone would ask if I "still feel safe there."

Safety, however, isn't something I think about often. The one time I screamed here (at the sight of a mouse scampering across my kitchen floor), two large men were on my porch in a minute, one armed with a rifle. I thanked them for their concern and quick response, and asked "Rambo" to please leave the gun at home next time. The gun was unsettling, but the incident reminded me that neighbors here do watch out for one another.

I know people associate the inner city with drugs, street gangs, and random violence. It is true that some pockets of the city—of any city—are dangerous places, especially for a single woman. But before I bought this house, I studied local precinct reports, talked to other home owners on the street, and felt confident that I was committing myself to a stable neighborhood.

When I approach my next landmark birthday, I'm sure I'll still be here, and I will think about my grandmother's advice to her daughters: "Never live in a house for more than ten years. You'll get too attached to it." I already understand her warning. I cannot imagine someone else owning my glorious fireplace.

But this is not the year to imagine the next owner. There are too many firsts still on the list, here in this house where the best of me becomes . . . well, becomes.

S U S A N   K A M I L

The Time-Travel Game

am sitting on a bench between
Seventy-second and Seventy-third streets in New York City, my back to
Central Park, playing the time-travel game. It is high noon on a brilliant
day in April, but I have played this game here in many seasons over the
past thirty years, whenever it seemed important to reconfirm the past,
the way people do when they show a child or a lover where they went to
elementary school or lived for the first time on their own. Yet no
member of my family nor any friend knows about this place; I come to
be alone.

The previous time I found myself here, staring across the street
at the apartment building where I grew up, was two years ago, in winter,
when I separated from my former husband. Today I am here because I
have fallen in love again and am thinking about remarrying.

• • • • • • • •

A black limousine pulls up to the entrance of the building and a well-dressed woman emerges carrying a big, beautifully wrapped box. The liveried doorman rushes to help her and, just like that, the time-travel game kicks in. The limousine melts away and in its place idles a black 1956 Cadillac. The elegant woman evaporates and in her place stands a dark-haired child wearing a navy-blue sailor suit and a matching hat with ribbon streamers that fall to her shoulders. Her father waves and slowly slides the big car into uptown traffic. A valuable piece of Chinese porcelain he has just purchased awaits him at Parke-Bernet; it is too delicate to be entrusted to the moving company unloading the rest of his family's belongings upstairs.

The little girl—me, of course—watches the car drive away, then turns and marches past the doorman and disappears into the lobby. I am about to learn at age six that there are few days more filled with dread than the day one moves.

When the elevator clanks shut on the third floor, the door to Apartment 3A is thrown open by my mother. She is a spirited woman under any circumstances, but today, her natural vitality has been charged by a newfound pride of ownership. Under a thick mop of dark hair, her brown eyes are flashing, and when a smile spreads across her lovely face, the heat of her considerable fire gathers on me, the surly one, the recalcitrant child who was happy to stay right where she was. I sense myself weakening, but the steel rod of my stubborn nature lets me dig in my heels. My mother, standing in the doorway, gets it immediately.

"What a little terror you are," she says, amused, and sweeps me down the long tiled gallery past a swarm of moving men and into a small room strewn with cartons. My room. "Time to unpack," she says, then promptly disappears. A trace of Chanel No. 5 lingers in the air. I realize that she expects me to cope with this mess alone. My mother is the daughter of immigrants, a seamstress and a housepainter. She grew up in the Tremont section of the Bronx and is now a successful fashion executive, wife, and mother of three, as well as the dazzled owner of an apartment on Fifth Avenue. If she can manage, so can her daughter.

Through the wall of the room comes the soothing voice of my governess, Betty, crooning next door to my two little brothers, made hysterical by the noise and disarray. Echoes of the loud army of movers are punctuated by mysterious thuds and thumps, the occasional sounds of splintering crates and, once, the shattering of glass. The moon is where I want to go, as far away as my imagination can take me. Little Rocketgirl hurtling through space. But just as I am about to blast off, she is there again at the door, my mother the field marshal. "Come with me" is the command now. "I have something to show you."

Back down the gallery we go, past castles of cartons, past the admiring looks of strong men hoisting furniture out of our way, through a maze of dark, still corridors that lead, finally, to the master bedroom. There the white light of late morning streams through huge leaded windows overlooking Fifth Avenue. Across this vast space, the skyline of Central Park West comes into focus through the dreamy trees of Central Park. "This, dearest, is New York," my mother says, her palm on the glass. "This is what I want for you."

My mother has more drive than the others in her family. My stout, dour Romanian grandmother refuses to leave the kitchen table when she comes to visit, her lips pursed around the rim of a glass of tea, resisting all efforts to draw her into our lives. ("Nana, come see my room." "I'm OK here.") And the top of my aunts' mountain is no higher than the second-floor window of a split-level in suburban New Jersey. But does my mother discuss the deprivation of her childhood with me? Never. I believe she cast away the last piece of baggage from that time the moment her fingers closed around the keys to her new home.

Now my mother's hand rests lightly on my shoulder. "Look," she tells me, and my eyes follow hers across the boundless, shining oak floor to the only object in the room: a tiny child's chair upholstered in bright orange silk standing in the far corner. It is my size exactly. "This is a gift," she explains, coaxing me toward it, "from the nice people who sold us the apartment." She lifts me up and places me in its little lap, then stands back, hands on hips, taking stock of what she sees.

"Princess," she says, "this is definitely a throne made for you. May it be the first of many." Her enormous exuberant laughter fills the room with gaiety and delight, gutsy laughter that challenges all comers. And from the moment that laughter rolls over me, I am anchored back on earth. Little Rocketgirl on her orange throne. I give up. I'm home.

The formal little Louis XVI piece remains in the very corner where it became mine. Growing up in its Lilliputian embrace, I participate in the mornings and evenings of my mother's days: watching her dress for work

("Always wear bright colors, Princess, they go with our skin"), sharing her breakfast tray of coffee, pot cheese, and dry toast ("Never be a pig, Princess, you'll get fat"), listening to her give phone advice to her many friends ("I know it's hard, but whatever you don't want to do, do it *first*"), watching her dress for a night on the town ("Wear simple gowns when you grow up, dearest. People should look at *you*, not at your clothes").

I adore her, of course. How could I not? We all do, my father most of all. Like her, he is a Depression child. The son of Austrian immigrants, he still has strong ties to the Lower East Side where my fearsome, humorless grandfather lives. Every Sunday, my father piles my brothers and me into the car and soon we are ambling happily through bustling Hester Street, Ludlow Street, Stanton Street. Here we will duck into a wholesale dry goods store to pick up a new bedspread or towels or sheets. My father gently reminds the owner who my grandfather is and, like magic, the price drops.

Then on to the fish market, where the merits of this or that side of smoked salmon are debated with the cousin of a cousin. Downtown, my stolid, impassive father comes into his own, liberated by the resonance of his past—so unlike my mother, who lives for the present and the future. They are opposites, to be sure, but on the many evenings that my parents sail through the front door en route to the Copacabana or the theater or the fights (my mother loves the fights), his eyes sparkle, his essential reserve overcome by his wife's enthusiasm for the high life.

Beside my mother, my brothers, and me, my father's only visible passion is collecting. Anything, everything, and our new place gives him wondrous license. One day a Louis XV desk arrives. A vast dining table is brought in and assembled leaf by leaf until the huge proportions of that room seem to shrink. Returning from school one day, I discover the library shelves filled with leather-bound books: the collected works of Shakespeare, Arthur Conan Doyle, Brett Harte. Old familiar furniture from our previous apartment vanishes, gradually replaced by sofas and chairs of rich brocade, velvet, silk. A man of few words, my father speaks through the objects he chooses.

Furnishing their lives slipcovers, for a while, the widening rents and tears in their marriage. Six years pass. I outgrow my little chair and learn that the perils of moving day are nothing compared with the complexities of approaching adolescence. The axis of our household shifts. My mother, who made certain she was home in time for dinner every night, is out more at client functions. Business trips frequently call her away, and Betty takes primary responsibility for running our daily lives. My father prowls antiques galleries and auction houses as if the act of bidding and winning empowers him in ways his marriage no longer can. He buys new andirons, another three paintings for the living room, more vases, lamps, statuettes. His romance is now with things, until finally, they cannot substitute for a partnership long since dissolved.

They divorce when I am eleven, my father moves out, and the next year my mother decides to marry the rugged, energetic man I am certain is the love of her life. I try to accept him because he is kind to my brothers and me, in a distracted way; we are ancillary planets in his new universe. And I see from my mother's behavior—the way her fingers lace through his when she greets him at the door, the way she puts her feet in his lap when they read the newspaper after brunch on Sunday—that her restless nature has settled down at last.

Their wedding ceremony is to take place in our apartment, and several of her close friends have congregated in her bedroom to partake in the joyful womanly rituals of matrimony. Paralyzed by ambivalence, I lean against a wall in the corner watching her luminous face as the double strand of pearls is clasped around her neck, the buttons of her satin evening suit securely fastened. By my side, knee-high now, stands the little orange chair, and in its lap sits a perfect spray of white roses. Is this really happening, I wonder. Then there is a knock at the door, cries of "It's time! It's time!" and the crowd begins to move.

"Wait! My daughter! The flowers!" My mother knows just where to find me, too. And when she turns in my direction, the radiant smile on her face seduces me from the shadowy corner of my confusion just as it always had, just as she knew it would.

Two years later, cancer takes my mother from us. Her last months are spent between the hospital and the hospital bed that has been set up in her bedroom by the great leaded windows overlooking Fifth Avenue. When I return home from school every afternoon I read to her—from J. D. Salinger or Saul Bellow—words that serve more to tamp down my terror than to anesthetize her rage. In the evenings, my stepfather sits by her bed, talking quietly or holding her hand until she sleeps. Once when I go to say goodnight, I open the door to see him leaning over the bed bars singing softly in her ear, and the sight of this drives me to the bathroom to bury my face in the towels.

During this time, I have my thirteenth birthday and instead of the pink princess telephone she knows I long for, my mother gives me a typewriter. "You'll need it, dearest" is all she says, then holds her arms out to me for a hug. Several weeks later, after the hospital gurney clatters down the long tiled gallery for the last time, I understand the gift. My mother has imagined the unimaginable—my future without her.

When the apartment is sold, my brothers and I move with our father to more basic quarters. The new space is too small to accommodate the prodigious amount of furniture we own, so much of it is sold, too. The Louis XV desk remains, though, and several of the paintings, lamps, side tables, and sofas. And, of course, the little orange chair. For the twenty-five years that our governess remains with the family, she keeps it in a corner of her room, covered with plastic. "A shrine," my brother once calls it. Then she, too, dies, and I take it for my own.

Today, the little chair stands by the piano bench in the living room of my country house in Connecticut, amid the cheerful disarray of antique American quilts, old rugs, and Shaker blankets I have collected over the years. When friends come to visit I watch as their young children, awkward at first in a strange place, run straight to it. One afternoon, my neighbor places her fidgety four-year-old in its seat. "This," she says to me as the child relaxes, "is a throne for a princess," and my heart cracks.

• • • • • • • •

The first time I found myself on the bench on Fifth Avenue was the first anniversary of my mother's death, but the grief was still too raw and I had to leave. Gradually, over the next three years, I stopped crying myself to sleep, stopped avoiding the fully parented homes of my friends, and began to heal. So when I was about to take my maiden voyage to Europe, or when I was accepted at the college of my choice—times when it's important to know you are walking into the future on solid ground—I returned to the bench and fared better and better.

Even after three decades, the time-travel game can call up snapshots best left locked away. But not today. Today I win, and walking uptown to meet the dear, dear man in my life, I consider the notion of white roses at our wedding. I am sure that white roses will be perfect.

Country People

DIANN   SUTHERLIN

Worldly Goods

hings were progressing pretty
much as I expected during the weeks following my grandmother's burial in
the remote Green Grove Cemetery in southern Arkansas. Her six children,
fourteen grandchildren, twenty-seven great-grandchildren, and assorted half
sisters and second cousins twice removed were alternately engaged in mourn-
ing the passing of the ninety-three-year-old matriarch and arguing over who
had done more for her during her last days and was, therefore, more deserving
of her worldly goods.

Mama Lillian had no savings account. No IRA. No CDs or mutual
funds. No Wal-Mart stock. There was no heirloom Waterford or Steuben
or silver tea service. No Chippendale or Stickley. Not even any Fiestaware.
Her '63 Chevy Bel Air had been sold nine years before when she developed
cataracts, and for the past three decades, she had lived off her modest Social
Security check with help from her children. She had nothing of monetary

value—nothing to amount to a hill of beans, she would have said. Certainly nothing to provoke the scavenging frenzy that followed her death.

The only exception, in her eyes, would have been the three-tiered, nineteen-bulb chandelier that had hung over the dining table. The chandelier barely cleared the bowl of mashed potatoes when the table was set. Mama Lillian had consolidated her Christmas money one year and bought the sparkling, dangling wonder from Sears, and she had thought it exquisite.

A month after my grandmother died, my mother, the executor of the estate, called me to say she was putting Mama Lillian's house up for sale. My grandmother had helped build the simple three-bedroom frame house with her third husband some sixty-five years ago. It was hammered together by necessity, guided by guesswork, and limited by resources, but it had suited my grandmother just fine.

My mother said, "Everybody's pretty well got what they wanted out of the house. We'll have a garage sale to get rid of the little bit that's left."

"Would anyone mind if I came down and went through the house one last time?" I asked. "I'd like to have something of hers. A memento."

"There's nothin' left worth diddly," Mother said matter-of-factly. "If there was, you know your cousin Vandy would have already gotten it, but you're welcome to come on down."

The following Saturday, I drove the two and a half hours from Little Rock to my hometown of El Dorado, collected my mother, and drove out to Mama Lillian's house on the Strong Highway. When her third husband died twenty-nine years ago, Mama was living down a blacktop country road some forty miles from this spot. Her children began badgering her to sell her house and move into town, to an efficiency apartment or maybe a retirement home. A widow had no business out there by herself with so few neighbors close by, they told her, but my grandmother wouldn't hear of it. She held out for five more years. When at last she relented, it was on her own terms. "I'll move," she said, "but I'm takin' my house with me."

The house movers wrenched my grandmother's home from its comfortable spot sheltered by sweet gum and dogwood, hauled it forty miles up the road, and plopped it down on a site right next to her oldest daughter's house on the highway. The year was 1969 and I was a junior in college. I still remember the sensation the first time I went to visit her after the move. It reminded me of the fun house at the county fair. The walls listed. The floors slanted. The bedroom door had to be propped open to keep it from slamming shut.

The transplanted house shattered my equilibrium, but my grand-mother took the move in stride, as she had so many other losses. Her first husband had died prematurely of a brain tumor, leaving her with five young children. Her second husband, my grandfather, died of pneumonia when my mother was only three. With six children to raise, she married a third time, to a man twenty years older with whom she would live for the next forty years. My grandmother was born of pioneer stock and had not been afforded the luxury of sentimentality. She seldom waxed nostalgic about the old home place, unlike my younger brother and sister and me. Our conversations were sprinkled with "Remember when . . ." We reminisced about the gnarled persimmon tree at the end of the lane and the abundant tea roses, daffodils, narcissus, gardenias, irises, and snowball bushes that hugged the old house, the big vegetable garden she planted every year with incredible tomatoes, squash, and fuzzy okra that we picked in the scorching sun.

The old place was an oasis in the midst of barren stretches of earth where things no longer grew. In 1921, oil was discovered nearby. Wildcat speculators from all over the country flocked to Union County, leased mineral rights from landowners, and sank wells in a frenzied quest for riches. At the time, the money from the wells had been a godsend for my grandmother and her neighbors, but by the fifties, gas had become so cheap that the proceeds from the wells barely covered taxes. In the end, only a few houses remained, dotting the landscape among the rusting derricks and loblolly pines. This was the place of my childhood memories, where oil wells pumped like tribal drums, lulling us to sleep on sticky nights as we lay on quilts beneath the breeze of the oscillating fan.

There was a comforting sameness to grandmother's house as predictable as the pulse of those wells. The candy dish filled with hard ribbon candy was always in the same spot on the coffee table. The dusty conch shell with the "Florida, Land of Sunshine" decal was always by the front window in case it needed to be propped open. Mama Lillian never felt the urge to rearrange things. With the exception of moving the house itself, once she had committed something to its place, it remained there.

While I was growing up, Sunday dinner at Mama Lillian's was a ritual. A smattering of relatives was always in attendance, as well as the preacher and his wife once a month. The menu was nothing fancy and it was always pretty much the same, except for the main course—fried chicken for ordinary Sundays, baked chicken and cornbread dressing for holidays. Mama Lillian took great delight in cooking and even more delight in watching the family enjoy the meal. There were always mashed potatoes, cream gravy, fresh corn, and purple hull peas (from the deepfreeze if they were out of season), turnip greens, and pies: pecan, lemon ice box, and sweet potato. If any of the parents chastised a grandchild for eating too much, Mama Lillian would say, "Let that baby eat whatever it wants—this is grandmother's house." In her eyes no child was ever too fat, too noisy, too slow, too stupid, or too messy.

The house was small, maybe twelve hundred square feet, but this was where all the family gathered to feast on Thanksgiving, Christmas, Easter, and the Fourth of July. On these occasions, with forty or more relatives congregated, people were found eating in every room of the house and spilling onto the porch with their plates heaped, weather permitting.

These gatherings were decidedly down-home affairs. There was no clever repartee around the dining table. This was not a sophisticated group; the majority of the clan still lived within a fifty-mile radius of their birthplace. Few had ever flown in an airplane, or wanted to. My grandmother had left school after the third grade to chop cotton. She was barely literate, managing to read the Bible, decipher dress patterns, and write an occasional letter. None of my aunts or uncles had attended college; most had not graduated from high school. They had married young, some of them often. My mother's generation were Bible-believing Southern Baptists and straight-ticket Democrats.

My grandmother didn't hold with evolution or astronauts. "God wouldn't allow men up there messin' around in his place," she told me once, explaining that the moon landing was staged in Hollywood. The only time politics reared its head was when my Aunt Clarice and her rabid third husband, Wayne, would come in from Baytown, Texas, with an ice chest of Pabst Blue Ribbon in the trunk of their Buick. By late afternoon, after a few trips to the car trunk, Wayne would have a serious buzz on and invariably launch into a tirade about the evils of integration, outside agitators, and how in blazes Arkansas could have elected itself a Rockefeller for governor.

Generally, the main topic of after-dinner conversation among the men was car engines. I suspected that they emerged from the womb babbling about plugs and points. There was always a malfunctioning vehicle and, eventually, the guys would meander outside to start gunning its engine and poking around under the hood. The women would sit in the front room and talk in great detail of births, deaths, illnesses, sewing, recipes, and church business.

Like many extended families, ours was composed of a lot of people with whom I ultimately would have very little in common except genes and a shared history. The history centered on my grandmother's house, where the back gate was fastened by a rusted horseshoe, where chickens nested in the old tires in the garage, and a tire swing was suspended from a sycamore tree. Grandmother's house was a tacky, tasteless, architecturally insignificant, thrilling old place held together by imagination, invention, and affection.

I had not been in the house since the funeral. My grandmother's last request was that her body be taken to her house for viewing rather than the funeral home. "This practice is highly irregular in these modern times," the funeral director had fretted. Some people were scandalized, but Mama Lillian wanted to be in her own house and her wishes were honored.

As we walked inside on my final visit, Mother looked a little peaked. I felt queasy myself. We stood there staring at the familiar celery-green-painted paneling and the yellowed lace curtains and we breathed in the enduring smell that came from years of cooking bacon and turnip greens. The furniture was gone. In the dining room, ceiling tiles dangled where the chandelier had been ripped out.

"See, not much left," Mother said as we walked across the cracked linoleum in the kitchen. All the matching glasses and Teflon pans and Corning Ware had been claimed, but my eye lit upon a blue speckled enamel bowl flecked with rust spots discarded in a trash can.

"This is the bowl Mama Lillian used to make biscuits in," I said. Cat head biscuits, she called them, because they were as big as a cat's head.

"Is it?" Mother responded. "I guess I forgot. She's been buying canned biscuits for years." I picked up the bowl and ran my finger around the bent rim. We always awoke to the smell of slab bacon frying and biscuits baking at my grandmother's.

Mother and I walked down the short slanting hallway to the back bedroom. In the closet, which had no door but bark cloth curtains gathered on a rod, was a box of patterns dating back fifty years. My grandmother had sewn for me throughout my life, my earliest memories being of calico sunsuits made from chicken-feed bags. I remember her bare feet working the treadle while her skilled fingers guided the fabric as it raced past the pounding needle. The patterns of my life were all there in that room with editorial notes attached. "No collar on this one" or, during the late sixties, "Can you shorten the skirt to fourteen inches, please?" which she did, saying only,

"Honey, are you sure you want your dress way up to there?" After I married, she even made my husband a corduroy suit.

Leaning against the closet wall was a framed picture of a rooster studded with dried corn and beans. I made it in vacation Bible school one summer when I spent a week with Mama Lillian. Apparently, it did not appeal to my cousin Vandy's artistic sensibilities. A cedar jewelry box with a broken hinge rested next to the rooster. Mother explained that all Mama Lillian's "good" jewelry—her peridot birthstone, her wedding ring worn thin, her Timex watch—had been grabbed. Left behind was a cheap, tarnished Old Faithful charm bracelet I had brought her from Yellowstone when I was ten. I put it in the bowl and tucked the rooster under my arm.

The rest of the personal things, her handmade clothes, her shoes, purses, and belts, would be sold for nickels and dimes. Strangely, her children had decided she should be buried in an expensive long blue organza gown they purchased from the mortuary—an outfit more suited to the blue fairy from *Pinocchio* than to Mama Lillian. I thought she should have been laid to rest in one of her own creations—she never even owned a store-bought dress while she was alive—but it was not my place to decide. Soon strangers would be wearing her clothes.

My grandmother, had she lived to be a hundred, would have garnered kudos from Willard Scott on the *Today* show. She taught Sunday school. Birthed six children. Raised two of her grandchildren and tended to several others. Up until her last brief illness, she had been independent, active, optimistic, opinionated, and involved. Although she enjoyed a trip to Six Flags Over Texas each summer and an occasional visit to see the Christ of the Ozarks statue in Eureka Springs, she had never expressed the desire to live anywhere else or do anything else.

Mama Lillian led what Plato would have deemed an "unexamined life." Unexamined by her, perhaps. I, however, scrutinized her life with reverence. She was a magician who made butter from milk, jelly from muscadines, quilts from tiny scraps of cloth. She even made the wart on my brother's finger disappear by rubbing it with a raw potato and burying the potato under an old oak tree that had been struck by lightning. I studied her every move, hoping to learn the tricks, but unlike stage magicians, she was more than willing to reveal her secrets.

My mother was growing restless and a little teary standing around in the empty, chilly house. "I think I'll go break off some of those gardenias and see if I can get 'em to root," Mother said. "They were always my favorite." The gardenia bush had been transplanted from the old place, along with the house.

"I'll be right out," I answered. In the fading daylight, I spotted a photo of my sister and me in matching dotted-swiss Easter dresses our grandmother had made for us. I laid the picture in the bowl and made one last walk through the front bedroom. In the corner where the nightstand used to be, a small wad of crochet thread perched on a sack of fabric scraps. I picked it up and spread it out. It was a medallion of cream-colored cotton shaped like a snowflake, about the size of my hand, and asymmetrical, having been halted abruptly halfway around. Mama Lillian had started this piece just before she became ill. She had told me she was going to make a tablecloth for my daughter, her namesake.

I stepped onto the front porch with the biscuit bowl, the Old Faithful bracelet, the Easter picture, and the framed rooster. I placed the snowflake in my pocket, careful not to unravel Mama Lillian's last stitches. Mother looked at my keepsakes in disbelief. "I tried to tell you there was nothin' left."

JOYCE ORRELL

Song of the River

smell a river and I am a child again. The river place was our lodestone. The romance of having it and the tragedy of losing it are woven through my life.

I was born during the Depression in an old South Central Texas farmhouse on a bluff forty feet above a bend in the San Antonio River. The music of the river and of the towering cottonwoods was mine from birth, as known to me as my mother's singing, and the fresh river smell was as sweet to me as the scent of my mother.

Among my first memories is the sound of the river rippling over the rocks and the sun filtering through the leaves. I can feel my mother holding my small body in the lapping water, her arms silky against my bare skin, laughter bright around me, the sound of loved voices, the feeling of happiness and safety.

Above, on the bluff, there was a dirt yard swept daily with a broom and edged in bright flowers. We tumbled and played on the hard-pan, and the yard was tightly fenced to keep five small children from the dangers of the river and its high, steep bank. The house lay low and bleached, sagging into the land. A porch ran the length of it, and bulging brown tow sacks filled with pecans leaned against the wall, a few sacks open for anyone to take a handful. Cane-bottomed rocking chairs and benches were piled with bridles, saddles, harnesses, and ranch tools. The farmhands and the men in the family would sit and make repairs while they rested or waited for meals. On our six hundred acres, we grew corn and cotton and raised cattle.

There was a water faucet on the porch with a wooden water bucket and an enamel water dipper beside it on a high bench; also a wash pan, a saucer with a bar of homemade lye soap, and a white towel, usually smudged with fresh handprints, hanging from a nail. The rough smell of horse sweat, the acrid smell of pecan shells, and the fragrance of leather hovered over the porch. Bees buzzed in the morning glories that climbed a trellis behind the water bench, and hummingbirds zoomed in and out of the blue trumpets, fighting for dominance. We played on this porch and soaked it into our depths.

I also remember a bed, high as a mountain to a toddler, the bed of my mother and father. It had a soaring carved wooden headboard, starched embroidered pillowcases with flowers as bright as those in the yard, cool and crisp to my cheek, and a quilt my adult mind cannot recapture. All the quilts of my childhood merge: the Butterfly, the Dutch Girl, Grandma's Flower Garden, the Double Wedding Ring, the Log Cabin, and many more. The bed was a soft, familiar spot where I sometimes napped. It sat catty-corner in the bedroom, leaving a little triangle of dusky space between the headboard and the walls. My little brother and I liked to crawl behind the big bed and hide.

When I was two or three, I had a passion for sweetened condensed milk. I clearly remember standing in the kitchen yearning for the rich taste while Mother was cooking. I reached up to the scrubbed pine table for the open can of milk. I can still feel the drips on the outside of the can as I clutched it and ran unnoticed to the shadowy corner behind the safe, high bed.

I don't remember going to sleep with the can clasped to my breast and smears of sugary milk and dust across my face, nor could I remember the terror of my mother when she could not find me, her fear of that high river bluff. I know, because the story has become one of the family folktales told over the years, that the house, the barns, the outbuildings, the river, and the banks were searched and searched again. Every available person entered into the hunt. There were shouts and grim faces as the Mexican hands on the farm, their families, their children, even neighbors summoned by the party-line telephone, gathered.

But I do remember, several hours later, the joy, the tears, the laughter, the hugs and kisses I received as I was passed back and forth among the adults, the prayers of "Thank God!" Someone had remembered the bed, found me sleeping in innocent and sticky repose, and brought me forth to the most jubilant celebration I have ever experienced.

We moved away from the river place when I was four, evicted without warning by a reprobate relative who owned the land my father and his father had rented and worked for nineteen years. We left the San Antonio River and the trees, the rich bottomland, the Mexican hands who with their wives and children were like our extended family, and moved to South Texas. The arid parcel of land that my father bought was next to the forbidding fences of the famous King Ranch.

Our home in South Texas, an ugly little four-room bungalow with a front porch, was a square divided into four equal parts. My first sight of that house remains imprinted perfectly in my brain: a gray, desolate building, no trees, no tidy yard with pretty flowers, just a ragged sweep of wine-colored bachelor's buttons. There was no lovely river bordered with cottonwood trees, no rush of invigorating oxygen from leafy pecan trees, no tall corn and thick cotton. I held my little brother Charles's hand and gazed. Standing in the bareness and dryness, looking at that little house, I felt my mother's heartbreak as my own. Suddenly, unable to bear the pain, and a child after all, I ran to pick the ugly maroon flowers, but I always remained as attuned to my mother as I became in that illuminating moment.

It was impossible for a farmer to scratch a living out of such infertile soil. We no longer needed the six teams of horses and mules. Daddy did not have farmhands. Mother lost the help around the house and the companionship of the women. We children lost our playmates and the interwoven support system that had sustained us all: the Mexican people depending upon us, and we upon them, and everyone upon the land.

Mother became depressed and the house became chaotic. We children scattered to the yard and beyond like baby quail and only returned at night to our baths in a tin tub. Then, one day, a neighbor brought a huge bouquet of Talisman roses and gave them to Mother. They sat in their vase and glowed in cream and coral splendor amid the debris and clutter of the little house that Mother was too sad to make into a home.

It was later, when I was older, that she told me what the roses did for her. She said she looked at the glorious flowers that made the bungalow seem so pitiful and she got up and scrubbed the place until it shone. She vowed always to have a house that could stand up to roses, no matter how small or how poor it was. My mother lived on many different farms after that, and she kept her vow.

Though we missed the river, we children enjoyed a large pond behind the house with high banks of wonderful white clay. The pond became the center of our world. We took the clay and created our own toys and baked them in the kitchen oven. My older brother, Lanham, was always inventive and clever with his hands. He made wooden boats that would propel themselves through the water using tightly coiled rubber bands cut from old inner tubes. He made up all kinds of mechanical toys. We had rubber guns and stilts and kites. We built wharves and docks and farms and houses and barns using sticks and stones and anything else we could find.

Life was hardest for Daddy: His line of credit was several hundred miles away. The work was done by horse and mule, a labor-intensive way of farming; he had to do it all himself and it was so unsuccessful. Daddy's partner, his father, had not moved with us, going instead to his daughter's house in town. Like Mother at the beginning, Daddy became immobilized by depression and finally saw the doctor, who prescribed a dose of whiskey every night. The whiskey fascinated us kids. We watched Daddy drink his allotted whiskey each night and begged for a taste. One night he lined us up—five in a row, the biggest boy, the three girls, and my little brother. He got a tablespoon, and one by one went down the line with a taste of whiskey for each child. We sputtered, we spat. One taste was as much of that particular drink as I ever wanted.

In the lean times in South Texas, Mother and Daddy, always sweethearts, clung to each other even tighter. After the bedtime ritual of stories and songs we had every night came my most loved lullaby. It was the sound of my mother and father talking over their day—never the words, I never heard the words. It was the melody I listened for, of Daddy's deep voice and Mother's silver tones darting in and out of the low notes in musical trills.

When the last baby came, Mother recovered slowly, but her health was diminished thereafter. Little Dudley was like a living doll lying in his crib, a sickly little doll. I adored him, but a dark cloud seemed to envelop the plain little box house, menacing the frail baby and Mother and the rest of us. Most of the time I never thought of it, but on some level of consciousness, the feeling never entirely left me: Tragedy and loss could strike at any time.

Often at bedtime I would crawl into Mother and Daddy's bed, lie back on the pillows and daydream and listen to the sounds of evening, Mother singing to the new baby, my older brother and sisters doing homework by lamplight in the kitchen, the night birds, the owl and sometimes the whippoorwill. And the sounds of the barnyard: the horses stomping or neighing, the cows mooing to their calves penned away from them, and the howl of the faraway coyotes. I would struggle to stay awake. Daddy would braid Mother's long, dark hair. The kerosene lamps would be blown out one by one. I would close my eyes and pretend to be asleep, one hand carelessly tucked under my cheek, the other clenching with all my might on one of the posts of the painted iron headboard (the big carved one had disappeared—probably gone to town with my grandfather). I would hear my mother say in her silvery voice, "Oh, Joyce has gone to sleep." Daddy would say, "I'll just carry her to her bed," and he would put his arms around me to lift me up. I would moan softly and hold on to the bed harder. Then Daddy would say, "She's sleeping so good. Just let her sleep with us tonight." The lamp would be blown out and the final wisp of fumes would drift for a moment in the room. I would smile in the dark and snuggle between the two people I loved best in the world, except for Charles. Maybe I loved them as much as I loved Charles. I would drift off to sleep hearing them talk over their day, the music of it.

We moved again when Dudley was two, and often after that, to one farm after another, becoming poorer each year. But wherever we lived, Mother kept that vow.

Because she loved red in her kitchen, Daddy made her a long red table with two red benches. There were three boys on one side, three girls on the other, Daddy at one end, Mother at the other, and starched tablecloths and napkins spread on the table. Daddy said the blessing three times a day while we all bowed our heads, even if the meal was only cornbread and milk.

On cold winter mornings, Daddy would get up first and build a fire in the tin wood heater. As we put on our school clothes, our front sides would burn and our back sides would freeze. Usually, we had biscuits and B'rer Rabbit syrup and milk. I detested B'rer Rabbit syrup. Some days

Mother would serve our own sausages or ham from our smokehouse with redeye gravy. In all the years since, I have never tasted anything better, but it was the coming together at that red table that tugs at my heart even now.

With six kids, it was hard to stretch the beds. Mother would put the three boys in one bed and the three girls in another, crosswise; more could fit in that way than up and down. On really frigid nights, Mother would take bricks or sadirons and heat them to put at our feet, wrapped in newspaper, which gave the room a scorched smell. One particularly cold night, with a Texas blue norther whistling through the half-inch cracks in our house, Mother and Daddy pushed two iron beds together where the eight of us huddled and shivered through the night, even with all the covers in the house piled on top of us.

Those six boys and girls now look back on rich, productive lives, four college degrees, thirty-two children, forty-three grandchildren. The river place was our start—even for the youngest who was not born there but was weaned on stories of that perfect time, that perfect place, that attainable dream. Our strength was that we could move on, adapt, somehow hold on to the unchangeable love and joy of our family life.

These many years later I still live in South Central Texas. I am now a widow, mother of three sons—a doctor, a youth minister, and a missionary. My five grandchildren are the ongoing stream of my life. I work in geriatrics with people of my parents' generation. In the course of my days, I cross the San Antonio River over different bridges going in different directions. When I smell the river and hear its song, I am a child again.

The Grandmother Who Could Do Anything

t happens every spring. Perhaps there is something about the way the sunlight strikes the land, as though coming through a great expanse of green water; perhaps it is the promising smell of the earth, damp from melted snow. Every spring, I am back to the 1940s with Grandma and her chickens.

That was when my mother's parents, Grandma and Grandpa Tucker, came to live with us in our fifty-year-old white house with its green roof and primitive plumbing and heating. (In winter, ice used to form on the bedroom walls.) The little house stood at the end of a dirt road that wandered out from town before melting into the wild Ozark countryside behind our few acres. I was about two years old when Grandma and Grandpa, who had always been tenant farmers, were told that the farm they worked was sold and they had to leave immediately.

There was no question about whether Grandma and Grandpa would come and live with Mama, Daddy, and me. We not only loved them, they could help us survive financially. Wartime prosperity had not yet come down our dirt road. Mama worked long hours as a practical nurse and Daddy, a salesman, went from job to job with long idle periods in between.

So Grandma and Grandpa came to cook, clean, wash, chop wood, and look after me so that Mama and Daddy could work in town. And even though Grandma and Grandpa were in their sixties, they did extra work that brought in money and made a real difference in the desperate circumstances that sent me to school in last year's outgrown shoes and sent Mama to pawn her wedding ring to make the mortgage payment.

Right away Grandpa built Grandma a chicken house where she installed the flock of fifty hens brought from the tenant farm. Grandma's hens not only supplied us with at least one meat dinner a week and all the eggs we could eat, but Grandma sold the surplus eggs for things that we had to pay cash for. And although I punched a schoolmate in the eye for even suggesting it, I confess that my identical dresses with a full skirt, yoke, and three buttons in the back were made by Grandma from the chicken-feed bags that came in pretty prints. The solid-colored ones became my underwear.

Grandma had an almost magical talent for making something out of nothing. Not only did she preserve every scrap of food she could for our hard winters, but she was a forager before it became fashionable. Grandma and I, carrying burlap bags, would wander along country roads, looking for early wild greens to bridge what Grandma called the "hungry time" between winter and spring. In summer, we searched for wild fruits to be turned into deep-dish cobblers and glasses of jewellike jelly. Late autumn found us wrapped in wildly patterned mufflers and mittens of Grandma's own devising, collecting black walnuts and persimmons. And as we walked along, Grandma would sing to me. I can still hear her voice, sharp and high with its Ozark twang as she sang "Barbara Allen" and "Go Tell Aunt Rhody."

Our bags loaded, we would go home where Grandma let me help her cook our "plunder," as she called it, just as she let me help her bake our breads and pies and cakes—cooking lessons I never forgot. Grandma also taught me to sew and do fancy embroidery. I felt she could do anything.

Grandpa's vegetable garden yielded produce for sale as well as providing us with fruit and vegetables for the year. But as much as I loved Grandpa and his perfect Peter Rabbit garden, I was most fascinated by the chickens because they were connected with Grandma, whom I loved totally.

Grandma called me her little shadow with braids, and often as I tagged along after her, she would turn and pick me up, saying, "Come to Grandma, Baby. Let's go visit Grandma's chickens."

One of our most important visits occurred on the first day of weak spring sunshine when Grandma let the overwintered hens out into the poultry yard. A speculative glint in her eyes, she would lean on the fence, watching the portly hens. Tentatively, they scratched the ground before they remembered with their dim brains the summer and autumn before and industriously settled down to work, scratching busily for bugs with their scaly yellow feet. When I saw Grandma watching her hens, I realized she was thinking about replenishing the flock, and I knew that I would get to accompany Grandma to the poultry house in town.

The poultry house both butchered chickens and sold replacement chicks, priding itself on offering a wide selection of breeds, something Grandma respected because she was always searching for the perfect chicken. Grandma and I would wander hand in hand around the wonderful, chicken-smelling building, looking at the pens of peeping chicks and reading brochures that described each breed in exhaustive detail.

Grandma would carefully study these brochures as she searched for a bird that could be used both for eggs and meat. Sometimes she would be persuaded by the literature (and, I always felt, against her better judgment) to select one of the new, high-stepping crosses that usually came in plain white. However, Grandma's real loyalty lay with the older breeds: Plymouth Rocks, Rhode Island Reds. Dominiques, and Buff Orpingtons. I believe she chose them because she loved their colors and histories and, yes, even their old-fashioned heavy, close-to-the-ground, comfortable look—very much like that of Grandma herself.

As soon as the chicks grew up and took on their duties as layers, we would have at least one that—no matter what the literature claimed—decided to go broody. This meant two things. First, it meant that this hen claimed a community nesting box as her own personal property and settled down to lay and hatch a clutch of eggs. It also meant that as Grandma's delegate to gather the eggs, I had to deal with what had formerly been a placid, easygoing hen now transformed by incipient motherhood to mindless ferocity.

For a little girl, gathering the eggs was often nerve-racking. If I avoided the wrath of a crazed broody hen, I might be attacked by a rooster seeking to defend his harem. Coming from out of nowhere, he would suddenly whirl down the chicken yard, wild yellow eyes starting from their sockets, wings flapping, and beak and talons ready. I never told Grandma how terrified I was because I knew she was not like Mama, who always tried to soften the harshness of life for me. I knew Grandma believed in meeting reality head-on. She once told me, "Baby, life just ain't fair."

Whenever she suspected that a hen was just looking busy but not producing, Grandma would snatch the hen up by her feet to see whether the egg vent looked healthy. Sometimes, the hen was lucky and passed inspection, but other times, that hen left the chicken yard still hanging upside down, swiveling her head curiously as she viewed her world from a new perspective.

What happened next was awful. Without ceremony, Grandma would march to the chopping block, flop the chicken's neck onto its surface, and with a single, one-armed blow of her hatchet, strike off its head. I can remember the first time I witnessed this and really understood what was happening. I must have been about four years old, standing with a finger in my mouth, watching the blade come down. With a thud it hit, the head remaining on the block but the rest of the chicken falling to the ground where it stood up and began racing unseeingly around the yard.

I guess I must have become hysterical because Grandma picked me up, pressing my face into the starched bib of her apron so that I couldn't see, saying, "It's just nature, Baby. That old hen—she lived a good life, better than most of us, and now it's over. She's just reacting. She don't feel it anymore." Yet no matter what Grandma said, I continued to sob.

That must be why the next time, Grandma had a clean trash can ready. After she chopped off the hen's head, she hurled the body into the can and clapped the lid on. I suppose she hoped that either the chicken would be quiet or I wouldn't realize what had happened. However, the chicken continued trying to escape and it was somehow even more terrible to think of that old hen there in the darkness, headlessly thudding against the walls of the can. Anyway, Grandma returned to her usual method, probably feeling that a country child had to learn to deal with the cycle of life and death just as it happened.

Death was certainly part of a chicken's experience. Yet just as Grandma dispassionately ended the lives of nonproducing hens, she fiercely protected the flock against predators—the raccoons and weasels that raided the henhouse in the middle of the night. I can remember my heart racing as I would awaken to hear the chickens panicking. The moment all the commotion began, Grandma would jump out of bed not even stopping for her slippers, grab Grandpa's shotgun, and take off for the henhouse. Back in the safety of my bedroom, I would sit hunched up in bed, listening as Grandma raced to the scene, shotgun in hand, knowing that in their bedrooms, Mama and Daddy and Grandpa also listened. Then came a couple of ear-splitting blasts, followed by more hysterical hen noises, and then, a dead silence. In the morning, I knew that there would be a lifeless raccoon or weasel on the woodpile waiting for further attention from Grandpa, who would tan the pelt and sell it.

The only predator that Grandma didn't shoot was Grandpa, and he was one of the hens' prime enemies. Grandpa's pride and joy—his vegetable garden—shared a six-foot-high chicken-wire fence with the poultry yard, and well within the range of the beady-eyed hens were Grandpa's lettuces, his favorite crop. The hens were also fond of lettuce and were always plotting to get over the fence and into the garden. Grandma periodically trimmed their flight feathers, but every once in a while an especially cunning hen would manage to escape the clipping, and the minute Grandma's back was turned would fly over the fence, destroying Grandpa's lettuce crop. Then Grandpa would come stomping into the kitchen carrying a dead hen, having wrung its neck with grim satisfaction along the way. An argument always ensued, but that chicken was still dead, its last happy memory being Grandpa's lettuces.

I guess that, like many people, I tend to romanticize the good old days. Yet I am the first to admit that those times were sometimes frightening to a child like me, who was very aware that the man who knocked loudly on the front door was the bill collector, a child who wondered whether she would ever have a store-bought dress or a pair of shoes that fit. Yes, times were hard, but I always felt very secure. Besides my parents and Grandpa, best of all I had my beloved Grandma, who always seemed to be opening her arms and saying, "Come to Grandma, Baby." With Grandma holding me, my face against the bib of her apron, I felt invincible, as if nothing could ever hurt me.

Spring will come soon with its watery light and earthy smells and I look forward to being engulfed in my chicken-yard memories once again.

Real Chicken-Scratch Cow-Pie Country

ow my Swedish immigrant family prized their farm spring, fed by the oak forest on an Indiana river bluff and spouting clear and cold into a mossy pine spring box!

They arrived at their homestead in 1880, and well into this century, there was a brick springhouse straddling the flow. In it my great-grandmother's eggs, cream, and butter crocks cooled in the year-round fifty-five degree water. Family legend has it she could dart out of the kitchen, down the steps to her natural refrigerator, and be back before the screen door slammed. A murky tintype shows her in child-frazzled matronhood; to me, she looks impatient to return to her backyard summer kitchen, an airy, barn-like dining gazebo with trestle table, black iron cook stove, and even a foot-pump organ for church choir practice.

Ever the Swedish peasant, she traipsed barefoot into her eighties. "Soles thick as harness leather," clucked the genteel great-aunts. I have wondered if it was she who handed down my mother's simple but memorable summer salad—peppery watercress from the spring topping chunks of iceberg lettuce with chopped hard-boiled eggs and homemade French dressing.

The first settlers must have looked eagerly for those green billows of watercress marking the cold brooklet that could make a family the envy of the neighborhood in the days before ice boxes. My hometown's oldest bird's-eye-view paintings show a scattering of farmhouses along our spring-rich river valley; not big, gushing artesian springs, just friendly bubblers flowing over blue clay hardpan down to a slow bottomland river of lily pads, bullfrogs, and sunfish plopping in the floating duckweed.

Although my wife and I still live in the old house (she's only the third cook in 112 years), the look of our shrunken farm's last three acres has changed. Today, our mowed grass riverbank is shaded by the tall, leggy, multitrunked willows common to the Middle West. They are nothing like the artfully pollard-pruned willows of my 1930s boyhood, with their squat trunks thick as wine barrels topped by a crown of ever-sprouting pole limbs, the European peasant's traditional wood supply. No one in the family remembers who trained them that way, but at least since Roman times, thrifty farmers have cultivated such waterland willows as a fuel crop.

Every fall, my farmer uncle Louie would take his bow saw and bald a few willow crowns for a winter's worth of quick burning wood for the cook stove and wash boiler. My reward would come when, out for a morning's sledding on a school holiday, I would smell the sweet willow smoke and drag my Flexible Flyer over for some of Aunt Hilda's Swedish pancakes—big and thin, to be smeared with grape jam, sprinkled with powdered sugar, and rolled up for tidy forking.

Another fascination to a small boy was Aunt Hilda's spectacular washday, a near-sanctified rite for housewives of the era. Together we would lift the cellar trapdoor and descend into a steamy uproar wherein great willow-fired copper wash boilers rumbled gouts of hot suds, lye soap, and bluing, surely God's cleanest smell on a Monday morning.

Even as a child, I envied Louie and Hilda's view of our own green-shuttered brick farmhouse with a gingerbread sitting porch, set on top of a knoll in a grove of huge white oaks. Seventy feet up to the topmost branches, it is home to screech owls and elfin flying squirrels. By moonlight on a windy winter's night, I am still struck by the shadows of the giant limbs moving against the snow. In autumn, a rain of acorns patters on our roof.

What a place for a Depression boy to grow up: a classic heartland home still so Currier & Ives–perfect that old people stop their cars to gaze and remember. I am pleased to preserve this latchstring haven for a large extended family, dozens of people long scattered from coast to coast. Many still show up every decade or so for a cup of coffee and a reminder of real plain-dirt, chicken-scratch, cow-pie country in an era when the word *country* has been so abused.

What a place to string a naptime hammock, with a choice of massive oak boles beneath a vault of forest shade. What a place to laze with a croquet mallet before electing the breezy front porch and a pitcher of lemonade, listening to the tinkling of Japanese painted-glass wind chimes, the coolest sound of summer. What sublime night sleeping, even in dog days, with a whippoorwill calling down the river and katydids stitchety-stitching a sooth-ing sound of bedtime peace. What gentle excitement to enjoy fireflies spark-ing in the soft dark, so many that it is easy to net a child's take-to-bed jarful, their tiny flashes bright enough to read by under the covers.

Uncle Louie's barn is gone now except for chunks of the concrete foundation, but I remember his hayloft—dim, and alluringly mysterious, a Carlsbad Cavern with twittering swallows and golden dust motes in the shafts of sun. Bats at evening would flutter out the high hay door like dark but-terflies, off to hunt moths beneath the streetlamps. We boys discovered that if you wave a white handkerchief under a streetlamp, you too could feel like a hunted moth with a swirl of bats around you. We fooled them every time.

Horseplaying in heaps of fragrant timothy hay was good fun, but you itched deliriously until you wallowed in the horse trough for relief. Our dammed-up spring was too icy cold for even a dip, although it remained our summer drinking fountain, cupped up in grubby-boy palms.

More luxurious was to collapse into a bin of cool, fresh-threshed wheat or soybeans, to roll and snuffle in near sinful joy, something like swimming in dense salt water and best done naked although, this being Indiana, it was hard to manage. And as every farm child knows, a pinch of tender wheat finally chews down to a surprisingly decent wad of gum.

Uncle Louie had springs too, but his were different—dark malevo-lent vagrants that trickled underground nibbling at his barn footings, chilling out his vegetable patch. The result was a cracked foundation and tomatoes so wilty that Louie finally took a long-nosed spade and trenched the hidden springs away from his barn and garden and made a respectable brooklet.

Right down the street, our home's attractions for boys included the storm-blasted ruins of the family apple orchard fit only for flickers' nest holes and the annual miracle of bee-humming blossoms. But the orchard was a middle, watchable distance from the kitchen window, just right for a Cub Scout overnight in my father's homemade, glued-together, make-do tent, the one that soaked up a wee-hours cloudburst to dissolve into a heap of sticky canvas and became a neighborhood joke. The largest geriatric Winesap boasted the most celebrated treehouse fireplace on the street (known informally as Swede Avenue), an old baking pan that roasted a summer's worth of hot dogs before burning through the floor.

When my grandfather's greenhorn family arrived in 1880, by way of the railroad and a fellow Swede's hay wagon, they found a mature oak-hickory forest inhabited by white-tailed deer. By the time I came along, this near wilderness had become as open and elegant as formal parkland, grazed to the nub by a herd of Brown Swiss milk cows belonging to a cousin of ours. In retrospect, it seems a Maxfield Parrish dreamscape, with me drowsing on the riverbank, listening to the distant purr of a farm tractor, watching the jiggling cork bobber that signaled yet another flopping sunfish or bullhead to be cane-poled into the tall horseweeds.

After sixty years I still love working the bottomland's pink-wormed black earth. It was long a Potawatomi Indian pathway, later a cornfield, then a wartime Victory garden so fertile that my fiancée and I once won Garden Club blue ribbons for Best Pumpkin and Best Gourds—just possibly because they were the sole entries in their categories, a crafty ploy that might still work for an upstart gardener.

Before mowers and gardens, there was also a glorious April sweep of violets and buttercups beside the river, self-renewing dainties that lured generations of pickers, especially on Mother's Day when children trooped home with mashed-stem bouquets for the supper table. Predictably, too, would come giddy squeals as a couple of young women scrambled up the bluff, flushed from an encounter with a tongue-darting garter snake.

Decades have passed since we awakened to the last rooster, not to mention a farrow of piglets squealing for their morning slops. Animals in general have become so scarce that once-reviled varmints are now tolerated if not cherished—a few woodchucks, weasels, and raccoons, the odd opossum, an itinerant red fox, subject of recent rumor. We even enjoy the relentlessly fecund rabbits, always a cozy spectacle as one's homecoming headlights sweep the kitchen garden to reveal several of them solemnly munching our lettuces and greens, planted partly for their benefit.

And let me tell you, nature has her own slow, healing timetable. For while our farmstead has become a rustic green island amid raw clay housing projects, the river forest, once lost to become grazing land, has restored itself, with so dense an understory that only winter gleams betray the apartment complex beyond the hill.

A few deer have returned to browse sweetly in the dawn. Even a pair of great horned owls, whose breathless hooting leaves city folks wondering whether they have heard or imagined, are back. Wondrously, too, the family spring flows on, diminished in force but still tingling cold and pure enough for watercress.

Yet some decade soon, I think, one metastasizing subdivision too many will seal shut the spring that cooled Indian throats, that charmed my boyhood. It will surrender its last Pleistocene dribble, leaving a damp place for marsh marigolds. The shimmering clear pools that delight bathing birds and night-tracking animals may become someone's handy trash dump. But still, rain falls, snowdrifts melt, and who knows where or when some lost freshet may emerge from the river bluff to sparkle in tomorrow's sun.

Loren Eiseley, the anthropologist and author, suggested that if there is truly magic in this world, it is in water.

I wonder if he once knew a spring.

Americans
Abroad

Under the Etruscan Wall

y house faces
southeast, toward a road lined with cypress trees, toward the foothills of the
Apennines, and toward Lake Trasimeno, where Hannibal defeated the Romans in 217 B.C. I am amazed at how often Hannibal comes up in daily
conversations around here; previously, I had not heard him mentioned since
World History in eighth grade. Now I know the weather conditions the
morning of the battle (foggy), the route and the number of elephants Hannibal took over the Alps on the way to Rome, even what the Roman soldiers
wore as they were driven into the misty lake and drowned.

Because I grew up in the American South, where hardly a day goes
by that the War Between the States is not mentioned, I am used to the past
intruding on the present. But the past in Tuscany goes back far beyond the
reach of my most indefatigable Georgia aunts: I am driving with a friend
and she points out the villa of someone she knows, saying, "That's where

Luca Signorelli died when he stepped backward on the scaffolding to get a better look at the fresco he was painting." She speaks as though recalling an unfortunate accident last year, not the fate of *the* Signorelli, who died in 1523.

I wonder if this is why I came here, why I instantly felt so at home in Tuscany when I have not a drop of Mediterranean blood. In the South of my childhood, every house contained a story; those who lived earlier seemed about to walk in the door at any moment. It is the same here, only the people of the Tuscan past stand against a mighty background of art, philosophy, history, and religion.

For three years, I have been a part-time resident of Cortona, which remains an essentially medieval hill town with layers and layers that peel back to pre-Etruscan times. Farmers still plow up in their furrows small bronze horses that Etruscan artisans made in the sixth century B.C. At the same time, the Tracy Chapman rock concert on a summer evening draws thousands to the parking area in front of the church where the incorruptible body of Saint Margaret of Cortona (folk rock pulsating in her bones?) has lain since the thirteenth century. The one-day photo service thrives in a dark twelfth-century rabbit warren of a shop with a new glass front, and there I receive faxes from my job in faraway California.

For me, buying a house in a foreign country was an audacious act. The end of my long marriage seemed to return me to the adventurer I was in my youth. When the smoke from the divorce cleared, I found myself with a full-time job, a daughter in college, a stash of stocks and bonds, and a new life to invent. I was in no hurry, but I had a clear desire to transform those static blue chips into something pleasurable—a house with land. I could hear the echo of my grandfather's voice, "Buy land, they aren't making it any-more."

In my (scary) freedom, I began to vacation in Italy. Since I teach in a university, I have three months off. For five summers, I rented farmhouses all over Tuscany. I tried Cortona, then Montisi, Florence, Quercegrossa, Rignano sull'Arno, Volterra, Siena, Vicchio—two weeks here, a month there. Always, I was drawn back to Cortona, to my first impressions of old houses tawny as loaves of bread and the bells of thirty-odd churches ringing over the fields. I thought that here I would begin to write poems not in the usual way, on a legal pad or a laptop, but with a pen and real ink in one of those handmade, marbled-paperbound books, a big one, with thick, creamy pages.

That fifth summer, I began to look seriously for a place to buy. I was no longer amused by the caprices of rented houses, however charming: sagging beds, no hot water, bats roosting in the fireplace, a caretaker who, uninvited, flies through the rooms shrieking and banging shutters whenever it rains. Because I was by then establishing a relationship that seemed permanent, the quest for a house was linked to whatever patterns Ed and I would create in the future. He shares my passion for Italy and also the university boon of free summers.

My daughter, Ed, and visiting friends drove with the agent and me over back roads that turned into paths, participated in discussions about how cow mangers could be turned into banquettes, cooled my enthusiasm for one enchanting place that had no access road at all and a family of blacksnakes guarding the threshold. We found several houses I wanted, but Tuscans hate to part with property, so owners often changed their minds. One ancient contessa cried to think of selling, doubled her price, and seemed cheered when we walked away.

By the time I saw my house, I had given up. I was leaving in two days, had thanked the local agent, and said good-bye. The next morning, I ran into him in the piazza. "I just saw someone who might be interested in selling a house," he greeted me.

Outside town, he took the winding road that climbs around to the other side of the hill Cortona is built on. He turned onto a *strada bianca*, a road white with pebbles, and after a kilometer, pulled into a sloping driveway. I caught a glimpse of a shrine with a ceramic saint and then looked up at a tall apricot-colored house with green shutters and tumbles of overgrown bushes and briars. I was silent as we drove up. There was a lovely wrought-iron fanlight over the door. The walls were as thick as my arm is long. Old glass in the windows wavered. I scuffed through silty dust and saw smooth terra-cotta floors in perfect condition. He showed me two bathrooms, rough but functioning *bathrooms*—after all the houses I had seen with no water, much less plumbing. No one had lived in the house for thirty years, and its five acres seemed like an enchanted garden rampant with roses and blackberries. Ivy twisted into trees and ran over fallen stone walls.

The agent shielded his eyes and surveyed the land. *"Molto lavoro,"* he pronounced, much work.

"It's unbelievably romantic," I answered. I already envisioned myself snipping sun-warmed herbs into a basket, setting a long table with a checked cloth under the linden trees, Ed roasting boar in the big fireplace. I wanted to hang my summer clothes in an armoire and arrange my books under a window with a view of the winding row of cypresses beside the road, each one planted for a boy who died in World War I. After weeks of looking at ruins with collapsed roofs or at tasteless modernizations, after miles of dusty roads, this house seemed to have been waiting all along.

The Tuscan sunlight pouring into every room warmed me. There is something especially beneficent about the Italian sun; it seems to seep farther in, clarifying the mind. I felt renewed, excited, and calmly right, and I suppose this is part of what it feels like to be at home.

In America I have bought and sold a few houses—loading up the car with the blue-and-white Wedgwood, the cat, and the ficus for the drive across town or across the country to the next doorway where a new key would fit. Choices were always practical, bound to graduate schools or jobs. But this time, the new door's iron key weighed half a pound and the doorway was seven thousand miles from home. The legal language and the baroque arrangements of buying baffled me. Currency rates were falling. My broker was selling my life savings and chiding me about *la dolce vita*. But three years later, I still feel stunned by my good luck, although I can also wake up thinking, What on earth have you done and why, when you could have had a cottage right here on the California coast where you would buzz up for the weekend?

One San Francisco August, I had looked for idyllic cottages and had even made an offer on a log house on the foggy Mendocino coast. I was instructed by how relieved I felt when the offer was turned down. I already knew what to expect from California, and from my home state of Georgia, which I also considered. I was running on instinct, and instinct said time for a new kind of home. Time for the unknown. Time to answer the question Dante faced in *The Divine Comedy*: What now to do in order to grow?

My little villa made of enormous stones perches on a terraced hillside covered with olive trees. Close to the house some intelligent soul planted fruit and nut trees—apricot, fig, plum, apple, hazelnut, almond, and many kinds of pears that bear in sequence. From summer through late fall, I find pears to pick and a reason to stock the kitchen with the local Gorgonzola, the perfect accompaniment.

A neighbor said, "Your house is only a couple of hundred years old— mine is a thousand." He's right, the house is not old by local standards. It is not the classic stone farmhouse called *casa colonica*, nor is it a real villa. Although there are fourteen rooms, none has the ample proportions of a house of the nobility. It might have been the country place of some genial

Cortona parvenu who brought his family here when July heat struck the stones of the town. The symmetrical house rises three stories with a fanciful iron balcony on the second floor above a double front door. From it, I train hanging nasturtiums, but I can imagine someone sometime stepping out to hear a lover sing "Ecco Maggio," or some equally corny popular song.

I bought the place from a doctor, who had recently bought it from five ancient sisters of Perugia. The doctor thought to make it a summer house, then changed his mind (turning a great profit, no doubt). I never think of him because he never lived here, but I often think of the five sisters. They must have been girls here; I can see them simultaneously pushing open the shutters of their five bedrooms and leaning out in their white nightgowns. This is the kind of fancy the house inspires. Why? Because it is a dream house. Not a dream house that has a perfect kitchen and ideal floor plan— I don't think dream houses have albino scorpions in the bidet—but it resembles a house from a dream, one where you discover a room you did not know existed, and in it a dry plant bursts into full bloom. Oddly, everyone who visits comes downstairs to breakfast the first morning and says, "I had the strangest dream." Here I have a recurrent dream of swimming without effort in a clear green river, totally at home in the water, buoyantly carried downstream.

Reality is just as remarkable. I am dazzled by the remains of a Roman road at the edge of my property. I follow that stony path through the poppies into Cortona for espresso. I am dazzled by the cistern near the well. When I shine a flashlight into it, I see a brick archway underground. The caretaker at the Medici fortress on top of the hill claims that an underground escape route runs from the fortress all the way down to the lake. He shrugs. "Possibly, your cistern was part of the passageway." How casual the Italians are about such things; that one is allowed to own something so ancient amazes me.

I am still learning to be casual about far more everyday experiences. Even the roof is extraordinary. I climb up the terraced hill and look down on the old tiles, formed over someone's knee and now alive with lacy gray moss. What else? The deeply satisfying tilt of the demijohn as I draw off some of my own olive oil for tonight's salad, oil from olives we picked and had pressed at a local mill. Also the thick, cool marble kitchen counters where the pizza dough never sticks, the small owl that lights on a windowsill and looks in, the straight stone stairs with a wrought-iron railing that kept some smith busy an entire winter.

Ed stripped and waxed each room's chestnut beams—some genius had slathered all of them with a sticky mud-colored varnish—and all the rooms are newly whitewashed. In one bedroom, a friend painted blue domes over the windows and filled them with Giotto-like gold stars. Walls are bare, except for a few of my daughter's paintings; tabletops are bare; casement windows are bare except for their sets of solid and louvered shutters. This house is now ready for long afternoons of reading or baking or putting up plum preserves—once we prune the olives and reset the stone terrace walls.

At least once a day, I go out on the second-floor terrace and look up the hill. I can see a section of Etruscan wall that has the exact orientation of the house. If the wall had not securely kept vigil over this land for twenty-six centuries, I would be afraid it might tumble down on us: blocks of stone as big as the Fiat I rent, blocks on blocks. Etruscan walls form part of Cortona's town wall, and a couple of Etruscan gates and tombs remain scattered about.

From its position, historians think this wall is a remnant of a sun temple. The name of my house is Bramasole, from *bramare*, to yearn for, and *sole* sun: something that yearns for the sun. I used to be surprised that everyone knew this house. "*Ah, Bramasole, si, una bella casa,*" they say. Delivery people, even from miles away, do not need a map. "*Si, si, la villa Bramasole,*" they say. They have picked cherries or nuts here during the thirty years of abandonment, or even earlier. They have gathered mistletoe from the almond trees at Christmas. Their grandmother picked figs every September.

One day in town, I spotted a postcard of the Etruscan wall said to be "in the locality of Bramasole." The owner of the shop, a lifelong resident and neighbor who lives just under the wall, explained that our whole section of the hillside was once known as Bramasole, not just my house, and long before my house existed. Perhaps the name goes back to the ancient purpose of this site, to the lost temple where people like me came when they were yearning for the sun.

Our English Year

n 1958, my husband won a
Fulbright Exchange grant to teach twelve-year-old boys in Leeds, and we
rented the Yorkshire house of the teacher with whom he was exchanging
schools. She described "Langford" so glowingly in several letters that we
imagined an elegant house set in an English garden, something on the order
of Shakespeare's birthplace. After all, the name of the village we were going
to was Burley-in-Wharfedale, and it resonated in our excited imaginations
like Stratford-upon-Avon.

   We arrived at the Burley train station with eleven pieces of luggage
and two small children—one still in diapers—exhausted, having left New
Mexico a week earlier. In those days, the exchange teachers sailed across the
Atlantic on the S.S. *United States*. We were picked up by a teacher who was
to drive us to our new home.

   The first houses we passed on Station Road were grand indeed, built of Yorkshire limestone—a soft beige yellow—and set in charming gardens. I expected our driver to stop any time, but he continued down into the village. Now there were smaller houses, closer together, with modest lawns in front and lots of red geraniums. Any of these would do, I thought, rapidly readjusting my expectations.

Our driver plunged ever deeper into the village, however. Now we drove past streets of coal-blackened row houses with tiny patches of grass in front. At the end of one street, he stopped in front of a grimy and dilapidated house, its front garden gone to tall weeds. I saw a worn plaque next to the door that said LANGFORD. My husband and I stared at one another.

It was a semidetached villa, our driver explained—two families side by side—whereas the terrace houses on the rest of the street were all joined together.

We entered a dark interior that smelled of mold. Although this was August, Langford was freezing. A coal fire had been laid in the tiny sitting room, and it proved to be the only source of heat in the entire house.

One step down from the sitting room we found the kitchen, which had a cement floor and looked out into a very small backyard, also gone to weeds. There was no refrigerator, nor were there cupboards or counters in the kitchen, only a stove and a sink.

Upstairs were two ice-cold bedrooms with small wooden wardrobes instead of closets. The toilet was in a separate room from the bathroom, and it flushed with a pull chain from a high wooden cistern.

Two other teachers arrived to prepare food for us, so my husband and I were unable to express our shock. My private thought was that we could never live here with two children, but I held back my tears until everyone had left.

Numbly, we sat around the table and sampled our first high tea. Platters of fish paste sandwiches and buttered bread were passed. Slices of fruitcake were passed. Slices of sponge cake were passed. A pot of tea was brought out from under a quilted tea cozy. My husband hated tea. The children had never drunk tea. But we all took what was handed to us. Todd, aged eighteen months, cried and was put to sleep in one of the freezing bedrooms. He didn't seem to mind the straw mattress or the dingy green quilt I put over him.

The next morning, we looked in *The Yorkshire Post* for rental listings. There were none. After the war, the housing problem in England was desperate for a full generation. So we agreed we would stay in this house for a few weeks, until we could figure out what to do.

Our four-year-old daughter, Jan, started at the village infant school. Every morning, my husband, Lenny, took the train, still pulled by steam engine, into Leeds for his own adventure. Because there was no refrigerator, I had to shop every day. Someone lent me a "pushchair" for Todd, and I began my daily rounds. In this way, I met the neighbors and the shopkeepers. Social life in the villages of the Yorkshire Dales was kept alive by the daily shopping ritual.

People started coming to our back door. Mrs. Crosby, the milk lady, pushed her cart there every morning, wearing brown carpet slippers because she had trouble with her feet. Twice a week, the butcher's assistant delivered meat on his bicycle. The coal man came. Smiling happily, he said we used more coal than anyone else in the village. We kept a fire going in the grate all day long, banking it at night. A coal fire is slow to start, slow to warm up a room, and very dirty. Everyone burned coal in 1958. The chimneys belched smoke that seeped into the houses and left black streaks on all the golden Yorkshire stone.

Neighbors came to the back door, too, introducing themselves and offering assistance. Alice Hudson, who lived next door in our semidetached villa, became our chief guide to village life. She worked as a barmaid at the Cow and Calf up on Station Road and knew everyone in Burley. It was Alice who taught me to ask for a "tuppence hapenny" stamp at the post office instead of saying "two penny, half penny" and bringing snickers from everyone in line. Taking Alice's advice, we bought woolen underwear at Marks and Spencer in Leeds and wore it constantly under our clothes, simply dressing for the outdoors indoors.

There were other visitors: the village window-washer, who invited my husband to join the Wharfedale Fishing Society, leading to jolly expeditions on the Wharfe River; the laundryman, who did our sheets and towels; Bobby Jones, the local police officer who rode over on his bicycle to see if we had "settled in"; a man from the British Immigration Service, who asked to see the "aliens"; children to play with our children.

Across the street, elderly Mrs. Thorne looked after Todd if I wanted to go to the nearby market towns of Otley or Ilkley. She brought out old greeting cards, on which he drew pictures, and served him milky tea and homemade scones. Mrs. Thorne rarely spoke to me about her past life, but in the course of the year I found out that she had lost a child of her own, been widowed, and worked as a nanny for several families.

A weekly back-door visitor for a while was Mr. Beaseley, a widowed insurance collector, whose two daughters played with our Jan. He had sandy hair and pale eyelashes and spoke in a thick Yorkshire accent. I served him American coffee and he helpfully explained how the National Health Services worked and told me about market days in the nearby towns. Then one day, with an intent look, he asked me if I wanted to go dancing Friday night at the Hare and Hounds. Had he taken my American animation for something else? I had to proclaim, "Mr. Beaseley, I am a happily married woman." After that, we talked only when he came to pick up his girls.

Lenny faced the hardest adjustment of us all. The twelve-year-old boys he taught had all failed the national education test then given to eleven-year-olds. A mere 10 percent of British students passed and went on to the elite grammar schools that prepared them for university. Lenny had imagined English schoolboys straight out of *Good-bye, Mr. Chips*. Instead, he saw the underbelly of the British class system, and the boys without futures came as a shock that strongly influenced him later on as a teacher and administrator.

But life at Langford was improving. The house was gradually filled with Penguin paperbacks, English magazines, and newspapers. We read *The Yorkshire Post* and the Wharfedale weekly newspaper. We listened to the BBC radio and watched BBC television. I laid some cheap linoleum on the kitchen floor. We bought an antique coal scuttle to take home and kept it by the fireplace. The children's toys spilled out of a box in the sitting room and my new blue-and-white dishes from Stoke-on-Trent sat on the sideboard.

Running up and down the stairs, walking to the shops, doing clothes in a wringer-style washer, hanging them on wooden racks, bringing in coal from the shed, I was in better shape than ever before. I lost ten pounds despite all the sponge cakes and Cadbury chocolate biscuits I devoured.

At night, we had high tea instead of dinner. We came to like tinned tongue and fish paste and even developed a taste for Spam, which the English adored. Lenny had lunch every day with his students and learned to drink hot tea with milk and eat hot custard sauce on every dessert. Sometimes we made enchiladas for friends who came to tea, using canned green chiles sent by our neighbors in New Mexico.

We became a tight family unit. We spent hours together in the little sitting room. We ate there, we talked there, Todd got toilet trained there on a blue china potty, we watched television there, we dried the clothes there in front of the fire, we entertained there. The rest of the house was too cold to venture into, except for sleeping. There was no privacy that year. If anyone wanted to be alone, well, they just couldn't.

One night, I watched the children lying on the rug close to the coal fire. They were snug in Dr. Denton's sleepers with the feet attached, and their faces shone in the firelight. Jan was talking about a nature walk she had taken with her class. Lenny was grading papers. It seemed to me we were amazingly resilient to be here at all. I marveled at us and poked the fire so it sprang up brighter.

The children called me Mum now, and they spoke with Yorkshire accents. Jan said "Good show," when Todd used the training potty for the first time. Todd pleaded for "sweeties" when I took him to the shops.

Months had passed since I had looked in the newspaper for rental ads. Langford had become home. Weekends we drove up and down the Dales in our secondhand Mayflower Triumph, exploring the Brontës' house in Haworth, picnicking at Bolton Abbey, having tea at the houses of new friends.

Before we knew it, it was summer. In June and July in north Yorkshire, daylight lasts until midnight and the dawn begins at 3:00 A.M. The children refused to sleep. They leaned out the second-floor window and called down to their playmates.

Suddenly it was August and we were standing on the front stoop with fifteen pieces of luggage, waiting for a friend to drive us to Liverpool, where we would catch our ship to America. The neighbors stood in their yards watching. Mrs. Thorne was crying. Our adventure was over.

Recently, I found a folder of letters I wrote to friends that year and they made me weepy for days. I started dreaming of Burley-in-Wharfedale at night. It isn't only the remembered picturesqueness of village life that moves me, or the sweetness of our neighbors. It is also the sharp memory of how young and optimistic we were, and how self-sufficient as a family. All we needed was one another to rise above the hardships and sustain the adventure. We felt that Yorkshire had been created for us, and that we would never grow old or die. The world beckoned in a timeless, limitless way that is lost to us now.

How glad I am that there had been no rentals in Leeds and that we spent the year in Langford. What we experienced was the day-to-day life of ordinary people in an English village. Underneath the grime, despite the cold, we had found a real home, and we had found each other in a way that will last all our lives.

Formentera Spring

he island of Formentera, the
smallest of the Balearics, lies off the Mediterranean coast of Spain, partway
to North Africa. For three and a half months in 1967, it was my home, and
although I have lived in different places since—and for much longer periods
of time—my stay in Formentera has come to occupy a disproportionately
large space in my memory.

For one thing, it was the first time I lived in a house that was my
own. As a college senior at McGill University, I had lived alone in a rented
room in Montreal, but this was a real house—not a suburban bungalow like
the one I had grown up in but an isolated farmhouse in open country. More
important, it was on Formentera where, as a just-graduated architect full of
dreams and ambitions, I first experienced what Louis I. Kahn called "the
essence of architecture."

It happened like this:

I had come to the Balearics in early spring, attracted to Mediterranean islands by memories of an earlier visit to Crete. I landed on Ibiza, a short boat trip from Valencia, where I had left my car. It was my intention to spend several days on Ibiza and then return to the mainland and resume my journey. This was my *wanderjahr*. After graduation, I had worked for seven months in a Montreal architect's office, had taken a freighter from Quebec City to Hamburg, and had traveled from there through Holland and France to Spain. After Ibiza, I had vague plans to drive to Greece.

Ibiza was a disappointment. The tall stucco houses surrounding the harbor were attractive, but the narrow, climbing streets were packed with visitors, many from the cruise ship anchored offshore. This ancient fortified town founded by the Carthaginians and invaded and occupied in turn by Romans, Vandals, the Byzantine Empire, Normans, Arabs, and lastly Catalans, was now firmly in the grip of German and English tourists, judging from the fashionable shops and restaurants. It was not what I was looking for.

It was early Saturday morning and I thought of how I would kill the rest of the day until I could catch the overnight ferry back to Valencia. I walked down to the harbor and along the stone quay. There were several boats tied up to rusting bollards, and a holiday crowd: townspeople, tourists, fishermen, yachtsmen. Out of the corner of my eye I caught sight of a tall, striking girl. She wore loose, patterned clothing and strode purposefully down the quay, her long, fair hair streaming behind her. She certainly didn't look Spanish. Perhaps a Californian or a Swede? She had the aplomb of beautiful women everywhere.

I watched her turn and jump aboard a large motor launch. When I reached the launch, I saw there was a battered, hand-painted sign attached to the handrail: M/N JOVEN DOLORES IBIZA-FORMENTERA 17 PESETAS. It was a ferryboat, apparently going to somewhere called Formentera—which couldn't be far since it cost about a dollar. I had no intention of approaching the beautiful Californian—I was too shy for that—but the scruffy *Young Dolores* appealed to me: It was exactly the sort of boat tourists would avoid. I too jumped aboard, carrying a canvas bag with my belongings. Five minutes later, the launch headed out of the harbor and turned toward the low, gray headland of a small island.

This was only the first of several chance events that day. After the boat docked at a rather forlorn wharf, I decided to find a village where I could get something to eat and a room for the night. There was no bus or taxi (in fact, there was only a handful of cars on Formentera), and most people simply walked away, including the beautiful Californian, whom I never saw again. I bought a soft drink from a stall and set off up the road.

The island was flat and extremely rocky, and the only vegetation appeared to be cacti and occasional olive groves. There were stone walls everywhere, and many isolated farmhouses, but nothing that looked like a village. (The chief village of the island—San Francisco Javier—was actually nearby, but I had taken a wrong turn.) The road was dusty and the March sun unexpectedly hot, and after more than an hour I became tired and sat down. My adventurous mood was flagging.

I saw two people approaching; they must also have come on the launch. We exchanged greetings. Michel and Maryvonne were Parisians. His surname was Mendès-France, a famous French family; I later learned that he was the son of the ex-prime minister. I spoke French, and perhaps because of the shared language (and French, the language of diplomacy, is particularly suited to socializing), or through politeness, they invited me to join them. They were heading for a beach which they had been told was nearby.

At the end of the afternoon, we went to a bar in a hamlet called San Fernando. Michel was to meet some French acquaintances here who had reserved a house nearby for a month. He told me they had changed their minds. Perhaps I would be interested, he said offhandedly; I don't think he was serious. But I was. Through fatalism—or was it just laziness?—I felt drawn to Formentera. Anyway, I had no pressing commitments and this austere landscape appealed to me.

By early evening, the friends arrived, a deal was struck, and I had become a householder. I invited Michel and Maryvonne to stay with me— it seemed like small repayment for their mediation—and they did so for two days before leaving. When I returned home after seeing them off on the motor launch to Ibiza, I had a brief moment of panic—What was I doing in this desolate place? Alone. Alone in my house.

The interior was dark, lit only by candlelight. (There was no electricity on the island except for a few public buildings that had generators.) There was very little furniture: several Lilliputian chairs, a couple of benches that did double duty as tables, and the bedsteads. White walls, devoid of adornment, completed the decor. To most people it would have appeared spartan and bare, but to a young architect who admired Le Corbusier and had been trained in the severe aesthetic of modernism, it was perfect.

In truth, it was probably the architecture of the Formentera houses more than anything else that had precipitated my decision to stay. It was not picturesque in the way of the white, sculptural villages of Aegean islands, or dramatic like the steep hillside constructions of Portofino. But I always found the picture-postcard beauty of such places slightly intimidating. The plain stone houses of this stony island were different. They had a quality that was found in the best of Hemingway's writing—which is what had brought me to Spain in the first place. Like Hemingway's stories, the Formentera houses were spare and unsentimental but oddly affecting.

This appeal was derived from clarity rather than contrivance, from satisfying function rather than from adding embellishment. The house I was in—my house—was almost childishly simple. The square plan was divided in two by a wall that supported the roof ridge. On one side was a long room resembling a medieval hall with a huge fireplace at one end; the space on the other side of the wall was further divided to make two equal rooms for sleeping. Outside there was a porch, and off it, an outbuilding containing the kitchen—a small, windowless room with some metal plates and utensils and a kerosene stove. One wall of the kitchen was dominated by a huge bread-making oven that I never dared to try.

The materials and construction were equally straightforward. The thick stone walls—thick enough to contain cupboards and niches—were plastered and whitewashed, inside and out; they were surmounted by a shallow, clay-tiled gable roof. The natural bedrock, which was at the surface, provided both foundation and floor. The small windows had no glass, only shutters; a pair of sturdy wooden doors led into the large room.

From the owner, a middle-aged woman to whom I paid the rent, I learned that the house was called C'an Pep Ferrer and had been built in 1884 by settlers from the mainland. It was basically a version of a common Catalan farmhouse, and was distinguished from the older houses of Formentera chiefly by its use of a pitched roof. The older houses, which dated from as early as the sixteenth century, had flat roofs. A curious feature of these houses was that different rooms had ceilings of different heights, the largest room being the tallest. This produced a staggered effect on the exterior, as if the houses were a assembled from different-sized boxes. They reminded me of some Cubist paintings.

Flat roofs in traditional buildings, whether in Casablanca or Taos, are always an indication of a lack of rain. This was the case with Formentera. Despite the fact that the Romans had named it Frumenteria, or "place of grain," through erosion and weather changes the island has become rocky and dry. In 1235, just after Spain took Formentera from its Arab occupiers, it was completely depopulated by a drought and remained so for almost a century. Throughout the Middle Ages, Formentera suffered periodic abandonment. The last great drought had been in 1823 and had destroyed the vineyards as well as the crops. Dry weather was a particular problem for the inhabitants because they depended on the scant rainfall for their water supply; there were no springs or streams. Each house had an underground cistern, laboriously carved from the solid bedrock.

The Formentera houses fascinated me. They looked so simple, yet the longer I stayed there, the more I grew to appreciate their somber beauty. What was it that made them feel so right to be in? They were all more or less similar—the roof shapes were the chief difference—yet each house had its own character. This was not architecture as I had been taught it; there seemed to have been no interest in originality. Nevertheless, as an architect I could not help but admire the results. I even started to admit to myself that these untutored builders might be able to teach me a thing or two.

But what? I was beginning to feel that there was a secret here to be unraveled. I started to walk around the island, sketching the old buildings, many of which were abandoned. I asked questions in my broken Spanish and made notes about construction methods and materials and island history. One house, called Es Castell, resembled a little fortress, with high-placed, tiny apertures. Pedro, the owner, told me that it had been built in the sixteenth century to resist the periodic raids of Berber pirates. A hundred years later, Spanish military engineers built five circular stone towers that dotted the coast of the island and served as platforms for signal fires to relay advance notice of approaching pirate ships to Ibiza.

I also made measured drawings of the houses: plans, cross sections, facades. It was while doing this that I came to realize that there was an underlying order to the size of things. Everything in the house, whether it was the width of the door, or the height of a windowsill, or the depth of a niche for storing water jugs, was dimensioned according to its function. A door was just wide enough and high enough for a person to go through, and no more. Ceilings were ten feet in the main room, eight feet in the bedroom, seven feet in the kitchen; niches were at different heights, depending on their function. A low wall beside the outdoor porch made a convenient place to sit. It was as if the houses had evolved over the centuries to fit the activities of their human occupants and become a sort of architectural clothing. This was my small discovery: that the essence of architecture—or at least of this architecture—was nothing less than its humanity.

As a student, I had built cardboard models and made abstract drawings, but in Formentera, I realized that buildings were always an intimate part of a particular place. Or, as I wrote in my diary: "The rock upon rock, a house. To build a house means to rearrange the rocks, and from the rearrangement, shade, coolness, rest. But remember that 'house' meant something to the Formentera fisherman—antagonists of the sea, of the pirates, of the sun—that it cannot mean for us."

By this time, the month I had decided to spend on the island had come and gone; it never occurred to me to leave. My lease ended and I moved to another house and continued my sketching and measuring. I met a Parisian who owned a piece of land on the island and who commissioned me to design a small house, which allowed me to put some of my new architectural lessons into practice. I took up wood sculpting. I made friends with a British painter and through him met other expatriates. I fell in and out of love with a willful Frenchwoman.

Eventually, my Formentera spring came to an end. I had to force myself to leave lest I stay forever. The motor launch took me to Ibiza and I retraced my steps to Valencia (where, of course, my car had disappeared) and thence to Paris. The journey back was uneventful.

Sentimental
Education

or two weeks, I scoured the
Paris dailies and queued up for one overpriced, undersized apartment after
another. Not until I chanced on the American Center's bulletin board did
the city yield what I was desperately seeking: *Studio d'artiste, Quartier Latin,
1,400Fr.*

As a graduate student in French literature, I could populate the
limestone building at 8 rue Pierre Curie with characters from nineteenth-
century novels just by looking at its garlanded facade. My twenty-two-year-
old heart pounded at the thought of a whole year among the rooftops in the
cradle of French culture.

I entered a tall, aristocratic foyer, loped up a winding wooden staircase (polished with beeswax to a squeak), and arrived at the second-floor
landing, where I rang at an intimidating set of carved twelve-foot-high doors.
Madame Villette—tightly wound and fiftyish—greeted me in two-hundred-

134

mile-an-hour French, gathered her keys, and charged up five flights, saying in several equally uncharming ways that I really shouldn't take the apartment if I couldn't afford it. I had sized up the facade; she had sized up my blue work shirt and jeans. It was the height of the sixties.

After four years of college dorms, anything that wasn't a box would have seemed exotic, but just beyond the small entry lay a space that would excite anyone—brightly lit with a tall ceiling that sloped up steeply to a roomwide skylight. Through it I could glimpse the serene lantern dome of the nearby Panthéon. Perfect for any self-respecting nineteenth-century consumptive and her tenor, the room was also modern in its openness and angularity. Next to the fireplace, a low doorway led to a narrow bedroom under the front mansard; a small kitchen (I had never cooked a meal in my life) led to a cozy bath. Through its windows, the history of Paris seeped into the apartment. I wondered who had painted and written and loved in this studio.

Before I knew it, I had committed to the full price. The apartment was mine. Madame left me alone there with the key and I exulted. One rarely realizes when life takes a turn, but clearly this was a commencement. I could see myself going to sleep under the night sky. I plotted my paths to the Sorbonne—the direct way down the rue St. Jacques, the historic way by Eglise Ste. Geneviève, the fashionable one down the Boulevard St. Michel. It was not so much that this was my first apartment but that its romantic character strummed my imagination.

I immediately expanded my French vocabulary at the hardware store. To my surprise, a previously unknown urge to decorate seized me: With Madame's blessing and her agreement to pay for the paint, I would shape the space with color, bringing out the existing architectural features. These were the first stirrings of a design impulse that two years later would land me in architecture school. I might be finishing a master's degree in French literature in this apartment, but its haunting spaces kicked my right hemisphere into gear.

I chose what-the-hell colors—an Yves Klein electric blue in the entry and a dark green soured by lime in the bedroom. I painted the main room what the French call a "broken white"—pure white shaded with pigment—and picked out the two beams crossing the lofty studio in black. I found a pair of gold bedspreads at Galeries Lafayette for the two daybeds and arranged them in a conversational L around a twenty-liter drum, which I turned upside down and painted Klein blue.

The tall, spare space triggered rumination as much as a dim gabled attic loaded with trunks would have. In the midst of painting a wall I would lapse into deep daydreams, as though my eye, without any objects to look at, simply rolled back and peered into my mind. On some days, I discovered, the studio seemed a bowl of light, and anything in the sky, whether the luminous blue of the Paris twilight, a passing cloud, or even an airplane, registered on the walls. In a space that wanted to stay simple and pure, I rewound a five-franc coil of wire from the hardware store into a shiny orbital sculpture.

The small undercounter refrigerator assumed I would make daily trips to neighborhood shops for fresh provisions. It dawned on me that I could take my meals into my own hands, and I discovered the *charcuterie*, the *boulangerie*, and the *pâtisserie*. I had an oven. All I needed was a match.

Soon an older woman entered my life—she was all of thirty-two—and she remarked that *bananes flambées* were very easy to prepare: sweet butter, bananas, sugar, cognac, all spritzed with lemon. I bought ripe bananas, went home, melted the butter, poured on the cognac and, not without hesitation, torched it. Buoyed by success, I went on to flame other fruits and then started combining them with reckless originality—and often sorry results.

With the American dollar still strong in the sixties, I had an advantage over French students for whom my apartment, though hardly luxurious, was unaffordable. The gentrification of Paris was eliminating artists, writers, and students from most historic districts, including the Latin Quarter. Hemingway's loosely structured bohemia of casual encounters and moveable feasts was a distant memory. My place became a way station for friends passing through (I learned from one how to avoid the draft; mine is the Vietnam generation), and I decided to share it more frequently with classmates. I invited some friends over for my first sit-down dinner.

Seven guests arrived on a Saturday night. The wine was breathing, the candles flickering, and the moon wended its way across the skylight, casting shadows. I planned the dinner as a four-course procession that would draw out conversation, which I increasingly savored in this intensely verbal city.

To my surprise and relief, the pepper steak *flambé* tolerated a large margin of error and even flamed on cue. I remember thinking, "This isn't so difficult." I glided through the endive salad, and went on to dessert. Nobody pointed out the culinary faux pas when I again pulled out the cognac to flame blood oranges. I wasn't trying to show off; igniting food was the only way I knew how to cook.

At home in suburban Pasadena, and then in college, everything had been handed to me; all I had to do was read, take tests, devour food, and hit the tennis ball with topspin. Now, while I was reading Flaubert's *L'Education Sentimentale* about a child's development into an adult, my apartment was leading me through rites of passage—decorating, cooking, entertaining— bringing me into a larger life.

But unlike rooms in many British novels that are worlds in them- selves, populated with books, paintings, and deep sofas, my minimally fur- nished aerie was really an antechamber to Paris. The city drew me into its highly magnetic field.

The first stop was obvious—the café. James Baldwin wrote in *Giov- anni's Room* that cafés provided people living in tiny apartments with the living rooms they didn't have. True: Even without speaking to anyone or making eye contact, I felt a social warmth in cafés, with tables and chairs grouped so that everyone seemed part of a company. But I also found cafés fascinating as spaces, especially those decorated with mirrors that doubled and tripled all the movement of Parisian streets, breaking the city into a real- time Cubist canvas.

At La Coupole, I watched Sartre dunk his morning croissant and tried it myself: soggy. I puffed on a few Gauloises. No one I knew really had the time to hang out for hours in cafés—not even students—but I certainly paused long enough to soak up Parisian sociology and fashion. Women walked in a structured, brisk way, their high heels clicking smartly. Men often ambled with jackets over their shoulders—a habit I affected.

The Cinémathèque on the rue d'Ulm around the corner from my apartment offered another kind of education and a special thrill when the films pictured the same streets I walked daily. In an upstairs room at the Foyer International on the Boulevard St. Michel, I heard Alain Robbe-Grillet read passages from his latest *nouveau roman*. When I was in college, Robbe- Grillet had been a distant and mythic figure found on book covers. In Paris, wearing a nondescript gray jacket and looking pallid, he seemed surprisingly ordinary, but his simple tangibility was, for me, extraordinary. I was no longer learning about something somewhere else, something that had always been a book or a movie or a painting away. I was *here*. The Latin Quarter was dense and palpable; Paris was proximity. Street names alone were a history lesson.

My sentimental education was not only verbal. My eyes drank in the architectural proportions of elegant French windows. I learned to follow a horizontal cornice line on its path across the columns and pilasters of a classical facade. I discovered the Latin Quarter had two dominant urban histories and two scales—the medieval one with the meandering streets, and the imperial nineteenth-century one with straight avenues plowing through the older, tighter fabric. Trees everywhere united the streetscape, softening the facades, giving the city the intimacy of a low and leafy canopy.

The city and my apartment absorbed my attention so much that my thesis—"The Composition of Decomposition in the Novels of Beckett"— migrated to the back burner.

Was it Apollinaire who shaved off his hair in Paris, making himself unpresentable so that he could work? How would *I* force myself to work? By April, the due date of the thesis was fast approaching and I realized I had to send myself into exile to finish. I arranged for a dormitory room in Poitiers where, with all my notes arrayed in front of me, I wrote my thesis flat out in a little less than two very intense weeks.

The day I returned to Paris, an American friend living on the stuffy Right Bank called, anxiously reporting that the Sorbonne was occupied. I quickly walked there and found groups of students camped out by the pale Puvis de Chavannes murals in the grand Richelieu Court.

These were the first rumblings of the famous Events of May, which paralyzed Paris and France and nearly toppled the Gaullist government. My apartment sat on the lip of the volcano. Around rue Pierre et Marie Curie (Marie had been added during the year), students erected barricades of granite cobblestones pulled from the street. Opposite my apartment at the Institut Pasteur, Eisenstein's *Ten Days That Shook the World* and *Battleship Potemkin* played over and over. With my thesis finished, I plunged into the crowds and debates. As an American, I remained a witness more than a participant, but I identified completely with my contemporaries and took my place behind the lines.

The Events really started as a kind of intellectual, urban sport, the students complaining about authoritarian institutions from government to school to job, and about the emptiness of consumer culture. At first, Parisians threw fruit to the students in the streets from their balconies, and refreshed them with water cast from pitchers, a surprisingly benevolent act similar to sprinkling flowers. The youthful camaraderie carried up to local residents, who were basically the same people, only older. For a while, what the government called riots were simply crowds of youths flowing through the streets not doing any harm. The very word *barricades* conjured up the romantic heroism of past revolutions in the same quarter.

Tensions escalated. Several store windows were smashed, and in an especially sad moment, the crowds pulled down a couple of the great trees along the Boulevard St. Michel. I was ashamed. The government, hesitant to respond to the provocations for fear of inciting a confrontation, finally called out its attack-dog police force—the CRS. We all took positions behind the barricades. Traffic was nonexistent, but in the middle of the night, with the City of Light blacked out, our faces reflected the colors of traffic lights implacably clicking red, green, yellow, red, green, yellow.

There was a sense of exhilaration and freedom along with the constant threat of a police assault. Leaving my girlfriend's apartment late one night, I headed up the street only to run headlong into students bolting my way, chased by the CRS shooting tear gas. A canister fell nearby and the gas lodged behind my contact lenses, stinging like acid. Eyes shut, I groped my way out, feeling the facades like Braille until I reached the nearest corner. I narrowly escaped being bludgeoned—and repatriated.

Like the Sorbonne, the national theater, the Odéon, was occupied by students, and it became Paris's largest parlor. In the darkened house with an empty stage, speakers harangued one another from the first balcony to the third, the second to the orchestra. Through friends I had met Mary McCarthy earlier in the year; she was then writing *Birds of a Feather*. When I invited her to the theater, she jumped at the chance of a student escort into the fray. From our seats we listened to eloquent and spontaneous orations. Sartre himself spoke at the Sorbonne to a huge young crowd craving leadership, but he deferred to the students. Events had superseded him.

The revolution gained momentum with worker support, and soon intensified into real riots. One evening, outside my building, I encountered a handful of students fleeing in my direction. I motioned them into the foyer and we moved quickly and silently up the staircase and locked the door, breathless. We didn't turn on the lights for fear of giving ourselves away.

The flames from burning cars reflected off low clouds through the wide skylight, casting unearthly shadows and setting every face aglow, as though we were sitting around a campfire. We went to the kitchen window and peered over the roofline. The CRS swept down the street behind their shields and we could hear bottles crashing around them. One of my guests threw an empty wine bottle. I worried that we would be caught and I worried for the police amid the shattering glass. But they turned a corner, and we moved back into the studio and sat down to coffee and wine. No one dared leave. For hours we talked, intense and serious. The sense of history that previously entered through the windows had this time run up the stairs and through the door. That night probably ranks among the studio's finest hours.

It was to be my last student soirée there. Summer occurs abruptly and unmistakably in the Latin Quarter, and what de Gaulle's government could not resolve, vacation did. We all drifted off. I had to resume courses back in the United States and confront the draft problem. I closed up the apartment, and with it, the year. I left behind my orbital wire sculpture. I surrendered the keys to Madame Villette who with a brisk handshake thanked me for paying my rent on time, even in May.

ELAINE GREENE

The Palazzo Years

ne Saturday night in August a few decades ago, my spirits were so corroded by envy that I walked out of a party to sit behind a tree in the backyard and cry. It was Europe envy. Several of the other guests—friends my age but richer—were comparing notes on their trips abroad that summer: the marvelous little towns in the Cotswolds they were clever enough to find, the terrifying hairpin turns on the Amalfi Drive, the delicious puréed-plum baby food you could buy in France.

At the time, I was a hardworking housewife in a small Brooklyn apartment with a husband and two sons, four and eight. We lived on a single salary and we didn't have two cents to spare for travel. A Bermuda honeymoon was as far afield as we had ever gone.

My guardian angel must have taken pity on me in the backyard that night because one week after the party my husband called to say that his company had offered him a chance to work in Rome for a few years. They

141

would transport the four of us and house us in a *pensione* for a month while we found a home. We would have six weeks to get ready. I said yes immediately and never looked back, even though something like stage fright woke me every day at dawn from then on.

Twelve weeks after the party, I was crying again, this time in the bathroom of a splendid apartment we had the great good fortune to find. It was in a Renaissance palazzo in Old Rome, between the Pantheon and the Tiber—the best part of town, although I had not yet recognized that fact. I was ricocheting off still another culture shock; naturally I had them all day long. This one was an encounter with our stout, middle-aged Neapolitan maid, Ascenza, about our dinner. She showed me a bowl of tiny, whole, big-eyed, silvery fish—dozens and dozens of them—indicating that she was going to flour and fry them as they were.

I consulted my dictionary because I had a question. *"Occhi?"* I asked. (Eyes? Meaning, Do you really think I am going to eat all those eyes?) *"Occhi,"* Ascenza answered grinning, and dug her thumb into one of the eye sockets so that a long string of black slime hung off the little head. She laughed loudly to encourage me, but I ran down the hall to the bathroom, my shoes making a soft clicking sound on the old hexagonal terra-cotta tiles.

I think I was the only one in the family who was homesick. My husband had a regulated life doing familiar work, and for the children, home was where *we* were. I relied on them for that. The first night we slept in the palazzo, when every sight and sound and smell was alien to me, I went into the boys' room twice to look at them, sleeping trustingly under the afghans their grandmother had made them and—they never knew it—making me feel safe.

The boys jumped right into life in Rome. The first week at the American school, our elder son, to whom I would never read *Grimm's Fairy Tales* because they were so violent, came home to teach us a new game. "I'll be Perseus and you be Medusa," he said, with head-lopping whacks of a make-believe sword. That same week, our little one demonstrated his skills in Italian schoolyard fighting (many Italian children attended the American school, especially in the early grades). *"Lascia, lascia, è la mia,"* he would say to his brother, grabbing his toys (Let go, let go, it's mine).

My husband and I were taking Italian lessons twice a week—we did that till we left Rome—but I could see I would be linguistically crippled for a long time. The children's school was largely conducted in English, and so was my husband's office. I was the one in the trenches, trying to find the

words to buy a pair of socks or a needle. It was my appearance in the deli-
catessen that stopped all business as the clerks leaned over the counter to
hear what came out of my mouth, my task to give instructions to Ascenza
("The thing most important is the to be clean," is the equivalent of one
sentence I'll never forget).

It rained all or part of almost every day for our first three months—
Rome-style two-way rain that comes down so hard it splashes back up at
your skirt hem from the cobblestones—and it was chilly indoors. The eigh-
teen-foot ceilings in the palazzo dwarfed me: It seemed I could only feel right
in the eight- or nine-foot rooms I was used to. When we visited St. Peter's,
I complained that it was a railway station and inferior to any good New
England meetinghouse.

Still I tried hard to feel the excitement of Rome. I would go to the
place—not far from our house—where Caesar was assassinated and silently
chant to myself, *Julius Caesar Julius Caesar Julius Caesar.* Nothing would
happen. My imagination was dead. I had never been without it before and
the loss was like a curse.

Then in mid-January the curse began to lift—on my birthday, three
months to the day after we got off the boat in Naples. The rainy season had
ended and the sun was out. Climbing the Spanish Steps, I noticed the historic
marker on John Keats's house. It said he had died there on February 23,
1821, and I thought, "Oh, the poor boy, how cold he must have been." My
imagination was back! And not through some ancient Roman evocation after
all, but through a tragic, recent (by Roman measure) young poet.

Two weeks later, there was another birthday—our older boy's ninth.
We told him we would spend it wherever he liked and he chose the Colos-
seum. You could go to the top level in those days, a broad grassy terrace
more like a sheltering room than the arena down below. No one else was
around. The boys played with their father while I curled up in the sun on a
big hollowed-out stone and fell asleep. I woke up thinking *Where am I?* and
then I saw. Gratitude and bliss flooded my mind, and Rome became home.

I grew to fit all the extravagances there, including our high ceilings—
grew to feel worthy and deserving of Rome. Like thousands of foreigners
over the centuries, I came to believe that Rome belonged to me. Exclusively.
I loved the details of our daily life. One lovely act was pushing open the
louvered wooden outside shutters every morning, letting in the city: the swifts
wheeling and shrilling in the brilliant blue sky, the operatic bustle in the
narrow cobblestone street off the piazza as the neighborhood shopkeepers

and market vendors went to work, greeting one another with that full-throated Roman cry, *ah-OH*; the Baroque church across the piazza filling our windows with a view of huge expanses of travertine—niches, pediments, pilasters, a dome, a lantern.

Our simple, beautiful, faded-ocher palazzo was built smack on the street in the 1480s—before Columbus, we used to marvel—and has stood there ever since, through all the glory and havoc and ordinariness of history. Simply walking into it was a pleasure. In summer, you would come from the brightest, hottest sunlight into the deepest, coolest shade through double doors that were high enough and wide enough to admit a large carriage drawn by two horses. Ten steps into the building under the stem eye of the *portière* and you were in a private world, protected and privileged. Past a wall studded with fragments of ancient sculpture was our elevator, an ornate freestanding cage from the turn of the century that still bore, in a little frame, printed instructions prohibiting its use by servants. The instructions were dated XIII—thirteen years after Mussolini had taken power and named his accession the year one. Of the almost infinite layers of history in Old Rome, that too has to be counted.

A bloodthirsty 1911 guidebook that we bought secondhand told of "an oubliette lined with sharp pointed instruments" that had been uncovered when the elevator was installed. In it lay "a mass of skeletons," one in armor with a dagger thrust deep into the helmet. We also read that the halls of our palazzo were walked nightly by the ghosts of two cardinals (their Berniniesque busts framed our apartment doorway). Members of the family that had built the palazzo and held it until well into this century, the cardinals were tormented by a matricide that had taken place in it—a marchesa murdered in the sixteenth century by her two sons because she refused to name them her heirs. My two sons found that fascinating, of course.

Like most palazzos (the word means palace or any large residential or government building), ours contained stores on the ground floor (a pharmacy, a mattress maker). Our landlady the countess occupied the second and third floors with her family and servants, and on the fourth and fifth, there were offices (a branch of the University of Rome, a notary) and a few apartments. From our kitchen, we could see the countess's kitchen with a gas stove and a wood stove. When I asked our maid the reason, she was surprised that I didn't know you need a wood stove to cook fish properly.

Our apartment had long been unoccupied so all the appointments, other than a few of our landlords' family antiques, were new—the beds and all seating slipcovered in a pleasant green cotton damask, the meter-thick walls painted a fresh creamy white (although there was a patch of fresco painting behind a new radiator that the painters missed but one of the boys spotted). We were also supplied with a new bathroom, and a bare-bones kitchen for a servant to use.

Why did I have a maid when I wasn't working? Because Rome was set up for that; when in Rome you *have* to do as the Romans do. There were no kitchen cupboards and the tiny refrigerator barely held one day's food; we never nibbled in the evening because there was nothing left in the house. The daily marketing took hours, with vegetables and fruit and fish sold in the Campo dei Fiori, our big open-air market, but chickens found in one shop, meat in another, cheese in a third, mushrooms somewhere else, and salt and sugar in two separate places. The laundry was done in the bathtub and dried on the roof terrace or, in rainy weather, draped on our tepid little radiators. The drudgery, had I undertaken it, would have been Brooklyn times ten.

And anyway, I liked being a signora, which literally means Mrs. and sociologically means lady. I wasn't in a Puritan society any more, where I had to labor to justify my existence. Being happy, that was my job (a very Italian attitude). During a brief moment in economic history—about twenty postwar years—it was possible to live like a baron in Italy on an untaxed average American salary. For the first time in my life, I had a dressmaker— two in fact, a cheap one and an expensive one—and a hairdresser. I went to classes at the Dante Alighieri academy, conducted in Italian for foreigners (meaning the teachers spoke slowly), where I studied literature and art history. I acquired some excellent guidebooks and tried to see all that was significant in Rome, although two years of almost daily touring—floating through narrow streets fragrant with coffee—was not long enough to finish.

Possibly the most subversive thing I learned when I was a signora is that while it had been fun in America to be told that I *am* a good cook, it was even more fun in Rome to be told that I *have* a good cook. She was Ascenza's replacement, Gisella, a Tuscan; finding her was another huge stroke of luck. She was an excellent housekeeper, the children liked her, and when she went out to do the daily marketing, she was better dressed than I usually was.

We had left New York with names and addresses of friends' friends in Rome and soon developed a social circle (new expatriates form alliances quickly). It included my husband's co-workers; movie people, some of them blacklisted out of Hollywood in the "Un-American Activities" hysteria; American Academy and Fulbright fellows; U.N. and State Department people; other parents from the boys' school. When my mother came to visit after six months, I was able to give her a ladies' luncheon with ten guests.

There were very few Italians in our circle—three, actually, all of whom we still see when we go back, all of them with an American or English family tie. Although we were friendly with some Romans, we learned that they do not invite outsiders into their houses—not even Italians from other families. But living among them was delightful anyway. Italians love life and they know it's short. They are not interested in making it perfect, just enjoyable on a regular basis. Part of the enjoyment is watching the human comedy. If Gary Hart had been a married Italian politician photographed with a party girl on his knee, he would have amused the nation for a day or two, then gone on with his career.

In time, we spoke Italian adequately, sometimes fluently. We never missed a chance to improve. Late one night there was a cinematic scene outside our window: a woman in a housedress loudly denouncing her grown son on the steps of the church. He said nothing, and the third person present, a *vigile*, the lowest order of policeman, just stood holding his bicycle and looking on in the harsh streetlight. The shouting finally woke me and I saw my husband at the window with the dictionary, looking up new words (*rascal, villain, pimp*).

We bought a small station wagon and crisscrossed the country on weekends and holidays, ranging as far as Venice and Sicily. One summer, we drove to Prague, another, to Holland. When we stood on the Janiculum, the hill overlooking the center of Rome, our elder son could name all the domes. His little brother became so acculturated that he used to yell *"Brutta figura"* (meaning, roughly, disgracefully inelegant) out the car window at women wearing slacks—not considered acceptable in those days. We were happy to think that all their lives, our sons would know that they can live anywhere, that people can be different and yet the same.

After we left, being homesick took on a new, reverse meaning for a while. Although my own country eventually became interesting to me again, the chance combination of a glorious day, an energetic street in an old neighborhood, and the sound of a Vespa can still stop my heart. When we go back to Rome every three or four years, I no longer feel the city belongs to me, but we make sure to pass "our house," and if we explain our connection to the *portière* he always lets us through the portals for a minute or two.

146

Husbands, Wives, and Homesteads

HELEN HENSLEE

Another Woman's House

lthough I always knew that my childhood home in North Carolina had not been built with my mother or me in mind, I loved it. So one day, when I was about five, it was with deeply wounded astonishment that I heard my mother, who was something of a stoic, suddenly cry out to me that she hated the house and all the furniture in it.

My father was a prosperous manufacturer of late middle age in 1930 when he married my mother, a pretty student nurse of twenty, and settled her in a small town in North Carolina in a house he had built for another woman.

The other woman had not lived to see the completion of the substantial structure with its green tile roof nor to receive delivery of the American Oriental carpets, heavy furniture, and dour draperies she had chosen. But everything had been dutifully put into place. So when my mother, newly

149

off the dirt farm of her own father, stepped along the arrow-straight front walk, up the stone steps between the big white columns, and through the broad front door—a bride—she moved into someone else's dream.

My father had married his first wife before the turn of the century, and in that relationship he was the farm boy and she came from money. Pictures of him taken at the time show that his face took on no more gravity for the camera than it wore in everyday life. His demeanor was serious, and in trade as well as at home he held his purse strings tight.

In our house, pictures of his first wife were not displayed.

During my childhood, my curiosity about this shadow of a woman who had furnished *my* home was constant, as my mother's must have been, but although I kept an ear out for whatever bits my father might happen to disclose, not many stories were forthcoming.

What *was* known was that my father had found his first wife very beautiful and took on a courtship almost biblical in its endeavor to win, wed, and handsomely support her. The couple had raised their two daughters and one son in a comfortable wood-frame house, but by the time their family was grown, my father's first wife, who had social ambitions, wanted something showier. They purchased a corner lot on one of the main residential streets of the thriving little Piedmont town and had plans drawn up for a traditional stone dwelling with wide oak moldings and generous-size rooms, including sun parlor, gracious stairs and hallways, three bedrooms, and two and a half baths. A two-story garage was constructed behind the main house of the same pale gray charcoal-flecked granite.

As the foundation was being finished, an opportunity arose for a local hostess to receive for tea, some months hence, a visiting contingent of Methodist bishops and dignitaries. My father's first wife most urgently wished this tea to serve as her housewarming event. To gratify her longing, my father, in an uncharacteristic gesture, opened his wallet to hire double crews of masons, plasterers, and carpenters. Hammers rang on the site for sixteen hours a day, and the housewarming seemed assured. However, this desire to shine may have been the undoing of my father's first wife, for even as the construction was drawing to a close, her excitable nature gave her no rest, and she died suddenly of a cataclysmic stroke.

For a time, my stunned father, in his grief, halted all work on the site. Two years later, well after the house had been finished, my father met my mother one Sunday in church. He spotted her fresh face with its high cheekbones and alert blue eyes during the sermon. Their courtship was brief.

He took the young woman on a merry round of restaurants, resort areas, and clubs, the sorts of places she had never seen and he seldom visited. After a wooing entirely out of character for both of them, they were married out of town and spent a brief honeymoon at an inn. My mother was now to be a full-time housewife. My father delivered her to her new home, which she had only once previously glimpsed.

It was not to her taste.

My mother had grown up surrounded by poor but honest country furniture: old washstands with pitcher and bowl, not for show but for use; a kitchen table big enough to seat ten children and their hardworking parents; quilts made by her mother and grandmother covering the beds; and rag rugs on the otherwise bare floors. One of the few things she brought with her into the marriage was a simple pine blanket chest made by her great-grandfather for her great-grandmother.

In her childhood home, there were country hardships. Food was prepared on a wood-burning stove—a blast furnace during summer canning time. Leftover ham from their own slaughtered hogs and baked sweet potatoes were kept in a food safe with vent holes punched in the thin tin doors. Butter and milk had to be cooled in a springhouse some distance from the main dwelling. And the toilet was an outhouse.

Of course the luxuries in her splendid new residence—electric stove and refrigerator, tile baths, cozy radiators in winter—were appreciated. It was the decorating that drove my mother wild.

She disliked the scratchy purplish plush that covered the living room sofa and chairs. The imitation Oriental rugs of that room appeared to her to writhe with creatures from the sea bottom. She told me that when she ate dinner seated at the dark mahogany dining room table, the gloomy matching pieces lined up against all four walls seemed to loom over her. On the other hand, if she served meals in the breakfast room with its one high window, she felt cramped.

The house, she pointed out to me, was filled with possessions accumulated by a woman thirty-five years her senior. There were gilded deer poised to leap on table tops, vases covered with paintings of flowers with which no earthly blossom could compete. One wall-hung etching drew her particular scorn. In it, a chunky maiden wearing a concocted Grecian dress was, with leaden gaiety, flinging a gauze scarf over the antlers of a stunned-looking moose.

There had been discussions with my father about replacing some of these possessions. But although it was clear that my father was not heedless of my mother's feelings, his frugality prevailed.

Given this impasse, my mother began to garden. The property was expansive. There were already beds of bulbs, handsome shrubs, various fruit trees, and, towering over all, six giant willow oaks. But my mother noticed the bare stone wall of the garage facing her as she did the dishes at the kitchen sink. In went a row of hollyhocks, and in front of those, Sweet William, ragged robin, and buttercups. She loved lily of the valley and these she planted across the yard under the pear tree to echo its white blossoms in spring.

And she began to sew. Colorful tablecloths and napkins brightened the dim breakfast room; needlepoint pillows softened the scratchy plush couch. A pair of walnut-framed botanical prints found for small change in an antiques shop replaced the moose and looked fresh and lovely on the wall.

At this time, my father's recreational delight was fishing. On weekends he took endless drives out into the countryside and up into the nearby mountains hoping to spot some chill haunt of rainbow trout where he had not yet cast a line. Often my mother went along. Her quick eye was not for icy streams but for old, locally crafted furniture.

Tilted against the side of a barn or thrown beside a shed, abandoned as old-fashioned and scorned by some farmer's wife, a seventy-five- or hundred-year-old cherry table or a walnut corner cupboard would sit among the weeds in wind and rain. Appealing to my father's frugality, she would implore him to stop and she would offer a few dollars for the discarded furniture and find some way to stuff it into the car. At home, she sanded, scraped, stained, polished. Invariably, my father's good-natured derision turned to open mouthed surprise when he saw the fine lines of the smooth finished piece. And because the price had been so modest, he could readily see a corner here or a wall there where the find looked perfect.

And so it went. The childhood and teenage depredations of my sister and myself eventually wore out the wool plush, snagged threads in draperies that had been made to wear like iron, and frayed first the carpet fringes, then the carpet itself—a period of time spanning doll buggies to lindy hops. Then my mother learned to upholster with the simple fabrics she loved, and to cut and line curtains, and at last experienced the delight of choosing her own rugs. Finally the great day dawned when my father accepted the fact that we were all too much for the small breakfast room. Down came a hated wall, in flooded the welcome light, and now hot biscuits and corn bread, fried chicken and rainbow trout, the garden's first tender green peas, and peach and cherry pies with fruit from the yard and crust as sculpted and rich as heaven's gate were enjoyed in a big family-style kitchen.

A home is, of course, a lifetime's work. It is often the creative result of a struggle between two people who have freely chosen to blend their lives but who couldn't possibly be more different in their points of view. I remember my father's final pride in his home, but I also remember bitter arguments and stubborn resistance on both sides all along the way.

It seemed to be the shared adventures that softened the differences. My father loved to tell about the time my mother found a tall, regal secretary with glass doors being used to store horse feed in a backwoods barn. She wanted it desperately, but there seemed no way to transport it over the rutted dirt path that led to the paved road. My father hit upon the notion that a mule-drawn sledge would do the trick, and so it did. Even more dramatically, he told of a cupboard discovered in the attic of a pre–Civil War house, its cornice nicked by Union Army bullets.

The appointing of the house did finally reach as close to a finished state as any lived-in house does. It was never so fixed, however, that a grandchild's toys or the framed snapshot of a daughter's growing family could not be accommodated.

Both my parents are gone now, and the furniture has been divided amicably between two households. My sister and I have homes at opposite ends of the country, she south, I north, but our visits to each other are made richer as we again admire the heartbreakingly lovely lines of old pieces made by practical hands for everyday use.

When my father found himself widowed again, for my mother died first, I recall that for days afterward, he wandered from room to room in the gracious home that she had made. From the kitchen to the hall to the dining room, he paced over the subtly patterned rugs, back and forth past her favorite tufted armchair, and paused to reflect over the warm gleam of the antique dining table. Everything was harmonious, everything was in order, everything was beautiful. Even so, my father said, he felt he was standing in a ruin.

MARYBETH   WESTON   LOBDELL

The Marrying Kind

have just received the blue-
prints for the new wing we are building. My mind is walking through the
plans sedately, entranced by the way the architect has translated our needs,
dreams, and what-ifs into sections and elevations. My mind is measuring and
checking, but my heart is racing up and down the stairs, in and out of rooms,
even jumping on the bed, like a puppy off a leash.

The two-story addition is a honeymoon wing, a place for my husband and me to be young to each other. It will also be a new space for
enjoying our children and grandchildren. The wing will be our retirement
center, too, with a sensible downstairs bedroom, two studies, and places to
make music, read, see home movies, watch birds in the garden, play games,
and roll back the rug for dancing. We are newlyweds in our sixties.

The wing will be attached to the house where I have lived for nearly
twenty-five years, twice as a widow. An old friend who allows herself to be

154

outspoken, as old friends are allowed to be, asks me if adding to this house is really a good idea: What about the memories, the risks?

Yes, my children grew up here and one of them still works here as a writer. Yes, I still feel the presence of the husbands I lost, and sometimes I talk to them. I am not as sure as my parents were that in an afterlife families will meet and recognize each other. But if we do, I think all jealousies will be washed away. Indeed, I can almost imagine my husbands (and children) talking music, news, and baseball, and laughing about how I never did learn to cook without burning something. The memories are complex but good ones.

My first husband and I both came from long-lived, long-married families. His parents had their golden anniversary the first year of our marriage; my parents followed suit and celebrated theirs, as had my grandparents. Because Bill was fourteen years older than I, we wasted no time. Within four years of marriage, we had two boys and a girl, and had moved into our first small house in the suburbs. He was at CBS; I was at *The New York Times*.

For a while, I stopped juggling and became a full-time mother with part-time writing assignments. By the time the children were in school all day and I was working again in the city, we moved to this larger house, one hour north of Manhattan. Bill was a big man and had the kind of personality that needed space. He needed a big kitchen; he loved to cook and he enjoyed shopping and preparing meals for our family of five, plus frequent guests. He liked big dogs, big books, a big desk, and had two walls for his elaborate music equipment, records, and tapes, all classical. He had a darkroom, and a screen for showing films to the children and for viewing documentaries as part of his work at home. At first, this house seemed much more his and the children's than mine, and sometimes I envied his domestic competence.

My bailiwick was my office in the city, where I was a magazine editor, the laundry room at home (I didn't cook then but I liked to iron and did most of the housework), and the garden, which I loved and which claimed all the leftover time our lively family and my job allowed. When we first bought this house, the only spot of shade was under a picnic table umbrella. Our two acres are now half wooded and we have herbs, wildflowers, a grape arbor, and places for croquet and badminton. Our daughter and her husband had a garden wedding here.

Then Bill died, ten years ago, during the night after a restful vacation day in my hometown in Texas. Death left no trace of alarm on his face, or in the way his hands curved on the sheet, but neither his great heart nor his newsman's curiosity could be awakened. He was buried in our family plot near my grandparents and mother. I had my name and birth date placed on the marker, too. I thought my life was over.

Three long years later, I was married again, to a man I adored and whom Bill and I had known decades before. At the wedding, my father gave me away as if I were a girl. My father had married again at eighty and he and his bride, then sixty-nine, were like a young couple. Their first Christmas card showed them on camels in Egypt, and they had thirteen adventurous years together. Their courage gave me courage about remarriage and about being a stepmother and friend to grown children.

It was in this house that Dad had met Lewis as a prospective son-in-law. He was amused that once again I had chosen and been chosen by a newsman who liked to cook and listen to music. On Lewis's first visit here, we rode bikes around the community lake and afterward, while I was changing, I suddenly heard a Mozart tape on the player and a percussion of pots and pans in the kitchen. It sounded so much like Bill at home that I burst into tears.

Lewis and I never really lived here. He was retired and we spent our first five months of marriage at his house on Cape Cod, swimming, biking, hosting friends and family, a life both romantic and familiar. We lived in Provincetown, or in his New York apartment. We rented my house to a young couple for several summers, and our families enjoyed it on fall and winter weekends.

The last months of our three years together were lived at the hospital, where Lewis battled cancer and where I slept in a chair or cot and went home to the apartment each morning to bathe and get messages, and to tell the portrait of his beautiful first wife, five years dead, that she could not have him.

His children and I grieved together at the nineteenth-century Cape Cod house Lewis had loved so. The next summer, his sister and I sadly sold it and sent the money and best furniture to his children. At his apartment, which I continued to rent, I packed up more things they would want (including the portrait) and bought what could not be shipped. When they visit, they still feel at home. I was glad I had not sold my own place and that my children could also come home. But two years down the road I still woke up crying, wherever I was.

You are so strong, friends said to me. Yes, I thought, strong like heavy dark andirons where fires no longer blaze.

By any measure, I was not alone. I never lacked for company, and I'm content with my own. Still I felt maimed, half of what I was. Life can be productive at any age, but the joy was lacking. Then a miracle: Close mutual friends introduced Leighton and me. He, too, was the marrying kind and wished for family life again. Within months, we had a church wedding with dancing afterward. We each have children in their thirties. I have three, Leighton has five, and all but two are married. Between us, we have thirteen grandchildren, so far. With an abundance of family and friends one to four hours away, we see our expanded house as their stagecoach stop, weekend retreat, and holiday gathering place.

The idea of adding to the house was born shortly before our marriage. Leighton, who has a city co-op but prefers country living, suddenly stopped playing the piano in my living room and asked, "Have you ever thought about breaking through this wall?" I was watering plants. Surprised by this gentle man's ungentle query, I froze in my tracks. "If we broke through the wall," he continued, "we could build a wing and connect it to this part of the house with a garden room. I don't want to live in your house. I want us to live in our house."

As I examine the blueprints today, I imagine stepping through the piano wall to a skylighted garden room with fragrant and flowering plants, then down two steps into our music–sitting room. It will have an L-shaped balcony and a curved bank of windows, floor to ceiling, that will spill squares of sunlight and moonlight onto a cherry floor.

A spiral staircase leads to two loft studies and a long view toward an open field and a windmill by the lake. In the foreground are tall pine trees planted twenty-five years ago. Leighton's electronic piano faces them. As a divorced man who had earlier divided some of the family pieces among his children, he brings a dowry to this marriage of things that have special meaning and that will suit the wing (and some of the original rooms) handsomely.

I am very aware how carefully, how respectfully, we must mingle our furnishings, books, and memorabilia. When I lived in my second husband's house on Cape Cod, I blithely set about making what I thought were loving changes, giving the place my own touch, perhaps putting on my own animal scent—an odd mix of Mr. Clean and Miss Dior. To my anguish, I saw in his face and heard in his voice what I should have known: that rearranging a room or pictures, even buying much-needed new curtains or dishes, must be done slowly, tactfully. Changes can imply criticism of a beloved person, or of possessions that in day-after-day loneliness have become dear companions. I wasted some beautiful Cape Cod days before I realized that time together was what he wanted, not housecleaning frenzies or shopping safaris or freshly ironed pillowcases.

House fixing will be easier this time because my husband and I will be building and decorating together, in our own new place, at his suggestion. Should two people take on a building project when they have known each other less than a year? Probably not. But we knew each other well enough to marry with clear-eyed certainty, and by building, we have come to know each other even better, in a hurry.

One brings a lot of self-knowledge and confidence to a marriage in later years. We are not new to family life or gardening or modest fix-ups. But having to talk about ceiling heights, window placement, preferences in wood grain, favorite colors and textures is drawing out memories we might not have shared. My delight in the spiral staircase in his apartment and in a house I once rented, his recollection of a summer library in Maine, influenced the design of the music room. Leighton's favorite shades of russet and green, which go back to his boyhood—Irish setter chums sleeping with him on a green rug by a hearth fire—will find their way into our home.

Shortly after our wedding trip, we had set up a joint building fund. We made legal arrangements that would be fair to our heirs (taking into account the unthinkable). We began interviewing architects and contractors. With no prior building experience—neither of us had ever selected a door-knob before—we find building together wondrously virginal. Our bathroom is the big surprise. Something small and simple, downright plain, we told the architect. What we learned about ourselves is that given half a chance to be hedonists, we just might. Because a bath has to start from bare tiles and we couldn't furnish it with anything old, we had to go shopping. What happened is that we ordered wildflower tiles, and a whirlpool tub big enough for two.

Having thought we had Puritan inclinations, we're also a little shocked that we're installing a small wet bar. As I recall, the conversation went something like this. She: "Wouldn't it be nice to have cold drinks here without walking all the way back to the kitchen?" He: "We wouldn't want a bar, would you?" She: "Of course not. A little refrigerator and sink behind a door." (Silence.) "For beer and wine." (Silence.) "Orange juice for the grandchildren?" He: "A juice bar, now that's a great idea."

The easiest rooms to furnish will be our studies. Leighton's desk is from his boyhood home in New Jersey; it was his father's. Mine was my mother's. We have ambitious plans, to write songs together, Leighton's music, my words. I know my musical mother would have liked that. We are not so sure that his father would have understood his son, a successful banker who upon retiring is becoming the musician he had wanted to be as a boy. Curious that a new wing can seem to have ghosts, just as an old house can.

I'm thankful that our bedroom will have some echoes of his parents' house—a rosewood dresser, a walnut chest. Alas, there will also be an array of electrical switches for a ceiling fan, wall lamps, and, of course, recorded music. I have never managed to fall in love with anyone who didn't need big speakers and miles of wires.

We are learning many new things together, even what to call the space that links the wing to the house. To avoid blocking upstairs cross-ventilation and light, the architect proposed a one-story connector. It's called a hyphen. It holds the garden room–passageway and has a double-width pocket door. On the blueprint, this looks like a practical way to separate the generations under separate roofs, and maybe it will be if weekending children and grandchildren stay up too late and loud (or if the grandparents do). But it may turn out to be the occasional center of the hubbub. Two granddaughters already see the area as a stage and the pocket door as the curtain, precisely as my sister and I did in our grandparents' parlor in East Texas.

I have a recurring dream in which I find new rooms in a familiar house, rooms I did not know were there. Now my dream is coming true. I see that a house can open its arms and grow, just as a heart can find room for another child, and sometimes, after pain and loss, can find room for new love. I see all this in the blueprints of our house.

Many couples our age choose to move away from where they lived and worked, if they have a choice, or to find a small place nearby. We prefer to be only one open door away from family and friends. We know how lucky we are to have survived grief and to have found each other. We know how blessed we are to have the health and means to build a larger house for a larger family. We hope it will be a spiritual magnet and bonding place for the next generations. Combining the first syllables of our first names, we call our home Maryleigh. We pronounce it "Merrily."

JACQUELIN C. DEVLIN

The Florida Dream

n 1951, when I was five and my sister was two, probably while we were outside making snow angels, my parents decided to leave Ohio and move to Miami. It was a paradise they longed for—warm weather, coconut palms, fruit to be picked from the trees, fish to be caught in the ocean. The islands in the bay beckoned them. Not to mention the lower cost of living.

In Florida, houses had no basements or attics, storm windows, or central heat. Cool terrazzo floors, jalousied doors, and Venetian blinds on the windows were the easy, carefree style down there. Carpets and draperies were kept to a minimum. Winter clothing could be dispensed with altogether. And it wasn't idle dreaming either; my parents had had a taste of it during the war.

Originally a farm girl from Delaware, my mother thought Army nursing would bring her adventure and excitement. Her sister Dorothy, also a nurse, had already enlisted and was having the time of her life in Puerto Rico, playing golf and going to formal balls when she was off duty. Later, she waded ashore with the best of them at Normandy.

It was more than my mother could bear. But when she signed up, she was sent to the Army Air Force Regional Hospital, formerly the Biltmore Hotel, in Coral Gables, Florida, an affluent suburb of Miami. Mom's claim to fame was meeting Eleanor Roosevelt when she came to console the wounded. And it was there that my parents met.

My father was an Army Air Corps pilot whose last flight over "The Hump" in Burma ended in an explosive crash. One of two survivors, he recovered under my mother's care with no more to show for it than a scar on his forehead and one arm that wouldn't extend completely. They were married in 1944 and rented an apartment close to the Biltmore.

The Biltmore had been (and is again) a grand hotel in the Spanish style, with Moorish and Italian accents. Its creamy stucco facade and tiled roofs rose above the royal palms, and its three-hundred-foot copper-clad tower, copied from one in Seville, stood out against the intense blue of the Miami sky. For my mother, it was the jewel in the crown of Coral Gables and she loved being there. Coral rock grottoes marked the widest boulevards, and magnificent banyan trees and lush tropical foliage made the town an oasis in marked contrast to the gritty, sun-scorched yards of the surrounding neighborhoods.

But after the war, they went home. They lived at first near the orchards of Mom's parents in Delaware, where Daddy attended agricultural school. A short time later, they bought a small cattle farm in Ohio near his parents. The farm, however, was only marginally profitable and the isolation made them restless. They moved to the town of Marion and my father apprenticed himself to a tool-and-die maker, but that did not satisfy him, either. Life seemed too constrained, too ordinary, and the cold weather made his bad arm painful and stiff.

And so we found ourselves driving south in our chalky blue hunch-backed Plymouth, pulling a trailer loaded with everything we owned. We moved into a house on Seventh Street, just outside Coral Gables. It was a boxy two-story frame structure not at all typical of Florida, and the landlord lived upstairs. There was a strip of vacant land behind us and the yard was scrubby and unkempt. The pines did not rise majestically like the Biltmore's royal palms; they encroached.

The best thing about the house was its flagstone porch. Surrounded by a high stucco wall and leggy lantanas, it ran the length of the house and had a ledgelike seat built into one corner. The flagstones were cool in the shade and hot as flatirons in the sun. But for my sister and me, that porch— our haven, our refuge—*was* the house.

We could scatter our dolls and play all day without worrying about the red ants that made the grass so treacherous. The ants came from the sand and could swarm over our legs without our knowing it. We had fractions of a second to squash or fling them from our skin before they inflicted their fiery bites and left us screaming.

It was on this porch that we watched our father relaxing with a cigarette, celebrating his graduation from the firemen's academy. One of us wore his smart-looking, navy-blue dress hat with the badge on the front, the other wore his black firefighter's molded helmet. He sat resting his elbows on his knees and blew a stream of smoke at the flagstones between his feet. "This isn't good for you," he said. "It isn't good for me." He offered us each a puff. We hacked, we cried, and Mom hit the roof. But neither of us has ever smoked.

Mom knew the Seventh Street house was temporary, and she didn't want to spend one extra minute of her life in it. She hoped we would be out by Christmas. When she realized we hadn't saved enough money to make that possible, she went back to nursing and hired Agnes, the first of several housekeepers.

We hated Agnes. She was a short, thickset, German-born woman who took the Christmas tree down on December 26. Being of German heritage herself, my mother believed in obedience, and she usually backed up Agnes's *Sturmführer* demands for neatness and order. But our trees had always stayed up until Epiphany.

Mom came home midmorning, after a shift and a half, to a sullen household. She heard our story. She looked at the living room, spotless now, the presents put away, the chairs back in their usual positions. We didn't know what was coming. She marched into the kitchen where Agnes was ironing: "Agnes, please put the tree back up." Agnes said the ornaments and lights were already packed away and the tree was on the curb. Mom hesitated. We held our breath. Then in a calm, level tone, she said, "That's a shame, because I want the tree back up."

Agnes did it, slowly, methodically, without any expression on her face. Janny and I retreated to the porch and watched her through the screen door from the safety of the stucco seat. When Agnes finished, Mom thanked her and told her she didn't need to come back tomorrow. We were struck dumb by the drama of it.

For Janny and me, living in Florida seemed to be one high point after another. A brush fire once swept across the lot behind us, threatening four or five houses. The adults brought their garden hoses to the backyards, carefully managing their concern. But we children ran and shrieked, consumed with excitement. The fire trucks came with flashing lights and sirens, men running and hoses dragging. There was a powerful swishing of water. Although Daddy wasn't on that truck, we associated him with the charged air, the rescue, the importance of living.

Soon after, we moved to Fifty-second Court. It was even farther from Coral Gables, but the neighborhood was one of evenly spaced, harmonious houses. They were built of stuccoed concrete blocks—hurricane safe—and had attached carports, or, as my mother would learn to say from her friends, porte cocheres.

My parents threw themselves into making this the house of their dreams. They painted it dark gray with white trim, unlike any of the others. Mom wanted Daddy to build a white brick planter between the living room and the dining room, and when the right bricks could not be found, she made them, using white cement and wooden forms he assembled for her. For weeks, the backyard was filled with narrow, hand-distressed, snow-white bricks. Together they made larger, light-gray bricks of ordinary cement, and with them Daddy built a barbecue pit with its own storage shed and a huge patio in a corner of the backyard. They surrounded it with banana trees. They went crazy planting coconuts.

For some reason, the coconuts didn't do well; we had better luck with the almond tree and the royal poinciana out front. A few years later, the four of us would spend hours under those trees, beheading iced shrimp that we had netted the night before from the causeway catwalk over Biscayne Bay. And still later, I would sit there working up the courage to ask a boy to the Sadie Hawkins dance. It took me three hours. But he was older and he waited.

If Coral Gables had banyan trees, so would my parents. They planted one in the backyard that grew to such gigantic proportions in the course of ten or twelve years that it threatened half the neighbors' septic systems, our roof, the patio, and the barbecue. Mr. Carvelli, the neighbor behind us, began to complain that it was shading his fruit trees.

By then, Janny and I had bedrooms of our own, but we had shared one for years while Mabel, a live-in housekeeper, was with us. We hid sometimes from Mabel in the hall closet behind the vacuum cleaner, where we sat on the Ball jars full of pickles. And shamelessly we let her worry about where we were. But Mabel could wiggle her left ear and she spoke English. (Dora—the housekeeper between Agnes and Mabel—had been *"buena"* but we never got much further than that.) And Mabel did not leave our employ when a burglar stole something from every room of our house, including the bedroom where she was sleeping at the time.

The burglary was not much of a financial setback. The car didn't start for the burglar, either. But soon after, Daddy started his own business during his off-hours. He had just been "promoted" to a job he disliked at the station downtown; there he watched indoor gauges and turned knobs instead of fighting fires. We girls suspected it had something to do with his wounded arm.

The arm that had built our barbecue, our patio, the arm that planted trees and dug wells and repaired washing machines, was, after all, technically disabled. But his new business—using the skills of a firefighter—was high-pressure cleaning and spraying, and it got him back outdoors where the action was. Still, he began to drink.

He and Mom continued to enjoy life, though, and Janny and I were always part of it. As a family we fished, swam, water-skied, camped, and sailed. When they gave a neighborhood luau, we dressed the part and learned to weave birds and hats from palm fronds. We helped take the doors off the bedrooms to use as tables on the ground, which we then covered with banana leaves, and we helped dig the roasting pit for the wild boar their friends had killed in the Everglades. More than anything, they taught us to give fully to the task at hand and to enjoy both play and work.

After the luau, Mom turned her attention to the inside of the house and decided it was time to bestow some style on it. She did everything in the front rooms at once. She had never considered white to be practical, but she covered our new modern furniture in a white fabric with abstract blue, purple, and fuchsia designs. She hung matching wallpaper on one wall and matching draperies on the windows. She sketched and my father made a kidney-shaped, glass-topped coffee table with curvy black legs underneath and gold screw caps on top. Mom's decorating made us famous on Fifty-second Court and the neighbors forgave my father for having a turquoise truck in the driveway.

But as Janny and I grew older, the house seemed to grow smaller—

too small to conceal the shouting and the anger of our parents. My father's drinking had grown worse. They fought over money and hours unaccounted for. He seemed intent on marring their success and happiness, and eventually my mother began to doubt their achievements.

She suddenly perceived the street out front, which had never drained properly, as a health hazard. She no longer noticed the gracefully curving sidewalks to the left, but only the barrier wall to the right that shielded us from the backs of the stores. Directly across the street, the Colemans closed in their porte cochere and air-conditioned their house. The landscape was changing before her eyes and she didn't like it.

And then the huge banyan tree in the backyard could be ignored no longer; it had to come down. I remember my father working wordlessly under the roaring drone of the power saw. He stole glances at Janny and me while we stacked the logs, as if he was taking one last look.

Light flooded into the back of the house and rearranged the shadows. We found ourselves turning around unexpectedly, looking for our bearings. The beautiful white furniture in my parents' bedroom had turned yellow, only we hadn't been able to tell before. The draperies were faded. Everything looked unfamiliar. And in the middle of our backyard lay a gaping sandy pit filled with roots and leafy debris.

The marriage ended. My mother, my sister, and I moved to Philadelphia and lived in an apartment before we girls left for college and started lives of our own.

Our memories of Florida are less painful than our parents'. I'll always remember parading our dolls around the block in a string of cardboard boxes, decorated like floats with toy umbrellas and hibiscus flowers picked from the bushes. I'll remember returning from Andros Island, riding the boom of a friend's sailboat through raised bridges, my white, freckled skin miraculously turned golden by the sunset. I'll remember swimming in the coral rock caves at the Venetian Pool in Coral Gables, and being kissed in the porte cochere.

Until it was no longer possible, our parents had sheltered us from bitterness and defeat. They did not make their pain our pain. We grew up happy, strong, and ready to flower like the royal poinciana out front.

With the exception of a few years in Indiana, my husband and I have raised our family in the Northeast. I don't recall talking very much to my children about living in Florida, but my newly married daughter wants to try it. Her husband has fond memories of the ocean, warm tropical air, boats, and game fish. It's a logical choice. Even with their combined incomes, they can't afford living in the Northeast. They have bought their first home in Cape Coral. It's not large, but they have three bedrooms and a nice lanai. They are busy planting citrus trees on a lot devoid of any vegetation more than six inches high. "It's not the same down here," she wails in a letter. "When you plant, you have to put in the dirt, too! All they have is sand! And watch out for the fire ants!"

I don't mention how similar their dreams are to those of her grandparents. For what are we without our dreams? And if they pursue them with energy and joie de vivre, even if those dreams never fully materialize, good things will come of them.

H E L E N   P A R K   B I G E L O W

Portrait of the Artist's Daughter

here is a huge uninhabited lot in the Berkeley hills, hidden from the street and from neighbors. It would be a dream site for someone who likes seclusion, dense trees, and a dazzling view of the entire San Francisco Bay, but the boulder-strewn property is what Berkeley people call a slide area, where the clay soil expands when wet and can slump and bring down houses. No one will build here again, but this is where I grew up.

A steep private driveway zigzags up the hill through a neighbor's property. I climbed it recently on a sunny morning, and halfway up I was out of breath, a huffing, puffing, middle-aged trespasser going back home. I live just an hour and a half away, but I have only climbed that driveway a few times—once to show my daughters, once to show my new husband, and once or twice to show a close friend. If the place were more accessible, I might go more often, to sit in the sun or the quiet fog and visit the memories there.

One recent morning, I had an hour to spare in Berkeley and this is where my impulse took me. Sun-warmed redwood trees filled the air with the pungent, dusty smell of my childhood. Even stronger childhood memories are triggered by another tangy smell which sprang to mind—linseed oil and turpentine. The first instant inside our front door I would always smell oil paint because my father, an artist, brought new work home from his studio when its surface was still glistening wet. He'd chug up the driveway in our old gray Ford convertible with the top down and a new painting sticking out. Carefully carrying the canvas up the steps by our terraced garden beds, he would ease through our wide front door and set it on the floor against a wall, asking anybody nearby what they thought of it.

My sister and I called our parents Deedie and David. He eventually became recognized as an important Bay Area figurative painter, but when we moved into that house on the hill in 1941 a few months before Pearl Harbor Day, our father, David Park, was just a broke thirty-year-old artist no one had ever heard of, with a wife and two girls in pigtails. I was eight, my sister nine.

Our big brown-shingle house was so steeped in what my parents called "character" that they didn't care how askew it had been made by the shifting ground beneath it. It was a Craftsman-style house built in 1929 by William Wilson Wurster, who later became dean at the School of Architecture of the University of California in Berkeley. I will never forget the first time we saw the place. Through overgrown shrubbery and the boughs of trees we saw glimpses of a simple two-story house with weathered shingles, big windows, a low peaked roof, and a huge porch on one side. It looked friendly and inviting, and not another building was in sight.

We reached the front door through a tunnel of greenery. When the four of us walked in, our footsteps echoed in the empty rooms. A grandfather clock stood in the corner of the living room, willed there forever by some previous tenant. We prowled around upstairs and downstairs, and when I overheard Deedie and David talking about where the piano would go, I ran to tell my sister we were going to move in. We would have separate bedrooms, *three* bathrooms, and a whole room just for doing our laundry.

Because the building was damaged, the rent was only $40 a month, which was a low figure even in those days. A few years later, with the damage worsening, the owner reduced the rent to $25, a story my parents gleefully told friends while showing off windows that wouldn't close and gaps at the front door that made keys pointless. It was more important to them that all our front windows had sweeping views framed by wild greenery. Who cared if we lived in the slide area and the rooms were drafty? "I'm a fresh-air fiend anyway," my mother would say.

We moved in, wound the grandfather clock, and hung paintings on the redwood walls. We scattered our Navajo rugs and filled the built-in bookcases. Deedie always kept a big arrangement of garden flowers like zinnias and marigolds on the grand piano, on a mat that hid the white rings made by leaking vases. My father made our living room chairs because we couldn't afford to buy any. With seats only a few inches off the floor, slanted backs, and angular wooden arms, they were so modern and bold and jutting that they reminded me of some of the Picasso paintings in David's books.

• • • • • • • •

I reached the top of the driveway and smelled the redwood-redolent air. Cement stairs led past the old terraced flower beds now sprawling with dry weeds. Ahead of me, broken slabs of concrete poked up through blackberry vines. Runaway growth covered the building site, making it appear too small to have held such a large house.

As I stood there in front of what used to be our home, my father filled my thoughts. He was a skinny man, not tall, with intense blue eyes. I never got enough of my father, but I never questioned his need to paint in every free moment. I grew up knowing that everyone felt the way I did— my sister, my mother, other relatives, and friends. He would come home lined with fatigue, having been on his feet all day in his studio, but when he'd see one of us or when a friend arrived for dinner, the way his face lit up with happiness, the way he grinned and hugged, made the whole world a better place for all of us.

I remember sitting on the staircase in my pajamas looking down at the living room full of people on evenings when David played the piano with an old family friend named Ann. My mother and other friends would sit around listening. Ann and David liked to play a certain Mozart piece, a duet for four hands, and they sat side by side on the piano bench in fierce concentration. They played until one of them would hit a wrong key, and then they'd stop, groan, and start in again.

Finally, David and Ann would make it through the whole piece. At the last note, they would raise their hands off the keys with a flourish, their faces turned to each other, beaming and triumphant. Everyone clapped and exclaimed and so did I, but then when I went up to bed I would feel curiously lonesome, wrapped in a bittersweet glow.

I don't know why that moment of loneliness came whenever the music stopped. Maybe I was confused by the love that showed between Ann and David. But what I remember best is the air charged with music as I climbed the stairs alone, while down below, the grown-ups laughed, glasses clinked, someone played an arpeggio down the keyboard.

One day a few years later, my mother filled every vase with flowers and my father washed all the downstairs windows. There was to be a party, a special one that only Deedie and David knew about. That evening, friends packed our living room. The atmosphere was thick with secrecy when finally down the stairs came my father with Ann on his arm looking like an Oriental princess in something long, something red and gold. She carried flowers and smiled at the crowd and at a man standing by the fireplace waiting for her. A gasp, then a delighted murmur rippled through the room as all of us realized what was happening. Ann was getting married, and David was giving her away.

The years we lived on our Berkeley hillside—from 1941 to 1951— are divided in my memory as During the War and After the War. Through the decade, Deedie's passion for the sun remained constant. Off the dining room was an enormous open veranda where she flopped down on a mattress, naked, whenever the weather cooperated and she had a day off from her job at the University of California Press.

During the war, David was operating a crane at a defense plant on the graveyard shift, midnight to eight, and he was always asleep upstairs when I got home from school. My sister and I had to keep quiet so we wouldn't wake him. I knew the graveyard shift was part of the war effort, but I didn't like telling my friends that they couldn't come over to play or even call me on the phone. We had a wartime Victory garden to supply some of our own food, we sat at the dining table and mixed smelly yellow coloring into bricks of lard-white margarine because butter was rationed, and we stood huddled in fear at the big windows during air-raid warnings, watching all the lights of the Bay area go off for the blackout.

Each weekday of the war years, my father got off work at eight in the morning and drove to my mother's office building. She stood waiting for him on the sidewalk, having taken the bus down from the hills, a thermos of coffee tucked under her arm. He would park near her building and for fifteen minutes before she had to go, they sat in the car talking. Then Deedie went to her office and David drove into the hills to our crooked, drafty house to sleep for a few hours.

David always left for his studio in San Francisco in the late afternoon before Deedie got home, and he taught evening classes until it was time to go to the defense plant at midnight. For the four years of the war, the only time my parents saw each other from Monday through Friday was that fifteen minutes sitting in the car drinking coffee from our old red thermos.

By the time I was in junior high school, I was torn between my need to be just like everybody else and my pleasure in being with my parents and their friends, which made me very different. And I had spent enough time at girlfriends' houses to discover that other people's mothers didn't lie naked in the sun, other kids didn't call their parents by their first names, other people's fathers didn't paint paintings or play Dixieland jazz at jam sessions in the living room.

I married young—at eighteen, to my high school boyfriend. We drove away from Berkeley in a flurry of wedding presents and suitcases, crossing the country to live in Ithaca, New York, where my husband was an undergraduate at Cornell. A few months after I left home, my father telephoned with bad news. The night before, during a heavy rain, he and my mother had been jolted awake by a terrifying noise. In their nightclothes they hurried down to the living room and saw bricks spilled from the fireplace. The glass in our big windows had snapped and great jagged pieces hung from the frames with slivers shot all over the floor.

"What happened then?" I demanded, imagining the entire building slipping straight down the hill.

"Well, we decided there wasn't anything we could do," my father said. "We went back to bed and made plans for the morning."

"Where was my sister, what was she doing?" I was frantic to picture everything. My father laughed. She had slept through the whole thing; they woke her with the news early in the morning. After telephoning friends for help, my parents and my sister moved out.

They found an apartment; a salvage company came to take down the broken house. In time, my parents bought a place of their own, another of Berkeley's brown-shingle classics on another steep hill, where they lived for five years until my father died of bone cancer in 1960 at the age of forty-nine.

When I got married and moved away, none of us knew that our house would break up, and that nine years later my father would die and we would never sit around our dinner table again, just the four of us in a home of music and paintings and people glad to be together. Some time during the year we lost the house, my father painted that dining room table with three people seated at it. In his painting, the chair where I always sat is empty; I know it stands for my leaving. This picture, *Table with Fruit*, belongs to collectors in Missouri, but it appeared at an exhibition of my father's work at the Whitney Museum of American Art in New York in 1988.

•   •   •   •   •   •   •   •

As I stood spellbound on my hillside, I noticed some pears on an old tree near the Victory garden and climbed across the blackberry vines and chunks of concrete to pick one. It wasn't ripe and I couldn't believe this was the very same tree, but we had had Bartlett pears growing right there in that spot. I bit into the fruit. It was dry, tasteless, hard. I didn't care. It was my pear, my tree, my hillside.

A car came into view and stopped below me on the driveway. When a man emerged and looked up at me, I waved, tossed the pear into the bushes, and hurried down the hill. "I used to live here," I explained, and learned that I was talking to an expert on my pile of rubble. In fact, he owned it, having bought our building site along with his house. He had explored it carefully and even knew my parents' names. He wanted me to answer questions. Yes, the second fireplace was in a den. No, I wasn't home when the house broke up.

After he left, I walked slowly down the driveway. I didn't want my visit to end, so I called up my favorite family memory. It was during the war when I was about ten. Housing was so scarce that friends and relatives often lived with us for weeks at a time. Despite the somber war news and the graveyard shift, nights would come when our home was full of martini-drinking people in animated discussions about politics, paintings, and books. Midway through the war, both my uncles, Dick and Teddy, were home on leave from the South Pacific at the same time. My Boston grandmother had come by train to see them, so we were a wonderfully big family.

One night, with many friends there, we all played what my parents called "The Game," a version of charades with costumes. I remember rummaging through the large coat closet in the front hall with my father and

Dick and Teddy in a frenzied search for costume ideas and props. Wonder of wonders, I was on the team with all three men. I was also in one of those ecstatic stages of childhood when all the grown-ups are perfect and everything that happens is just exactly right. I must have been radiant with happiness, with my golden hero-uncles safe and *home*, with my grandmother all the way from Boston, for there in the closet my father was suddenly grinning at me. He nodded as if he knew every feeling I was having. As he nodded, he said, "Yup," and I thought I would burst with joy. That's all, just "Yup," just a moment in a closet to remember forever.

J O H N H O U G H , J R .

Mary Small's House

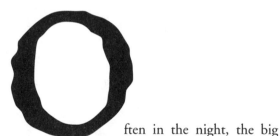ften in the night, the big house would shift its weight and a shudder would run through it, a window would jiggle. My mother saw a ghost once, a young woman who glided into her room in the middle of the night and stood beside the bed, eyeing her benevolently. My father did not wake up. The ghost left as it had come, through the open door and down the narrow hallway where the family photographs hung. My mother wasn't surprised. None of us was. These old rooms swam with a residue of life, the invisible accumulation of centuries; a ghost was bound to show itself sooner or later.

The house had its own smells, like all old houses. There was a dry fragrance of old wood and the peaceful, foggy-summer essence of mildew. All the rooms smelled like that except the kitchen, which in my mother's time was redolent of coffee and overripe fruit and the good cheap casseroles she improvised to feed the seven of us. There was a tiny pantry with a

174

mullioned window whose bubbly panes trapped the morning light, seemed swollen with it. The pantry smelled of potatoes and onions.

Built in 1690, this was one of the original houses in the seaside town of Falmouth, which is spread across the southwest corner of Cape Cod. The rear wing—dining room, kitchen, and pantry, with rooms above—had been added later, but was very old, even so. A greenhouse had been built off one side and a porch the whole length of the other, modern-day amenities that softened the austerity of line, the Yankee spareness of the tall shingled house.

We moved into it in the summer of 1955, when I was nine. We had been living in a drab little place on a shadeless quarter acre on the other side of town. The new house was three times as big and older beyond reckoning, and we were all in love with it. It had character, my father said. I imagined treasure buried in the cellar, jewels concealed and forgotten beneath a floorboard.

The ceilings were low, the lintels not always precisely horizontal. There was a fireplace in every room, upstairs and down, except the kitchen. The living room fireplace was a cast-iron maw opening out into the room, with two brass knobs on top. There were deep closets, and recessed cupboards large enough for a child to crawl into. The cellar was as dark and dank as a medieval dungeon. The attic was framed with hand-hewn timbers, its sloping roof perforated with a galaxy of black square-edged nails. I'd never seen nails or timbers that old.

The house did need work. Ceilings were cracking, the kitchen plaster was crumbling, the white paint was peeling off the outside trim. Window shades were in tatters. Sheets of wallpaper hung loose in the upstairs hall. But we didn't care. These were trivial blemishes, a price you paid for such uniqueness and antiquity.

The neighborhood was sprawling and rich in idiosyncrasy like the house. There were wild tracts of field and thicket, marshes and ponds. There were long steep hills perfect for sledding, and a field where the neighborhood boys played ball from March till World Series time. The foundation of a barn, our own granite ruin, nestled in the hillside below our driveway. Best of all was the railroad line in the back of our house, beyond the stone wall.

Trains! I put pennies on the rails, and crab apples. The pennies spread to surprising shapes, smooth and paper-thin; the apples disappeared under the wheels as if vaporized. For years, the early commuter train woke us for school. The outbound trains blew for a crossing as they passed our house; the Budd car had a brassy snarl that flared out behind it and hung there as the train sped on. Waking, I'd feel our bull terrier, warm and solid against me in bed. My sisters would be stirring in the next room. I'd hear my mother come down the hall to feed my baby brother, her bare feet thumping, the thumps reverberating in the limber plank flooring. She had pretty feet, pretty almond-shaped hands. She was prettier by a mile than any of my friends' mothers, a brown-haired beauty with a generous mouth and mild blue eyes set wide apart. My father's pride. She would pick up my baby brother, and if I hadn't yet rousted myself she'd put her head in the door. "Wake up, child," she'd say. "It's a *beautiful* day."

·   ·   ·   ·   ·   ·   ·   ·

I came home with my wife and stepdaughter for one last Christmas in 1986. My mother, who was sixty-three that winter, had just come home from a hospital in Boston where she was recovering from surgery. She had managed to do some Christmas shopping over the phone.

We live on Martha's Vineyard, a forty-minute ferry ride from the mainland. We came over late in the afternoon. There was only family at the house, not the usual old friends coming in for whiskey and eggnog and the conviviality, near to euphoria, we all felt at Christmas. No visitors this year, my father had ruled, and there was no arguing with him. Not then, not later. He watched over our mother with a private, growing desperation that none of us could ever penetrate.

She was enthroned on the sofa, wrapped in her bathrobe. She looked good, considering what she'd been through. Her hospital pallor had a creamy, vital radiance. Her blue eyes shone softly. She hadn't lost a lot of weight, but she seemed faintly diminished overall, as if the removal of a lung had shrunk her half a size. Her voice, too, was smaller, and scratchy, like an old record.

"You look great, Mom," I said.

She sat up straighter and put a hand to her chest, affecting surprise. She always had a touch of the performer in her.

"Do you think so?" she said.

"You know you do," I said.

"We're going to *lick* it," my father said, with a suddenness that quieted the room. He had been sitting gloomily apart in his captain's chair by the fireplace.

My mother sent him a grateful smile. The doctors had given her hope: a 40 percent chance, maybe 60. Willpower and family luck, which had never deserted us, would put her over the top. Anything else was unimaginable.

"Presents," someone suggested.

Our mother stood up. "Now," she said.

"Mary Small, you sit down," our father said.

Small was her middle name; this was his endearment for her, especially when he was being bossy. Once in a while, she would swear in his presence, just to get a rise. Mary *Small*, he'd say, sounding scandalized.

She listened to him most of the time, but not always, and not now. Now she glided to the presents in their usual corner as if she hadn't heard him. She chose two large boxes and came back with one under each arm, performing, showing off her spryness after surgery, her resilience against cancer.

A fire burned in the fireplace. Under the mantel shelf hung an age-blackened Revolutionary War musket, purchased by my great-grandfather a century ago at a house sale. The fire perfumed the room with its smoky sweetness. There was the Christmasy fragrance of evergreen and, still, that summery faintness of mildew.

The months passed. My mother began to drive and take little strolls. Often on weekends she and my father came to the Vineyard, where my father had inherited the country house that had belonged to his grandfather. The house was a quarter of a mile from ours, up a dirt road through the woods. My mother walked the dirt road. She read in the sun of the warming spring and took on some color.

Then, late in the summer, I rode the ferry over to Falmouth on a weekday morning, entered the house alone, and found the breakfast dishes unwashed on the kitchen table. There was no sound but the soft, nervous buzz of the fluorescent light. I turned off the light, went through the dining room, and called up the back stairwell.

"I'm up here," my mother answered from her bedroom. Her voice was tiny, distant-sounding.

I climbed the stairs, went down the hallway past the family photographs. My mother lay in the bed with the sheet pulled up to her chin. The shades were drawn.

"What's wrong?" I said.

"I'm just resting," she said. She smiled. The smile was tender. It was sad. "I think I won't go to lunch," she said.

My heart sagged, and I felt light-headed, as if I had walked into a dream. I had come over for a dental appointment and lunch, a twice-yearly ritual since I settled on the Vineyard. My mother loved to eat out, loved the specialness of it. Life's little adventures delighted her. She loved snowstorms and rough ferry crossings. She never forgot seeing Gregory Peck in a restaurant, their gazes locking for a long moment that became legend in the family.

"The car keys are on the mantel," she said.

"How long have you been lying here?" I said.

"Just a little while."

"Should I call Dad?"

"Heavens, no."

I stood there in that dream, in the muted light of the small square bedroom.

"You go on," my mother said.

"There's nothing I can do?" I said.

She smiled again. "What could you do, child?"

I didn't know.

"We'll have lunch another time," she said.

"Soon," I said.

"Soon," she agreed, smiling again.

I went back down the hallway, stopping to run my gaze over the wall of pictures. They hung randomly, a hodgepodge of eras and generations. Me and my Little League teammates in 1956, the year we won the championship. My father, a darkly handsome United States marine, in about 1944. My mother and her sisters, little girls in chiffon dresses and ankle socks, with their regal-looking grandmother in a big shadowy room in York, Pennsylvania. My brother and two Pennsylvania cousins on a long-ago summer day, good-looking little boys with tans and freckles, this house behind them with its long ell and broad slant roofs rising against the cloudless sky, ageless-looking, as if the summer made it young again.

When I was a kid, the wallpaper in the hallway was a sad, ashy brown. There was a bald spot in the stairwell, a jagged eye of grainy, grayish plaster that watched us go up and down the stairs for years, to my chagrin. The disrepair had not dimmed my love for the place, but it had become an embarrassment. We were in an affluent neighborhood, and friends who lived nearby looked at the peeling paint and crumbling plaster and decided that the Houghs were poor. Most didn't care, but I heard remarks and intercepted a knowing look or two when the subject of family wealth came up. I ignored them gamely, but the idea preyed on me. *Were* we poor? It did look like it.

One night, I asked my mother. My sisters were in bed, and my father had gone back to the newspaper office. My mother would read by the fire till he came home.

"Heavens, child," she said. "We aren't *poor*."

"Then what are we?" I said.

"We're comfortable," she said.

Comfortable. I liked it. It had scope and nuance, it went beyond a gleaming kitchen and fresh paint and furniture that didn't wobble. It went deeper.

"The Burroughs are rich," I said.

"Well, Mr. Burrough owns the cement-block company. There's more money in that than in a small newspaper like *The Enterprise*."

I knew my father was smart. He could quote Dickens and Stevenson and recite "The Highwayman." I knew he was able: I'd see him at the typewriter he used at home, the keys spitting words as fast as he could speak them. I'd see him in the office, his tie loosened, his sleeves rolled, a busy man, an important man.

"Your father's doing what he wants to do," my mother said. "Someday, we'll catch up and the house will be beautiful."

She was right. The town grew, the newspaper prospered, and the house came into its glory. The kitchen was renovated, at last. All the walls were repapered in old-fashioned pinks and blues. The trim was repainted. The floors, molasses-dark in the old days, were stripped and stained to a hard bright honey-gold. The rooms took on a stateliness, a soft-spoken and venerable elegance. They looked antique instead of merely old.

•   •   •   •   •   •   •   •

My wife said the house seemed smaller after my mother died. What I remember is the silence, so immense and so heavy you felt you could scoop it in your arms. I remember, too, the drawn and half-drawn shades, a new penchant of my father's that kept the house in a permanent twilight, gray in the winter, whiskey-brown on a summer day.

After a few years, the neglect began. My father had taken to escaping every weekend to the Vineyard, recentering his life, easing into retirement. Dust gathered in the old homestead, and the mildew finally had its way, blooming gauzily on baseboards and closet doors. Once again, paint flaked from ceilings. The grounds grew shaggy and too deep in shade. My father stuck it out for six memory-haunted years, then sold the place and escaped for good to the island.

I slept in the house for the last time on the September night of my thirtieth high school class reunion, a few weeks before the new owners took occupancy. I stopped in before the reunion, arriving at the golden hour of the evening. Crickets whirred in the tall grasses that choked the old barn foundation. Voices floated on the bike path where the railroad line once ran. Beyond, a car muttered, a dog barked. What had been field and thicket when I was a kid was all tract houses out there now, on half-acre plots.

The key was in its hiding place and I let myself into the kitchen. The pantry shelves were bare. I opened the refrigerator; my father had left a bottle of champagne for the new owners, a young couple with children. The refrigerator woke when I opened it, began to hum.

I carried my bag through the dining room, the living room. The window shades were gone, and the empty rooms drew in long shafts of sunlight. The light bathed the golden floors, it lit the far walls. The house was full of sunshine.

I climbed the stairs, went down the echoing hallway to my parents' bedroom. *I have some hard news*, my father had said over the phone. My mother had died of an embolism, a sudden but merciful end. The cancer had jumped to her liver, was on the move again.

Some hard news, but now the room was ablaze with the flame-yellow light of September, and I realized that the silence had thinned, as if the sunlight had burned it away, leaving instead a feathery hush, like the expectant quiet in a theater before the curtain rises. I walked all through the house, visited every room. For the first time in seven years, the memories all were painless.

I got back from the reunion late and slept on a cot in the front room downstairs, which had become my bedroom when I entered my teens. Outside, across the narrow road, a streetlamp shone down. The lamp was an old friend of mine.

One night, when I was about fifteen, a blizzard hit unexpectedly. I remember doing my homework and listening to the radio and watching the snow come down in the milky halo of the streetlamp. The windows rattled, snow peppered the glass in wind-whipped volleys. There would be no school tomorrow. The steam radiator clanked and hissed, and I felt as pure a contentment as I have ever known.

My mother came in to say good night. From my desk, I saw her go to the window, lean with both hands on the sill, and watch the spinning clouds of snow in the lamplight.

"Think how it'll look in the morning," she said happily. "It'll be up to your waist." She turned and gave me her smile. "You can sleep late and have oatmeal for breakfast with butter and brown sugar."

"Sounds good," I said.

"It'll be divine," she said, still smiling.

And it was.

See You in My Dreams, San Francisco

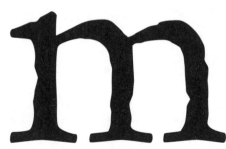y mother never liked to dawdle. When she decided to do a thing, she did it.

After two years with an illness that was consuming her bones, she was told that she would be confined to her bed. The last time I talked to her, the unspoken text in her weary voice went something like this: "For thirty years I cooked the meals and cleaned this place, I weeded the lawn and deadheaded the flowers. I am not about to lie in bed!"

That night, she died.

It took me the next five years to say good-bye, and in the process, I had to give up the house where I was raised, speak commandingly to my father, and understand my mother, perhaps for the first time.

We buried her in the roiling ocean facing the Golden Gate Bridge. The wind was in our faces as my father, brother, and I squatted with the small silver-foil box of ashes on the rough stony shore. When my father spilled out the ash, the wind lifted it. A little got into my nostrils. I sneezed.

It felt so lonely there on the edge of the West. Even the bridge and its great city seemed to have been tucked into a corner of the sky. Crouched on the rocks in silence, passing a bottle of wine, we three felt about as significant as fiddler crabs. But it was not so much the immensity of the surroundings that cowed us as it was our own intense embarrassment. We did not know what to say or do.

In the past when conversation flagged, we always counted on my mother to galvanize us. We often called her Mater, the nickname I had devised to needle her about the incongruous combination of formal politesse and forthright Kentucky grit that characterized her whole being.

We survivors might have talked about the house. We had spent more than thirty years in the place. It had been home base to my brother and me even after we had completed the journey from prep school through college, when summers were spent climbing and working in the Sierra Nevada. There was always the house, always the ride from the airport, winding back along the creek into Hillsborough, where no sidewalks or streetlamps or shops were allowed and where big old trees of every description leaned protectively over the road.

Our house was a refuge I could retreat to after whatever harebrained scheme I had just perpetrated. I ran there after dropping strings of firecrackers on the roofs of passing cars, after almost being expelled from school for promoting the Vietnam Moratorium, after being picked up by the Fresno cops at 3:00 A.M. for hitching home from the High Country.

Every single time, Mater was there to take me in, dressed in her at-home clothes: powder-blue shorts, white shirt, and white sneakers, or her quilted pink dressing gown. There was a spot on the stone stairs at the front door that had been worn smooth by all the occasions on which she had stood there waving good-bye or hello.

Now that she was gone, what would become of the house? Where would my father live? How could he be taken care of? Who would do the laundry? Who would cook? Who would care for the garden? It began to dawn on me just how many things Mater had quietly dealt with.

She was the heart of that house, and her moods were its heaven and its hell. If she had too many martinis, even the dog shared her moroseness. If she won a battle with the school board, even the doors seemed to swing happily on their hinges.

After her death, my father moved into the bedroom that had been mine. There he set up what amounted to a separate apartment, complete with sofa, bed, and desk. He had always delighted in quoting Satchel Paige: "Don't have no truck with the social scene. It ain't restful." Now, he seemed to have gone Paige one better: Have no truck with nobody, not even your kids.

We tried to interest him in something.

"Want to go out for ribs?" He loved ribs.

"No."

"Can we help you clean out the old dresses and give them to the Goodwill?"

"No, not yet."

He had put himself and the whole house into suspended animation. The Nicaraguan woman my mother had hired still appeared once a week to wash the whites and sweep up the dust bunnies. Certain things clicked on as always.

Still, I no longer experienced the present in its rooms. The clank of the old stepstool unfolding in the kitchen made me think of my mother making the chicken gravy, scraping the pan, and stirring in the milk. The swish of the swinging door to the breakfast room reminded me of how my father would enter, sheepishly, half an hour late after evening rounds at the hospital.

Sitting in the breakfast room now, waiting for my father and brother to come down, I seemed to hear the questions she had often asked me, her elder son, when Dad was late again. She would be nursing her third martini, we would be waiting at the table: Why couldn't he come home on time? Why didn't he pay attention? Why didn't he speak to her? Didn't he love her?

There was never any answer to these questions. Really, they were none of my young business, but she couldn't help asking them, and they still echoed loudly in my head.

I acquired the habit then of constantly disagreeing with my father and had never gotten over it. Immediately on my mother's death I thought he would sell the house and immediately I was against it. Being my father's son, however, I did not say so. I simply looked gloomy whenever the subject arose.

Every time I spoke to him from New York I'd ask, "Are we keeping the house?"

"At least for now," he would answer. But he was afraid of its running down, concerned that the gardener could not manage, worried that the dog was spotting my mother's white rugs.

During the next five years, I visited my father close to a dozen times. On each occasion, I found him still holed up in the room that had once been mine. He was obviously unhappy but unable to let go.

I tried to release him. "Come up to the Sierras with Sam and me," I said, tempting him with his three-year-old grandson's first visit to the High Country.

"No," he said. "I'm too old. I couldn't take the altitude at my age."

"Nonsense, we'll ride you in on horseback."

"No," he said. "You go ahead."

That was his response to everything, "You go ahead." It made me furious. *All right*, I thought, *so be it. I've done all I can. You stand guard over the remains of the family's life.*

Suddenly, in the fifth spring after Mater died, he told me on the phone that he was getting married.

My brother and I called each other in shock. My brother said, "Once again we're the last to know."

"I'm glad for it, if it makes him happy," I said, but what was in my heart was the thought that now he would definitely sell the house.

My brother and I flew out together to be co-best men. Why couldn't our father have let us know sooner? Why did he never talk to us? Why did he pay no attention to us? Didn't he love us? The record played over and over in my head as I flew west, until all at once it occurred to me that these were my mother's questions.

My father was changed: He was happy. His bride was a delight. She had been his patient for many years. He had saved her life. A romance had blossomed. They were in heaven.

My brother and I waited with our father in the cinder-block basement office beneath their church, trading lame jokes about the advice we might offer him on his wedding night. They held the reception in the magnificent backyard of the old house, beneath the immense Monterey cypress tree. The cast of characters was the same as ever—all those Hillsborough folks that Mater used to admonish us to be "sweet and charming" to—but it was obviously a different play.

In my toast, I wove his favorite sayings into a poem of praise to their new happiness. "Patience is a virtue," I reminded him, noting how it had taken so long to come to this moment. I told them that after all these years of telling his kids to "use good judgment," he had at last done so himself.

We stuffed their getaway car with about a hundred helium balloons, delaying their departure briefly. Then they were gone, knots of colored balloons rising in their wake and sticking in the branches of the fir trees. I stood there laughing on the front steps and realized I was standing just where Mater always stood.

Before many months had passed, my father called to say that he was selling the old place. He called on a Wednesday to ask us to be there on Friday and clean out our things by Sunday. Or, if we didn't want to, we didn't have to come at all.

"Here we go again," my brother said.

"What are we? Last on his list?" I said.

We went to his wife's house in San Mateo, where they had lived since the wedding. When my brother and I arrived, I found on my bed a copy of the real estate agent's beautiful broadsheet about our house, with a color picture and text describing its virtues and its offering price.

"Jesus, Jeff, did you get one of these?" I asked, walking into the bedroom he was to occupy.

"Yeah," he said.

"Jesus," I repeated. I didn't know what to say. It was so painful to look at. I didn't like to think that my father's wife had made us feel this way on purpose.

The next morning was eventful. My brother developed a 102-degree fever, nausea, and chills, and took to his bed. My father found a sudden wealth of small chores he just had to do all by himself, and went to his office.

I spent the next day and a half in the old house alone. Everywhere I opened a drawer or a box or a file, raw memories protruded: a baseball chewed to rags by the old dog; the halter rope that I'd removed from my horse's neck the moment after we had her put to sleep; an old ice ax and gaiters with which I had climbed the Palisades Glacier in the Sierras; the maps from a family vacation to Montana during which my mother had swum the Deschutes River in her underwear; my father's college copy of *Cyrano de Bergerac*, our common hero.

By the afternoon of the second day, my brother had recovered sufficiently to come to the house. Our father briefly joined us. We stood in the dining room, in the avocado-green breakfast room, and in the kitchen, fingering silver of uncertain use; set after set of glasses, goblets, and parfait cups; china, flatware, pots and pans.

There was an undeniable pleasure in acquiring some of these objects. I prized most the forgotten things that had fascinated me as a child. There was a little ivory nymph on a green jade pedestal that had once sat on my mother's dressing table. The fake Mesopotamian lamp and Greek black-figure vases that my aunt Mamie had bought back at the turn of the century from her world travels had always delighted me with their promise that the place called "abroad" really did exist.

At last, there was nothing left to mark, nothing left to pack, nothing at all to do. In the backyard, the westering sun lit up the bulk of the cypress and filtered in among the sweet gum trees.

The three of us walked out into the yard. Evidently, we would have to talk to one another, although it was as if each of us had been wrapped in cellophane, unable to touch.

On the brick terrace beside the creek, I invited my father to sit. He said no. He paced back and forth on the moss-covered bricks. I asked again. He walked away toward the pool.

We all knew that we would never meet in this spot again.

My father absently picked up the pool skimmer and began to sieve out mayten leaves. He acted as though he were sleepwalking.

"What the hell is he doing!" I hissed.

Jeff shrugged.

I was livid. I went over to him, took him by the shoulder, and said firmly, "Come over here and sit down. This is the last time."

To my amazement, he did as I asked. I think that it was the first time I had ever addressed a direct command to him.

I told him, "I just want to say that I am not angry at you for selling the house." As I said it, I knew that I was lying. "But I'd like to know why you did it."

Some part of me wanted to shout, You don't care! You're selling it for that new woman! You're betraying us!

I had expected an evasion, but he said plainly and without rancor, "After your mother died, this house was never the same to me." It was clear that we had kept the house going, all of us, as though somehow if we went on sweeping and dusting and rooting for the 49ers, she might return to us. But it was no good. We had to let her go.

I suddenly knew that this is what she wanted us to do. She never liked to hang around. She didn't give two hoots for this house that we were all agonizing about. She had made a home *for us*. For all she cared, she could have made it in a tent in the Sahara.

A whole different picture of her began to form in my mind. Instead of the bitter woman sitting alone in the breakfast room with her oily martini, listening to the hall clock tick, I saw the woman whose gumption made us proud: the one who supported a fired school superintendent for no other reason than that she agreed with him; the one who stood waving on the front step and gladly let us go. The least I could do was to let her go, too.

The next morning, when the New York–bound plane started its take-off, I felt for a long time that it was stuck to the runway and could not rise. When we were finally off the ground, I said to myself the little mantra that I have said for almost thirty years now: *See you in my dreams, San Francisco.*

The phrase no longer comforted me. In the past, I had always known I would return. I finally had to admit that I no longer lived anywhere near San Francisco. At the same time, I had the sensation that a tether had broken, and I was free, launched into light.

This year, two years after the wedding, my father will turn seventy. He recently told me that he has begun to take an exercise class, to keep in shape for his bride.

I laughed out loud.

"What are you laughing at?" he asked.

"Oh, nothing," I said, just as he would have said to me. But I was so happy to have my father back again instead of that old man holed up in the haunted house, and rid of the old house itself.

To hell with hiding in the shadows, I thought he was saying: It is not too late to live.

ANN   PRINGLE   HARRIS

Claire's List

ntering into a second marriage after a first that ended badly was not easy, but I was assured that in my new family there was a place all ready and waiting for me: I would be number 147. My new husband was number 24, my new stepdaughter and stepson-in-law were numbers 71 and 145 respectively, and my new step-grandson, aged six months, was number 146. That I should be surprised at this quantified record of blood relationships and conjugal alliances was equally surprising to my husband-to-be, who had, after all, grown up with it.

I was joining the archetypal southern family, extended beyond belief and sometimes beyond reason, a loose-knit but ironbound association of people who not only know the names of all their first and second cousins, but also the names of their cousins' children's children. In the case of my new husband, this knowledge wasn't hard to come by because it was all set down in the family list, beginning with number 1—my husband's paternal grandfather, born in 1859—and continuing into the 1980s, listing births and deaths and cross-referenced as to marriages and offspring. The list was started, and meticulously kept up, by my husband's aunt, Rosa Claire Harris (number 7), Miss Claire to several generations of children who had been in her fifth-grade class at the Roxboro, North Carolina, elementary school. Claire had counted heads in the classroom for most of her life. Keeping track was in her blood.

My first post-engagement visit showed me that I was not simply a number to my new southern relatives. I was "honey," "sweet Ann," and a dozen other terms of endearment. I was the somewhat awkward recipient of prolonged bear hugs from ladies and gentlemen I had never seen before. I was briefed on the exact degrees of kinship among the various Harrises, Michies, and Armstrongs I was meeting for the first time. I was told they all hoped to come to New York for the wedding. This last was a bit of a shock. Our wedding was to be a modest affair, appropriate to two people marrying for a second time in later life. Once, I had marched down the aisle, carried flowers, cut into a two-tiered wedding cake, toasted a happy future that had bafflingly eluded me. Could I tempt fate that way again? Should we settle for just living together?

It was too late, because I had already responded to Claire's request for information for the family list. I had given the day of my birth (the year wasn't required) and admitted that it had taken place in St. Louis, Missouri, to which Claire promptly replied that I would be the first person in the family to have been born west of the Mississippi. Was this a way of saying I was a Yankee? It didn't seem likely, in the face of the warm reception everyone had given me. Anyway, I thought to myself, I *am* a Yankee.

Although Claire, at eighty-five, wasn't coming to the wedding, it seemed that almost everyone else was. "There won't be anyone to sit on my side," I complained to my husband-to-be. Whereas he had relatives in depth, I could produce no aunts, no uncles, and precisely two cousins, only one of whom was a viable attendee. "You have your three wonderful children," he told me, striking, as he so often does, exactly the right note, "and I have only one."

I had learned from my first family-in-law the New York kiss, two cheeks that pass in the night. There may have been a warning in this, but I wasn't old enough or astute enough to catch it. Having grown up Anglo-Saxon, I wasn't too clear on where reserve stopped being reserve and became distance. By the end of the marriage I knew, but even after that bitter lesson I wasn't yet ready for the all-encompassing embrace of the South. In the Middle West as it was when I was a child, we decided at about age twelve that we were too old to kiss our parents, and terms of endearment stuck in our throats unless we were carried away by passion.

The most striking and, as I see now, the fundamental contrast between my first and second marital families, though, was in their concepts of shelter. My first parents-in-law thought of the home as an expression of one's taste and knowledge, and in order to make this expression as eloquent as possible, periods were researched, decorators consulted, and whole seasons devoted to an exhaustive exploration of the home-furnishings market. A change in family size or discretionary income was a signal for a total review of one's household furnishings, and when the youngest child was grown, it was not uncommon to move and start again from scratch, as my first parents-in-law did when all their children had left the nest.

In my second marriage, I found something I used to dream of in my early childhood, when we moved almost every year: a homestead that had been continuously lived in by members of the same family since the day it was built. This rambling, rock-solid frame structure was three stories high and a good fifty-five feet deep, but the first thing you noticed about it was a pillared veranda that ran the entire width of the house and turned the corner at each end, one end being a screened-in porch, the other a glassed-in conservatory. The house was built in the early 1900s by my husband's grandfather—Papa to his entire clan of eight children, their spouses, and nineteen grandchildren—and was currently lived in by Claire and her older sister, Mary Page (number 5 on the family list). They occupied fifteen or so rooms full of furniture ranging in period from post–Civil War to Early Depression, with a few modern pieces added as the need arose.

The overall decorating rule was to keep everything. Oriental rugs consorted with solid-color broadlooms and country florals. Victorian cut-glass bowls, etched glass goblets that were all the rage in 1912, and watery pastel tea sets hand-painted by ladies of the Old South shared shelf space in the large, bow-fronted china cabinet in the dining room. Old-fashioned potato ricers, wooden butter paddles, and enameled graniteware coffeepots—the kind in which you steep the coffee grounds with eggshells—sat side by side in kitchen cupboards with stainless-steel saucepans and glass ovenware of more recent vintage. In the bedroom assigned to me on my first visit, I found hanging by two prongs from a high, walnut headboard a rose-colored, shirred-silk bed lamp, circa 1932. When I pulled a chain, the light went on and turned the pages of my book pale pink.

On our trips to Roxboro, it became clear to me that if Papa had been the patriarch of this family, his fourth daughter, Claire, had succeeded to the role, playing it as family archivist. On every possible wall and table surface in Claire and Mary Page's house, there were framed pictures of many of the people on Claire's family list. My husband and I would occasionally see some of them. If we didn't, we would learn from Claire who had visited recently, who had gotten married or had a baby, who had taken a new job or another degree. Now and then, we also learned who had licked a problem with alcohol or survived financial reverses, because Claire adhered to the truth as strictly as she adhered to proper English grammar.

"They don't ask about *my* family," I would occasionally point out to my husband after one of these visits, and he would reply that Claire and Mary Page had never met my family. That was true; my little tribe had gathered for the wedding and some later interfamily events, but I had never succeeded in transporting my three children from California, New York, and Massachusetts to North Carolina. It would not, in any case, have sufficed. You could no more grasp the character of these two women (or the character of my three children) in one visit than you could grasp the character of a great wine in one sip.

But if it was true that Claire and Mary Page didn't know my family, it was also true that I had met only a fraction of the people whose recent histories were being summarized for my benefit, and I felt ambivalent about what this family represented in my life. Though I was close to my parents and my brothers, the moving about that we did in my childhood had meant that we were mostly out of touch with whatever remnants of extended family we could lay claim to. As a child, I made up for this lack by imagining myself a part of families in books—Galsworthy's Forsytes, Mazo De La Roche's Whiteoaks of Jalna.

Yet when I finally joined such a family, I felt that I might be submerged by the sheer weight of genealogical data. I jokingly threatened to write a letter to my sister-in-law that began, "Dear 26" and ended "Love, 147." My husband simply laughed and said that his daughter and one of her cousins had already played that game. Nevertheless, I began to feel a sense of gratitude on our visits to the homestead as I looked at the family pictures and the souvenirs and the gifts, and sometimes saw in my mind the people who had posed for them, chosen them, given them. They taught me that despite the teasing I took from my children, I had been right to save their letters and programs and report cards and the handcrafted gifts they had made for me in school. Someday, they or their children or their children's children would thank me.

As the years passed, Claire grew a bit vague about the family visits and family photos; she also became a bit deaf. Now it was Mary Page, the quiet one, who kept up the conversation and told us who was doing what. Both sisters had broken one or more bones, and getting them out of the house and down the broad steps of the front porch was difficult. In the house, the chores they had done on their own—Claire cooked, Mary Page cleaned—were done by people who came in by the day. Pretty soon, there were also people who came in by night.

"They don't want to leave their house," everyone said; "they've lived their whole lives there." Because home for me was a series of snapshots—a stair landing in St. Louis, a sunporch in Kansas City, an attic playroom in Evanston, Illinois, a room in Maplewood, New Jersey, where I lay in bed for a month with scarlet fever—I could admire and envy Mary Page and Claire's rootedness in the home place, but only with the greatest effort could I empathize with it.

When we last saw the two together, Mary Page was ninety-seven and Claire was ninety-three; each of them weighed about a pound for every year. We took with us our two grandsons (numbers 146 and 156), who were then six and eight. The boys immediately set out their cars on the floor of the front hall, alternately pushing them about and running up the front stairs, which mysteriously converged with the back stairs on the second landing. Claire and Mary Page, unmarried and childless, weren't fazed by any of this, continuing the family summary once they had established just whose children these were.

In August 1992, Mary Page died. Claire, who seemed hardly to comprehend this loss, went reluctantly to a nursing home nearby. The house would be sold, its furnishings would be cataloged by members of the family. One square piano, one oak dining table with ten matching chairs, one dozen silver goblets, three walnut bedsteads—there were more than two thousand items to be divided among the family according to a complicated scheme that took into account generational seniority, degrees of kinship, and personal choice.

Not quite all two thousand items: Claire, it developed, had made specific bequests to surviving members of her own generation, as well as to nieces, nephews, and children of nieces and nephews. She had provided a careful description of each item she wished to bequeath so that there would be no errors or omissions. My husband received a needlework picture of red birds perched on a branch of pink-flowering dogwood against a background of light green. "We don't have to hang it," he said, but I tried it out over the dresser in our bedroom and it's still there.

We went to see the house before it was sold. With its furnishings either removed or grouped together for easy inspection, it showed its age. The cream-colored wainscoting in the dining room was chipped; there were oddly spaced squares and circles and rectangles where pictures had hung on the cream-and-green scenic wallpaper for years. On the breakfast table, where there had always been coffee for late risers, along with Claire's homemade marmalade tart with a satiny sheen, there was now a random assortment of kitchen utensils: a wire whisk, a rotary flour sifter, an enameled dishpan. Yet a sense of the life that had gone on in that house, of the people who had lived in it, remained. It was still, as it had been since I'd known it, a house that people came to not because of obligation but because they wanted to be there.

The last entry on Claire's family list was for triplets born in 1986 to a great-niece. As I leafed through my copy of this four-page document, I began to understand what it represented. It wasn't an attempt at control, as I had first thought. Nor was it only a testament to Claire's love of clarity and order, although it was certainly that. In its truest sense it was, like the house, the visible sign of Claire's concept of the family as extended, inclusive, important. To a question I had once posed in exasperation—"Who cares whether number 23 and number 63 got together and produced number 65?"—the answer was now achingly clear: Claire did.

Visiting Claire in the nursing home, we sensed that she didn't know who we were. Certainly she was not the brisk, no-nonsense woman I had met a decade earlier. She hadn't been that for some time, and yet she seemed frailer, vaguer, more confused here in the home—gracious as always, but attuned to other voices than ours. It's the house, I thought; she's out of touch because she's not in her own house. An unexpected wave of loss swept over me and I reached for Claire's hand. Instantly, her expression became attentive and alert. "Your hands are cold!" she said in a crisp, semiscolding tone, but as she spoke, she gently covered my hand with hers.

After we left, I felt a sad sense of finality. Claire had made her last entry in the family list. She had stopped keeping track. Yet I kept remembering that momentary sharp look, that quick gesture, those words—"Your hands are cold." They seemed to be telling me something different. Eventually, I thought I knew what it was and my spirits lifted. Claire had not stopped keeping track. It was just that at that moment in her life, I wasn't number 147; I was one of her fifth-graders who had come to school on a winter morning without mittens.

Children
and Elders

Grandma and Mrs. Spangler

did not think it out of the ordinary that I had my own patch right in the middle of my grandmother's garden. I did not think it at all remarkable that she tolerated my frequent forays across her vegetable rows to pick my flowers. The garden was, after all, ours.

Grandma was not a schnoodle, mind you (the word—her own invention—meant without substance, like a combined noodle and *schnitz*, or dried apple). She snapped out Pennsylvania Dutch diatribes to my grandfather as sharply as she snipped her strong crocheting thread when she was angry with me. She slapped my hands hard when I played with the fly on my new overalls. She always told me not to be so *schusslich*, flitting from one thing to another. And she did insist that we finally eat Gus, my Easter duck, when he was big, ornery, and not appropriate for town. But the garden was different.

The yellow and orange flowers of my calendula bed were rampant. They nearly covered my grandmother's red beets and threatened even the green beans in our long strip of backyard.

Part of my success was the sweet limestone soil washed into our little Pennsylvania Dutch valley from the worn-down Appalachians. Added to this felicity was a temperate climate, soil husbanded by German farmers who distrusted machinery, and moderation in everything from summer's length to gardeners' expectations.

The lettuce and parsley were planted first. Grandpa would double-dig a patch of ground the size of a split-open burlap bag. I would hoe. Then Grandpa would put small shovelsful of dirt into a wood box with a screen for its bottom. Grandma would shake the box to sift the soil, just as a child sifts beach sand. Of course she, in her gray dress with her gray hair plaited at the back of her head and encased in the starched-mesh prayer bonnet of the Plain People, had been to no beach in my lifetime. The plain Brethren were in the majority in our town. Not as strict as the Mennonites or Amish and not as high as the Lutherans, they were serious, unworldly, pacifistic; they were against pretense and against brightness in everything but quilts and flowers.

When the loam was as smooth as sand, Grandma would shake the leaf lettuce seeds from a jar with a punched-hole lid. I would lightly rub my hand over the soil so that the seeds were slightly covered. Then she would spread the burlap bag over the patch. I would put four stones on the corners and hop up and down, laughing at the birds' frustration. Grandma would tell me, "Don't be so *schusslich!*" and we would move on to the beets and carrots and peas.

Then came my calendulas. We always debated whether to plant in rows or just broadcast. With a child of six or seven doing the sowing, it was a moot question. The result was always a profusion of cheery and serviceable rather than elegant flowers.

As I remember it in the 1950s, our whole neighborhood was cheery and serviceable. All along Cherry Street stood white frame double houses with wooden porches and pillars and wooden railings separating the two front doors. Maples lined the street, houses hugged the sidewalk to leave plenty of backyard space. In back were the sweet or sour cherries that gave the street its name, and this is where the gardens grew.

Even at a young age, I was amazed at how my flowers took over the middle of the garden before the vegetables even looked respectable: before our first tomatoes were marbles on the vines, before the peas had to be collected in a colander every evening, before the beets recovered from Grandpa's merciless thinning.

And with the first flowers, I had just begun: I would later rub the crinkly brown seed heads in my hands to scatter the seeds in fallow nooks for surprise flower shows. I would point to a corner and tell Grandma to keep her eyes peeled. I never guessed till I had my own house and my own impatient gardening children what quiet weeding and tending must have been carried out when I was away.

I was a veritable Johnny Calendula-Seed. While my much older brother was brooding over his latest Hardy Boys mystery book, crouched in the crotch of the huge cherry (planted at my father's birth and in its maturity pierced with a spike by my grandfather to give it iron), I was running around throwing more seeds at random. When my father came home from a long day's work and walked to the leaf pile by the alley to look for fishing worms, I whispered of future surprises. He winked, and then together we dangled long night crawlers into a can while I hoped that this would be the night I was old enough to go fishing on the Swatara Creek in a boat.

Another of my favorites, the tulips from the border, usually came with my birthday—a time of sunny spring days, presents, and a bouquet from Grandma. One spring, I was beset with chicken pox. Tulips were popping and I was stretched out on the couch day after day in what my mother liked to call "the land of counterpane."

Someone who didn't know better might have predicted two or three sick calls each day from Grandma and Grandpa, who after all lived on the other side of the same house. But there was a decorum I vaguely perceived. My grandmother had a strong sense of the space that belonged to her daughter-in-law, who had moved here all the way from Canada with her whole family in a Model-T Ford. "And they have a *king* up there," Grandma exclaimed of the monarch the young Canadian girl had no regard for, having gladly left the harsh prairies of Saskatchewan and a depression even worse than the one in the United States.

So Grandma's visits to my home were friendly but brief and formal. Though young and as selfish and unthinking as any other child then or now, I remember being strangely touched by the rare appearance of my grandmother in my sickroom that spring. She came bearing a concoction of eggs, milk, sugar, and vanilla to build me up, and a huge bouquet of tulips.

In normal times, I would have liked the flowers but, *schusslich*, would have quickly passed on to other things. This time, the flowers became the center of my sickroom and the heart of my grandmother's love. I watched the fringed, frilled, gaudy parrot tulips open. Then I watched unhappily as the petals started to fall while my health (complications had developed) did not return. I crept over to the desk, retrieved paper clips and tried to fasten the petals back on the stems. When my mother came into my room and saw the clips, she laughed and ruffled my hair.

Sometime later after I was well again—certainly weeks, probably months, maybe even years, time being what it is to a child—there was an urgent late-night call up our front steps from my grandpa to my father. "Your mother's sick." A flower basket on the front door the next morning announced that a Brown had died.

I grieved with a child's single-minded intensity. I grieved long after the rest of the Browns looked to the future. I ignored the garden, both in final bloom and when blackened by frost. The following spring, Grandpa tilled the garden one last time to plant it over with grass. In angry fistfuls I helped broadcast the seed and turned to memory for golden calendulas.

•　　•　　•　　•　　•　　•　　•　　•

In the neighboring house lived Mrs. Spangler, a stout, solid, no-nonsense sort of woman. Gravity had very plainly had its cruel way with her. Anything that could sag and jiggle did; anything that could turn down did, including the corners of her mouth. In addition, she was not Plain, but Lutheran, and therefore wore housedresses with patterns and colors, not to mention curly hair right out in the open for anyone to see! Nevertheless, I somehow felt she should, like my grandmother, have fussed over me; instead she kept her distance, until a picture I found in a newspaper made us friends.

The entire valley that constituted our county was served by only one newspaper, with columns on which neighbors visited whom, what myriad cantatas and oratorios were to be sung in churches plain and high, new recipes for shoofly pie, and articles, as my mother repeatedly said, "not *on* but *in* Pennsylvania Dutch." She arranged with the local stationer for delivery of *The Philadelphia Inquirer*, a paper from a city 150 miles away by road and a hundred years away in outlook.

To a very young reader, *The Philadelphia Inquirer* didn't offer much more than the funnies, but in one particular Sunday paper there was a beautiful pen-and-ink drawing that captivated me. It showed a maple-shaped leaf pinned down by toothpicks to soil. The leaf's veins had been slashed and little plants sprang up from the gashes. I studied the drawing, entitled "Propagating a Rex Begonia," again and again. I became obsessed with the idea of having a leaf so I could do the same.

I went next door to the half of the house where my grandfather now lived alone. He was at work, but if there was a rex begonia to be had, I was sure it would be on Grandma's windowsill. As I surveyed the quiet house I saw that the sills were bereft of plants. There was only a planter from Grandma's funeral on the kitchen table. I poked in its mundane ivy and pothos and saw only the cudlike remains of my grandfather's chewing tobacco. I was shocked at his transgression: Grandma never even allowed him to chew in the house, never mind spit. I was furious that things were not as they were *supposed* to be.

I stomped the few blocks to the Main Street five-and-ten to find the plant, and saw only philodendron, ivy, and wax begonias. I walked home angrily and put the newspaper clipping in my red leather scrapbook, along with pictures of fighter planes with jaws painted on the nose and my Shredded Wheat Straight Arrow cards.

A short time later, I remember sitting by Mrs. Spangler's grape arbor, carefully pulling apart her bleeding-heart flowers to find the bow and fiddle inside. I knew I shouldn't be on her property, but the dangling flowers were irresistible. I glanced up at the nearby kitchen window as I furtively dissected flowers. Then I saw it. As big as life in Mrs. Spangler's kitchen window with the African violets was a rex begonia.

For any other reason, I would have been the picture of caution and agonizing indecision. But I jumped up and ran over to rap on the back screen door that led to an enclosed porch. In a minute, she was there and let me in.

I was amazed to see Mrs. Spangler's back porch. It was lined with tables full of chocolate-covered candies, row after row gleaming in the dim light. It was as if I had discovered a gingerbread house right out of a storybook next to my own ordinary house. I stared in awe, forgetting my mission. Mrs. Spangler brusquely explained, "It's opera fudge for the church to sell." With her chocolate-smeared hands, she popped a rich chocolate cream into my mouth.

I tried to indicate my thanks while thinking of how to get another, but she made it clear it was time for business. I murmured, eyes to the floor, "Could I have a leaf of the begonia in your kitchen window, please?" She said, "Whatever for?"

I did my best to explain, desperate to escape. Mrs. Spangler began to melt, only a little mind you, just as she later told me her candy tended to do in June. She took me into her kitchen and pinched off a leaf. Then she asked me did I know that African violets started from leaves. I knew no such thing, but coveted leaves from her blue, pink, and white flowering plants.

Mrs. Spangler treated me with kindness and Germanic reserve. She gave me careful instructions. She warned me against burning south windows and cold northern ones. I had one violet leaf per color and one rex begonia, one candy only with no exit treat likely. At the screen door she asked, "Where's your dog? I haven't seen her around."

Our Tessie was a beagle-basset mix who led a miserable life trying to get down two flights of stairs before her bladder burst while waiting for preoccupied children and their absentminded mother. She was a sight, with sad pop eyes, her tail, stomach, and ears dragging the ground as she waddled through life. Only her name was perky: Tessie, after a tennis star we had read about in *The Philadelphia Inquirer*.

I politely answered Mrs. Spangler, "Oh, she's fine. She's in the house, I guess." And she asked further, "Whatever made you call her Bessie?" I shrugged off the misunderstanding with, "It's Tessie, after a lady tennis player." Mrs. Spangler surprised me by suddenly popping a bonus candy in my mouth while hustling me out the door. It was only later when I heard a neighbor talking about Bessie Spangler that I realized she thought we had named our comical waddling dog after her. How I regretted the hurt and the imagined cruelty.

No cuttings ever had such attention as the four she gave me, and the day I found the first rootlet, the first speck of green that wasn't algae, was the day I had before me a glimpse of a whole new kingdom.

As I shared my triumph with Mrs. Spangler, so began a new relationship. She was not the missing grandmother I probably sought, but was a complete other experience, rewarding in the best way—unexpected love. On my morning runs between the houses, she instantly stopped sweeping to talk with me about my project. Afternoons, we sat on the front porch together to wait for Mr. Spangler to come walking home from Main Street, where he caught a ride to work at the chocolate factory in a nearby town.

Many a summer night I spied Mr. and Mrs. Spangler outlined through the window by the light of a cut-glass Victorian lamp. Once, they were having a particularly acrimonious argument over whether Pennsylvania

Dutch words were foreign and therefore ineligible in their nightly Scrabble game.

I recall Mr. Spangler's retirement at sixty-five from the chocolate factory after forty-five years of work. On the last day, he went out and bought a new Studebaker and got a driving lesson from the salesman so he could drive the car home. Then off they went in January to Miami, "Just to look, mind you, not to swim."

I ended up a small child who felt immensely rich, with a million little sprouts of plants, mad to propagate everything that grew. I had plants and flowers everywhere, enough to take with me to fill the windowsills next door when we moved there to keep Grandpa company.

And in the midst of all those little plants and big changes was the stanching of my secret, silent tears by a woman who lived in a gingerbread house that lured a child from the dark forest. But there was no wicked witch inside—instead a gruff guardian, protecting me a little longer from the wicked witches of reality and loss.

This Is What My Uncle Taught Me

he house sits on a little hill and a road runs in front of it. Massachusetts farmers, like all others, needed to live as near as possible to their lifelines. In the lament my wife and I make to each other a couple of hundred times per vacation, as cars shoot past—"If only we weren't so close to the road"—lurks one of the last half-century's most salient demographic shifts in Berkshire County.

On the other side of our road, a semicleared field slopes eastward, down to a fringe of trees beyond which are a dirt road, some cottages, and a pretty lake. You can't see the lake from our house, but you know it's there, like a friend reading silently in another room.

I've known this house and land for all my fifty years. For forty-five of them, I was a favorite nephew to a favorite uncle—the magnetic, gregarious, and grouchy bachelor who bought the place in 1940, just before I was born. For five years, I've been inheritor and owner.

The first forty-five years, I hung out at the place—as a baby escaping New York's summertime polio epidemics; as a child on school vacations scraping and bruising myself with joyful abandon, shooting birds in the meadow and then crying about it, swimming across the lake, occasionally helping my uncle with one of the less onerous chores; as an adolescent waiting on tables at my uncle's adult camp down on the lake (his livelihood); as a young man stopping in from time to time, introducing my girlfriends to my uncle; then looking after him as he got older.

What a change the past five years have made! Especially for a lifelong apartment person like me. If through marriage and parenthood I didn't achieve maturity, I may have through such physical and psychological challenges as putting a new cover over the cesspool.

Where at nine I caught frogs in a small spring in back of the house, I now muck out the mud. If I don't, the water will back up and creep into our cellar. My seven-year-old son catches the frogs. Where I used to eat tomatoes warm from the vine, I now shell out thirty bucks for rototilling. My four-year-old daughter will get the pick of the crop in August. Where I once heard only the wind sighing around the eaves, I now hear the water pump clicking on in the cellar while my wife takes a shower, or the furnace firing up, or the crunch of gravel as a repairman turns his truck into our driveway. Who says we get deafer as we get older?

When I took over, the look of being put-upon and beset, which my uncle often wore around his house—and which had always amused me— suddenly seemed less like a colorful idiosyncrasy. It quickly became less charming and more alarming that a marble dropped in the dining room would race downhill toward the kitchen. The house typifies the New England telescope farmhouse—big front part built around 1810, a smaller addition behind that, and a still smaller one behind that—and it turned out to be literally coming apart at one of the seams as the rear section sank downward on rotten sills. We had a new foundation poured and the sills replaced.

The flaking paint lost its quaint appeal almost overnight. We had the barn-red clapboards stripped and stained putty-green, with the trim remaining red, in homage to the past. Indoors, we laughed less and worried more when we woke up with paint chips from the ceiling in our hair. They might contain lead. We had kids. We had the whole indoors repainted. The marvelous attar of woodsmoke in the living room, which I remembered so fondly, betokened soot and structural problems, we learned, and the chimney needed repair inside and out. Blown fuses, occasions of much hilarity in my feckless youth, changed into an occasion for middle-age anxiety, a visit from the electrician, and a new circuit panel.

There has been more, much more—floor refinishing, a new refrigerator, a tremendous amount of furniture rearrangement, and plumbing galore—and it has all been a lesson in responsibility. But not, ultimately, anything unexpected. It's not surprising to a man in his forties to find that home ownership appears as a major landmark along the road of adulthood, and it's a tedious tic to complain about the burdens involved, especially when shouldering the burdens has paid off so handsomely in so many ways. The feeling that my family and I have of *belonging* in this house easily outbalances the work, the anxiety, and the dollars and cents required to keep it up.

"Come on, Willy, let's go gather some kindling," I say to my son. Out of the house we go, to the apple orchard, through the white gate that still has a bullet hole in it from the time when, at the age of eight, God help me, I was taking target practice with a .22 and foolishly stepped back and tried to shoot the rifle without resting it on one of the gate boards. The hole is no more than a half inch above a cast-iron hinge and what would have been a very dangerous ricochet. I tell Willy about this soberly, we both shake our heads.

"Elizabeth," I say to my daughter, "do you know that your great-grandmother once sat in the very same rocking chair you're sitting in on this very same porch and, after I had said to her that where I was going was none of her business, told me, 'Little boy, that is rude. You must not say, *It is none of your business.* You must say, *It is none of your affair.*'"

I tell my wife, "This is what my uncle taught me," as I lay a fire in the fireplace or make pancake batter in the kitchen or play a song on the guitar or stake the tomatoes in the garden. "Thank you, I'm glad you like what we've done with the place," I say to someone who has just dropped by, wanting to see the house after many years of absence—a distant cousin maybe, or an old friend of my uncle's who first came to the place four decades ago. "And I'm even gladder to hear you say that it still feels like the same house, for all the changes." And it's true—we've tried hard not to lose the atmosphere of warmth and welcome that my uncle gave to the house, the atmosphere of sociability and security. Downstairs, the dining room still has the same dark paneling, the kitchen—despite the new refrigerator—still looks rustic (to say the least), the living room still seems to encourage relaxed conversation, with its big fireplace at one end and three wide, south-facing windows at the other. And upstairs, the bedrooms still offer refuge and privacy.

And the bittersweet still grows at the edge of the field on the hill above the house—we ritually cut some and take it back to New York every fall—and the brook beyond the bullet-hole gate still sounds like a faint chorus of children's voices, the sun in the afternoon still illuminates the mountains to the east, and the carpenter bees and the bats and the butterflies, and the very stones in the driveway, seem like old friends. With some luck, they'll be old friends to my children's children, and to their children, too.

Neither the lessons in real estate responsibility and the suffering that accompanies it nor the feeling of continuity and family history that hovers around our country house has come as a surprise. If I hadn't anticipated this reward, I'd have sold the house and found another, closer to the city, smaller, and more manageable.

What has proved amazing and enlightening to me about this marvelous legacy is, in fact, opposite, or at least complementary to the experience of permanence wrapped up in it. It is precisely the accession to the house, the keeping of it in the family, the succession of generations that have brought to me a deep and personal comprehension of human *im*permanence. My grandparents were here. They are gone. My uncle, my father, my brother were here. They are gone. I am here, and I shall be gone. Then my children will be here, and then they will be gone.

From time to time, this feeling, like a thunderbolt, has literally stopped me in my tracks as I have walked around the place from one occupation to another. I come upon my son swinging high in the tire swing in back of the house and I realize there is no still place in the spinning world. A strong breeze stirs the trees, and apple blossom petals fall like confetti around my wife and daughter as they wander by. They pause and laugh and I think of snow falling and the stillness of winter. After a bright morning, high clouds blow in and dim the sun. The brook runs dry in autumn. The embers from the fire turn gray and cold.

Whatever sadness such intimations of mortality bring on nearly always gives way to a more profound sense of joy. "Death is the mother of beauty," I and many other sophomores learned from the poet Wallace Stevens in college, but I think I never really knew what he meant until now. Until this house devolved to me and I began to truly understand what time is. Until the sense of the past, so palpable here, told me why I must cherish the present—the perfect arc of the swing, the sharp coldness of the stream, the dance of the fire's flames—before it vanishes forever.

What I Knew at Eight

y sister and I wake up when the sun streams across our beds. We chatter, keeping our voices down because we have not received the signal that we can rise. We arrived at our maternal grandparents' house in the Guilford neighborhood of Baltimore last night. It is summertime in the late fifties. Our tired mother, who drove the distance from Chicago in a Nash station wagon with no air-conditioning, was eager to get us into bed without much fuss, but if all is right with the world, our grandfather will remember our summer vacation rituals. Then we hear Grandaddy's footsteps in the hall. He explodes through the door.

"Let's go wake up Uncle Geerison!" he shouts. He is making a mockery of our Midwestern *A*'s, which he thinks an abomination. "No! No!" Anne and I correct. "It's Uncle *Ga-a-a-a*-rrison!" Grandaddy nods in satisfaction. Perhaps he will cure us yet.

We throw on robes. The three of us traipse up to the third-floor bedroom, where Great-uncle Garrison snores loudly. We pounce on Uncle Garrison. We pummel him. We pull at him and still he snores. We grow rougher, and finally he pretends to rouse himself for the first time, but only reluctantly. "Up and at 'em!" Grandaddy commands his visiting brother.

"Now let's go wake up the morning glories." We fall in behind Grandaddy, collecting the broom, the rake, the watering can along the march to the garden. We call upon Susie Morning Glory to waken her companions. We sweep the birdbath vigorously and refill it with Willie the Watering Can. (Willie weeps copiously when we go home, our grandfather reports in his neatly typed letters.) We look for Tommy, the blinking box turtle. I was chided for screaming the first time I met Tommy. Grandaddy said that was hardly a gracious way to greet Tommy, who was more than two hundred years old and whose intentions were friendly, he was sure.

Breakfast was sautéed fish from the Chesapeake and homemade biscuits. Everything was always fresh and steaming in silver serving dishes on a massive Empire sideboard. Grandaddy sat at the head of the table, taking enormous satisfaction in the summer's gift of three weeks with his granddaughters. Mother was smiling too. She was happiest as the instrument of these reunions.

After breakfast, Grandaddy would go to his downtown law office. We were free to explore the house, most especially the kitchen. This was the domain of Dotsie and Celeste. These two African-American women had everything to do with the smooth, cheerful management of that establishment. Dotsie was keeper of the house to my grandmother, keeper of the cookies to us. The cookies were large and good and they never ran out. Celeste was the laundress with the gold-toothed smile. From how many scoldings did she rescue us? We came in with grass stains and dirt on the hand-smocked dresses my mother had made. Celeste was only amused. She had our dresses washed and ironed again before anyone noticed.

I was summoned to my grandfather's third-floor office once for throwing a temper tantrum at Dotsie and Celeste. "Close that door," my grandfather commanded. "Sit down." I did my best to preserve my dignity as I clambered into the big chair with the hardwood seat. "I don't ever want to hear you behave like that again, young lady. Do you understand?" I hung my head and swallowed hard.

"It's bad to do that to anyone, but especially to the servants," he continued. "They don't think they can talk back, though you very much deserved it, Missy. We are all very dependent on Dotsie and Celeste here. It's hard work to keep a house like this running. They deserve your respect. Besides," he added, "that's no way to treat someone you love and who loves you."

I felt the first tear splash on my knee. My grandfather rose. I waited for the inevitable spanking. Instead, he walked to the door. "You stay up here and think about this until you are ready to come down to say you're sorry," he said, shutting the door. I knew in that moment what it is like to experience both the wrath and the mercy of God. I made my abject apology to Dotsie and Celeste. They absolved me with hugs.

Thanks in no small way to Dotsie and Celeste's competence, the house at 212 Chancery Road was a sociable place. What a collection of friends and relatives came through that dark-green door! Aunt Jenny and Cousin Ika, two spinsters, arrived in black dresses with bits of "family lace." Aunt Jenny carried the Dreaded Black Bag. The DBB, as we learned to call it, was a weathered medical bag discarded by Great-uncle Jack. In it, Aunt Jenny placed sterling-silver instruments of torture such as oyster forks, fish knives, and crab picks. These were for our manners lessons.

For poor manners we could be sent from the table. This was the threat, though it was never carried out, but once we children caught Great-uncle Garrison in some minor breach of etiquette. We summarily ordered him to his room, where he was to be given water without bread and bread without water, a torture we learned from James Thurber's magical tale, *The 13 Clocks*. "Fair is fair," we giggled, and he was banished, crying crocodile tears all the way. We were, however, merciless.

Mr. Tyson, a neighbor, lamely toddled over from the house on the corner. I remember coming down the stairs to join a party when I was very, very young. Mr. Tyson pulled himself up on his cane and bowed. "Good heavens, Mr. Tyson, you don't have to stand for the girls. They're just babies!" my mother protested. "And if I don't, how will they ever learn?" replied Mr. Tyson with weighty authority.

When dinner was called, we would rush into the dining room. Uncle Mason, a prominent surgeon noted for his delicate work on cancer of the neck and head, was a graceless carver. He looked as though he might put his foot on the meat. This made any prospective patients anxious, including family members, so he was directed to sit at some distance from the carving tools.

My grandmother presided over the dinner table. She communicated with Dotsie and Celeste in the kitchen by means of a buzzer that was hidden under the Oriental carpet. The buzzer had a habit of migrating during meals. As the dinner wore on, Ganny slipped farther and farther down, tapping her toe frantically in a search for the errant bell.

Around the table we repeated the old family stories. Had we heard about the night Mother's brothers, Garry and Mason, put a live goose in Ganny's bedroom? Tell us again about the day they stole all the carved wooden fig leaves that concealed the genitals of the marble statues in the Baltimore Art Museum. Did we remember the one about Mother's last date with Armstrong Thomas? (Armstrong urged her to have a banana split at a local soda parlor. She didn't want to go. Armstrong insisted. Mother played drunk.) Or about the time Mother's friend Judy placed Alka-Seltzer tablets in the chamber pots in a convent?

There was also the story of Great-uncle Jim and his son Spencer. After riding through the country, young Uncle Spencer and his cousin Henry took a notion to go skinny-dipping on horseback. Spencer slapped Henry's mount, sending the horse galloping through town with a stark-naked rider. Uncle Jim, trying to be stern, couldn't deliver a punishment for laughing. "Get out of here, son," he guffawed, "and if you tell your mother I laughed, I'll whup ya."

The evenings, when guests were gone, were quiet times for reading aloud. My sister and I meandered over to the house next door where Mr. Oates read *Uncle Remus* with a different voice for each character while we shrieked with laughter and held out our palms for fireflies. Or Grandaddy would read yet another chapter in an endless series of Oz books. Then, upstairs for bath and bed. There were lots of kisses at bedtime.

I remember my grandmother less well than my grandfather. She developed a brain tumor when I was very young, and before it took her there were three brain surgeries and sixteen years of slowly failing. So much of what I do remember are nightgowns and quilted Daniel Green slippers, trays of medicines, a thermal pitcher with a bent plastic straw, Sucrets, a weak voice, and a succession of nurses. I will tell you what I remember most about my grandmother, though: I know she loved us.

I know because one year she had deteriorated badly over the winter. I was too young to understand how sick she was. When two days passed after our arrival and she had not performed her usual ceremony, I tiptoed into her darkened room to ask, "Ganny, when are you going to open the toy closet?" I know she loved us because she slid out of bed and onto the floor, then hand over hand and baluster after baluster she began to haul herself up the stairs to the third story. I know because when my own distressed mother came running upstairs to stop her, my grandmother said, "I don't know how much longer I am going to be around. I want my grandchildren to remember that I loved them." And I do, Ganny. Forty years later, I still do.

I know my grandparents loved each other, too. I know because I remember incidents like this: We are assembled on the front lawn. My father has arrived for his short vacation. He is taking family pictures. My grandmother has one arm around my little sister; the other is resting on a cane. Her head is shaved from her latest surgery. There is a scar. There is a dent in her skull where they went in to cut out the bad spot. My mother is concerned. She whispers, "Daddy, do you think we should take pictures of Mother when she looks like that?" Grandaddy pats his daughter's hand. He looks across to my grandmother with a shining admiration. "Anyone who can go through what she's gone through and smile that way looks mighty fine to me!"

My grandfather died in 1956. Ganny was put in a nursing home, and my mother closed 212 Chancery Road. Only in our memories would we open the dark-green door again and walk into my grandparents' house on polished wood floors, passing through rooms darkened by awnings against the summer heat. We would have to consciously call back the high-pitched drill of the seventeen-year locusts outside, the scratchy feeling of the grass mats that covered the floor on the screened-in side porch, and the living room's horsehair sofa, remembering how uncomfortable those surfaces were to the bare thighs of girls in short dresses.

Grandaddy's death was the first I encountered at close range. Only very slowly did I understand my loss. "Mommy, do you think Grandaddy is in heaven?" I would ask for months after.

"I am sure of it," she would answer.

"What does he do up there, Mommy?"

"Oh, I guess he stands up at the Pearly Gates and invites people in. I imagine when Great-uncle Garrison went up there six months after Grandaddy did that Grandaddy said, 'Hello, Garrison. What took you so long? Come on in here and have a glass of sustaining punch.'"

I was only eight years old when my grandfather died, but think of what I had already learned in that house on Chancery Road. I had learned that someone loved me, really loved me. I learned that children are important and old people wonderful. I learned to spend a little time in the garden each day. I learned respect for nature. I learned that worker and employer, we need each other to get along. I learned to open the door and set another place at the table. I learned to keep the family stories, that what's inside is more important than your hairdo, that if I wrote a letter, somebody would answer. I learned perhaps the most important lesson of all: Take care how you are remembered.

By the Beautiful

Sea

s a small child in the thirties, the product of divorce in a time when divorce was rare, I spent five summers at my grandmother's house in Deal, a summer colony for Jewish gentry on the Jersey shore that was modeled after Newport. Young as I was, I fell madly in love with the big Victorian sun-bleached clapboard house, and with the pursuit of pleasure, glamour, artifice, and yes, I admit it, the underpinning of it all: wealth. I dreamed, and still dream, of blue skies, slinky dresses, and someone to pay the bills and pick me up if I fall. As the world grows harsher, visions of Deal, where big houses rose beside the ocean and snobbery was the most cherished comfort, leap into my mind surprisingly often.

My grandparents, who had moved to New York City from Peoria, Illinois, with money made originally in the family distillery and later invested in the stock market, bought the house before my time. But in my time, after my parents' divorce, my grandmother's chauffeur, Ray, used to pick me up at the end of June and take me to Deal, where my widowed grandmother would oversee my summer life.

My older sister was in camp, and my mother, dating, stayed in the city during the week. I remember the trip through the Holland Tunnel—a nightmare of congestion as endless lines of black, square-topped cars with running boards inched toward their destinations. My trunks, filled with red-and-white-striped shirts, red shorts and white shorts, organdy party dresses, and white Mary Janes, were sent on ahead.

After several hours, we arrived at the graveled driveway where the house rose out of blue hydrangea bushes in the middle of four acres. It overlooked a lush, deep front lawn and round beds of red geraniums and of pansies in many shades of purple. Beyond, the Atlantic Ocean roared, making the air pungent with salt. Deal streets, wide and clean, were shaded by fine old trees, and the houses, all versions of my grandmother's, were partially hidden by high walls or hedges. Deal was splendidly quiet. The grass was shiny, green, and thick, the curving driveways meticulously kept.

The car would pull up to my grandmother's front door under the porte cochere. I would step onto the broad veranda that encircled the house. Ray would unload the car and take the suitcases up to my bedroom past silent, cool, formal rooms on the first floor. My grandmother, the Peoria outsider yearning for full acceptance in Deal's summer social set, had called upon a decorator, Mr. Russell, to achieve the English country-house look popularized first in Newport and then in Deal. Mr. Russell filled the center hall with chintz-covered chairs; in a small den, a yellow antique Chinese Chippendale secretary had dark-red Chinese figures. In the living room and library, my grandmother insisted on deep-blue carpeting and worked with Mr. Russell to acquire a mix of eighteenth-century French and English pieces, bright lamps, low, springy chintz-covered sofas, and silver bowls filled with fresh flowers on cluttered tables. In the formal dining room, a corner cupboard held blue-and-white china, elaborately scrolled, and blue goblets.

My grandmother kept me at a distance, but on one occasion that I remember quite clearly, she took me with her to the market. Meeting a friend, she introduced me by name, omitting the words "my granddaughter." That would have underscored the fact that she was aging and no longer A Great Beauty. She dressed youthfully, believing "You're never too old to look young": Mae West's philosophy, actually.

Every day or so, the gardener would bring in baskets of peonies and roses, and my grandmother would spend hours at a time making artful arrangements. I also remember her standing in the linen closet, wrapping the "good linens" in blue cheesecloth to preserve them. From dust? Mildew? Yellowing? I never knew. I remember hearing the clacking of her satin mules as she paced in her bedroom until dawn. An insomniac, she disregarded the early bedtime rule for children, and nearly every night I was sent off with Ray to the amusement park in nearby Asbury Park.

Ray, whom I loved more than family, would point out the flagpole sitter. He would watch while I rode the merry-go-round or would accompany me to an early movie. The silver screen, as integral to my developing personality as my grandmother's decor, the life in her house, and my parents' divorce, helped shape my ideas about the world. A seductive blonde, Jean Harlow, set the style for would-be sirens such as my mother (and later, me). By the hour, I would pretend I was Harlow or Claudette Colbert or Carole Lombard as they portrayed saucy society playgirls in bias-cut gowns.

Tap-dancing Shirley Temple was too young for my taste. I preferred to watch Fred and Ginger gliding into the starry night, and I imagined a future that never came to pass: debonair men so overcome by my loveliness they would burst into song.

On the second floor, I occupied the "lavender room," one of six bedrooms. The walls were lavender, and the bureau and desk were painted lavender and trimmed in cream. All the bathrooms were room-size with windows, small white tiles on the floor, and a wicker *chaise percé* to hide the toilet. Farther down the hall, in the screened sunroom, I listened on the radio to Edgar Bergen and Charlie McCarthy, Phil Baker, Jack Benny, The Singing Lady, Uncle Don, and Little Orphan Annie, and like most thirties children, I sent away for an Ovaltine shake-up mug. On the small Victrola, I played Gershwin, Irving Berlin, and Cole Porter, whose lyrics all contributed to my sense of romance.

The Deal house was the family's center. Aunts and uncles, cousins, my mother and her younger brother, Billy, flocked to Deal on weekends. Uncle Billy, a dapper Yale graduate in his twenties, liked to reminisce about the suite of rooms he lived in at Yale, which were cleaned daily by a chambermaid. Billy and his friends ate in a palatial college dining room at tables set with fine silver and linen. Years later, *The Great Gatsby* reminded me of my uncle, a playboy who spent his days in Deal sailing or driving his new light-blue Packard up and down Ocean Avenue for all the world to see. Like some of the prosperous Gentiles who set the standards, Uncle Billy drank—

so excessively that his earliest offers of marriage to three well-born young ladies were refused. Uncomfortable with children, Billy gave me short shrift and I hated him until he died, decades later.

One person I remember vividly is the cook, Mrs. Breuch, a German version of the *Upstairs, Downstairs* Mrs. Bridges, presiding over the kitchen in her starched white uniform. Although my fare was broiled lamb chops, baked potato, string beans, and junket, Mrs. Breuch spent most of her time slicing and dicing and forming butter balls for my grandmother's elaborate parties.

A curious child, I was always watching, always listening. The Deal house trembled with excitement when the king of England, Edward VIII, married the scandalous American divorcée Wallis Simpson, for whom he had renounced the throne. The house buzzed with the latest gossip of the Royal Family, especially the little princesses Elizabeth and Margaret Rose, with whom I still identify. The house shuddered over the Lindbergh kidnapping, clucked over little Gloria Vanderbilt's custody trial. Although Adolf Hitler had become chancellor of Germany and the Nazis were erecting the first concentration camps, the Deal house remained indifferent. The residents felt themselves to be more Episcopalian than Jewish.

In the early forties, when my grandmother could no longer afford the upkeep on the Deal house, she sold it for the dismayingly low price of $5,000. An auction brought only $2,000 for the furniture. My grandmother spent her final years in a Park Avenue hotel and her constant companion, to the family's horror, was an Arthur Murray dance teacher. Today my mother, just turned ninety, is an exemplary great-grandmother. I am a divorcée with three grown children and two grandchildren. They would have loved that house.

Camp Colors

When my two sons went to their father's beloved summer camp in Massachusetts in the late 1960s, we thought we were giving them an experience to treasure, a part of their patrimony, but they hated it. The elder, a fifteen-year-old camper-waiter, ran away after a few weeks and spent the rest of the season in our summer house. The younger, eleven, didn't run away but he sent us a postcard that still makes me feel guilty: "Dear Mom and Dad, Every day seems like a year."

I guess my kids didn't need that particular experience, but I can't imagine who I would have been if I hadn't gone to summer camp. To me, it was a true home, one of the places where I was formed. Of course time has revealed that I am exactly like my mother when it comes to family matters—dealing with grown children, for example (don't ask questions, don't criticize, don't complain)—but my Catskill Mountain summers, six years bridging the Depression and World War II, were the font of my taste and my life as a citizen ever after.

Any one of a thousand sights and smells and sounds may unexpectedly take me back to camp. Sometimes, I get a poignant whiff of some combination of hot meat gravy and brown-soaped painted tables that catapults me to the sunny mess hall, where we stood behind our chairs every morning and sang a hymn that began, "Rouse, O Spirit, our endeavor/Keep our thoughts free, our hearts pure," to the tune of the "Ode to Joy" from Beethoven's Ninth Symphony (followed by the scraping of a hundred chairs).

My first summer in camp, about ten of us twelve-year-old girls (it was essentially a girls' camp with a few cabins of boy siblings) were taken to visit the nearby farmhouse of the camp owner, an excitable middle-aged artist. Daddy D——— usually painted the pair of mountains that dominated our landscape, now a famous ski area but in the thirties and forties just a pretty part of the hinterlands. The paintings were mostly purple and green, and those were our unusual camp colors, a matter that was largely theoretical because we never wore uniforms and never had "color wars," the athletic competitions popular at the time but sneered at by our progressive directors.

Although even twelve-year-old campers looked down on Daddy's paintings, his house was another matter. I had never seen such glamour. In the living room were two black concert grand pianos with their curved flanks fitted together so the performers faced each other; floor-length red curtains that closed; a wall of books; a low, deep divan covered with floral tapestry throws. Leaning against the divan's dozens of cushions the day we were there, wearing an embroidered silk kimono and smoking a cigarette, was Aïda, a daughter of the extended family. Her name meant little to me at the time, nor did her cousin Siegfried's, but the decorating changed my life.

A standard was indelibly, irrevocably established. I instantly preferred this decor to my own living room's brown upholstery, net tieback curtains, and vase of beadwork flowers with their dusty metallic smell. I wanted to live in a warm, *brainy* room like this one.

At the end of that visit, after Aïda and her husband, a concert pianist and teacher, played a thundering piece for us, we were seated at a long table under a grape arbor and served something amazing and perfect that I had never had at home, have never had since, but can still recapture with all the applicable senses: fragrant, cool, lavender-colored junket with no watery residue. There was no arbor in my backyard; the only structure was a hexagonal spiderweb arrangement of wash lines on a fixed pole. And instead of lavender junket on our dinette table, only boring red Jell-O with sliced bananas appeared. My poor parents had sent me off for enrichment, not to have my head turned—if ever there can be the first without the second in the life of an adolescent.

Enriching it certainly was. Even now, if I hear two bars of Debussy's "L'Après-midi d'un Faune" I am back on a grassy plateau on a starry Sunday night. A weekly calming event after parental visits (many parents, including mine, came up nearly every weekend) was a classical concert on the public address system, which also delivered our various bugle calls to wake up, go to sleep, appear for meals, write letters, jump in the pool (the same as the call to charge in old-time movies about the raj). A tacit Sunday evening competition among the senior girls was to be genuinely moved to tears by the music. Part of the game was to have your tears noticed without saying anything about it, and another part was not to reveal that you noticed someone else's tears.

Show me a pair of "rhythm slippers," soft T-strap sandals with tops and soles made of thin, taupe suede, and I can smell the dusty, unwaxed floor of our dance classes, the only place the middle teens wanted to be. How grudgingly we would allow ourselves to be pressed into playing tennis on the cracked concrete court or rowing on the small weedy lake. (Teenage girls who have no access to horses, which we did not, want to be dancers; I believe this to be a rule of life.) And our camp directors clearly had similar values. They didn't dredge the lake or build a new tennis court. They hired a bona fide member of Martha Graham's or Hanya Holm's troupe as our dance counselor every summer.

We not only wanted to endlessly exercise, practice, and perform; we also wanted to wear our leotards all day long. We sent home for yard goods so we could make ourselves bias-cut tie-on skirts like Martha wore, and we gathered the ends of our hair into a long scarf (or rag), then looped the knot under and tied it into a pageboy just like she did. But only the counselor strode around the rocky, hilly paths carrying a tom-tom—a privilege of those who had trod the true boards. "Martha would love your feet," spoken by the dance counselor the summer I was fourteen as she firmly clasped my arch, is still the most thrilling compliment I have ever received.

We also had a dramatics counselor, usually a speech major from one of the New York city colleges, to teach us Stanislavski's acting exercises (much later to become known as "the Method" and another good way to make yourself cry) and to direct performances of short plays. This counselor would also put on poetry readings: lots of Edna St. Vincent Millay, Amy Lowell, Sara Teasdale.

And there was Kahlil Gibran, another memory trigger. Just say, "The thorn bush by the wayside is aflame with the glory of God" or "Work is love made visible" and I am once again wearing my white middy and white shorts and fidgeting on the wooden bleachers that faced our outdoor stage (hard-packed earth on top of three stage-wide stone steps, like a Greek temple). I was amused when Gibran became fashionable in the sixties—I still hear passages in do-it-yourself wedding ceremonies these days—because that old humbug was a regular part of our bizarre, supposedly Jewish services every Saturday morning, along with some Old Testament readings; a Bach air for strings or woodwinds played by musical campers; a hymn, the tune perhaps by Haydn, the text nonsectarianized if necessary; a tiresome little sermon on a subject like the interlocking of responsibility and privilege; then a rousing Hebrew song. "Play ball" was the real amen of the service because the next activity was always the parent-counselor softball game—among the stars were my father and my uncle—with everyone cheering them on. Then our parents would visit our bunks and surreptitiously hand over salamis, the only thing I used my scout knife on, and boxes of chocolates.

My parents raised the money to pay the camp fees for me and my younger sister by renting our beachside house in New York City's borough of Queens and moving into Brooklyn with my father's sister and her husband. They were a happy, boisterous foursome, with no kids around during the week and lots of weekends at the camp's guest lodge. They had no idea of the extent of the bohemianism, radical politics, and "free love" notions their four children were soaking up from the counselors, and we knew enough not to tell them, ever. They had learned of the camp through Aïda's husband, who gave my Brooklyn cousins piano lessons once a week. This connection was enough of a recommendation, and obviously we were happy there.

The camp was run by two formidable women. One, a Dalcroze music teacher and mother of one of my bunkmates, was large and she always wore simple, ankle-length peasant dresses that my mother said had to be homemade. She taught us wonderful songs—very old English songs, entire Gilbert and Sullivan operettas, American folk songs, rounds far more interesting than "Row, row, row your boat." I'll never forget her saying that although it would be hard to learn the Elizabethan love song that she was teaching us, we would then have it forever. Not only was that song waiting in my memory when I had children to sing to, but the larger lesson, in the rewards of hard effort, has given me a lifelong strength.

The other director was a distinguished specialist in early childhood education—a small, tough, frizzy-haired unmarried person who wore short shorts and wire-rimmed glasses. She gave those responsibility/privilege sermons I found so boring, but in my first job as a junior writer on a teen magazine, I was given an editorial to write, and what do you suppose came out? It was like taking dictation.

The shared attitude of the directors toward the campers was interested, serious, and stern. One or the other was likely to call you "uncooperative," a major sin. We addressed them by their nicknames in the progressive-school style of the day, and we all longed for their approval. Lucky people got that, although no one ever rated anything as personal as a hug. I was too rebellious and quick-tempered to have a really high approval rating, but they liked me for my ability to play "Turkey in the Straw" on one of the camp's three upright pianos—sometimes for a full half hour—to accompany the Virginia reel. They also liked me for putting out the camp newspaper, printed by some means I half remember that involved trays of gelatin and purple ink. And they must have trusted me, because when there was a slightly retarded girl in our bunk one summer, they put me in charge of her.

Naturally, our counselors, as close in age as older sisters, were more accessible than the directors. They were idols, mentors, sometimes with a vocational edge: If you wanted to be an artist, for example, you had a crush on the painting counselor. Although a sorority girl slipped into the staff mix now and then, I best remember the radicals—the one who played a guitar and knew union songs, the one who taught us to sing the "Internationale" in French.

Some of the grown-up things the counselors did, like smoking cigarettes and having a lover, we didn't have to think about until the comfortably distant future, but I could and did adopt some of their political sentiments right away. I did boycott silk stockings in favor of horrid lisle because of the Japanese invasion of Manchuria; I did give part of my allowance for Spanish Civil War relief; I did frequently argue about politics with my father, a businessman and Roosevelt Democrat.

When as an older camper I became the postmistress, I discovered that three copies of the *Daily Worker*, the newspaper of the American Communist party, came regularly to our camp. Unlike Russian Communists of a generation before, the recipients of this newspaper were not potential over-throwers of any government; they were innocent, passionate, 100 percent American believers in the perfectibility of human beings. They had a quasi-religious faith in cooperation and responsibility, in a future world *in their lifetime* where everybody would work their hardest and consume only what they needed. It sounds like fairyland today after the genocide and war, stupidity and greed we have witnessed since—not to mention the failure of the Soviet Union—but it was an essential part of that dreamy world. Of all the things I miss about the days when I was young, such pure optimism seems the most irretrievable.

DALE MACKENZIE BROWN

Rearranging the Furniture

often dream of the house I grew up in. Walking toward it, down my old street, I am reminded of its secrets. And then I go inside. For a long time, I used the familiar rooms to play out my anxieties, but now that I have arrived at the latter part of my life with many accomplishments behind me, I am just as likely to dream of my boyhood home in a fulfilling rather than disturbing way. It has become a warm, enfolding place that offers up its hidden treasures.

As a boy, I lived in dread of the walled-off eaves on either side of the room in which I slept. They were the abode of a monster who could come through one of the two small doors to get me. Under the eaves were stored the things nobody could bear to throw away. Even on the rare occasions when my mother went in search of something, with me peering tentatively over her shoulder, she could not dispel my fears of what lay hidden there. The 100-watt bulb in the shadeless lamp she held did little more than

226

carve a hole in the overwhelming blackness, producing shadows that loomed and moved.

I don't think it should come as any surprise that the riches I dream of lie in the eaves. Rummaging unafraid in the larger, better-lit eaves of my dreams today, I turn up fascinating letters, precious jewelry, valuable furniture, even a forgotten room hidden in a corner. I awaken refreshed.

Our house was built in 1934 by my grandfather, a kind but taciturn man with white hair and a fine face who loved me at a distance and delivered his blessing on his deathbed in 1941: "The pride and joy of the Mackenzie family" is what I remember him saying. Twice he had brought his lumberyard and mill back from the brink of economic collapse, but when the Depression came, he found himself too old and too poor to triumph again. He lost both the business and the dwelling that was part of it. Somehow he managed to scrape together enough money to buy a lot and a half nearby and give us a new home.

Pa, as I called him, saw to it that our house had a certain middle-class distinction. It was quite smart for the Bronx. Set back from the street and standing three stories tall with a tapestry-brick facade and two-car garage, it lay at the end of the trolley line in an area that was only then beginning to be developed. One entrance on the garden side opened to Pa's ground-floor office where he carried on a vestigial business; the other, up an outdoor flight of stairs, led through a tiny hall into the living room.

Mother and I lived with Pa and her brother, Archie, while my father tried to make a living playing tuba and string bass in a traveling dance band. He was a handsome man ten years younger than Mother and she had hoped that marriage would help her escape her mother's grip, but my birth had brought Mother home; there would have been no way to take me on the road.

She walked into a trap when she moved back: Her aging father and helpless brother needed her, all the more because her mother had recently died. From everything I heard about my grandmother she was a remarkable woman: intelligent, well-read, witty, outgoing. Why she married such a detached man as Pa is not clear, but in her frustration she turned to her children and controlled them. When she died, Archie could not bear her abandonment of him and took her wedding ring, which she had pointedly bestowed on him in the hospital, and slipped it on his finger to wear for the rest of his life.

My mother and Archie were much attached; I suppose the word for them today would be codependent. She was two years older than he and she protected him while they were growing up. They were both hard of hearing, the result, they said, of having had malaria as children, and it made them diffident. They wore startled expressions on their faces as though they never knew what to expect next.

Archie always had a difficult life. His earliest photograph shows him sissified in a Buster Brown suit, his cherubic face framed by a big picture hat. He was not helped by being named Archibald, which schoolmates used to torment him.

Pa, reserved to a fault and determined too, had silently intended for his son to take over the business. He long denied what might have been obvious to all: Archie was not the kind of guy to sell lumber to builders. He wanted nothing more than to be a decorator; my grandfather would not hear of it and kept a sign on his mill that read A. T. Mackenzie & Son.

During the Depression, Archie couldn't get a job; he didn't even try. As a result, he had too much time to worry and complain. Only a good movie starring one of his favorites, Joan Crawford and Greta Garbo, seemed to lift his spirits. He would tell Mother over breakfast how beautiful they looked, what they said, and what they wore. In a very good mood, he would blow smoke rings for me between gulps of black coffee, but most mornings, he wakened with a headache, complaining of how awful he felt and even threatening to stick his head in the oven and end it all. Yet Archie had a sense of humor and a way with words and he could get people laughing—largely with the gallows humor of the Depression. I remember a Christmas when Archie and Mother could not afford presents. Undefeated, they did up boxes of all sizes in wrapping paper and ribbons and placed them under the tree. We would never have a more bountiful-looking Christmas.

Archie was our biggest secret, although everyone must have known that he was gay; still, there was no word for homosexuals in those days that was not demeaning, and besides, one never talked about such matters. His friend, a department store furniture salesman and a frequent visitor on weekends, was known to me as Uncle Charlie. Nothing more was said. To me, the greater secret was that Archie powdered his face before leaving for the movies or a cocktail party—he used a puff just like my mother's—and put clear polish on his nails as well. I would have been mortified if my friends found out, but they laughed at him anyway and I despised them for that.

Just how poor we were was another subject to hush up. We lived surrounded by the trappings of the 1920s, when my grandfather had money,

a large motorboat, and two Packard cars, and my grandmother spent that money liberally to make her home a showcase. Though the boat and the Packards were swept away in the undertow of the Depression, the furnishings survived to put a good face on things.

My uncle identified with his mother—worshipped her, he used to say—but he saw no need to perpetuate her memory by letting our home become a mausoleum. He set about updating it. Mother joined right in, and if I had to pick their most positive quality, I would say it was imagination. They were forever rearranging the furniture in the living room. The Duncan Phyfe settee, as we called it, had only two spots where it looked good: at the end of the room opposite the fake fireplace, and in front of the double casement window. In truth, I can't begin to count how many times that well-built sofa, which must have weighed a ton, was shifted.

A lot less bulky were the ornate twin mahogany bookcases, the grandfather clock (it ceased working, it was moved so often), and the desk shaped like a spinet, and they cropped up all over the room. The radio, a piece of furniture in its own right, standing on thin legs with a lift top that concealed a Victrola, could not be moved until my grandfather died; he was very hard of hearing and kept his chair pulled up against it. Even the 12- by 20-foot silk Chinese rug would be turned around, no mean task since when rolled it was the size of a huge cannon. Yet somehow Mother and Archie managed to swivel and unfurl it so the design seemed suddenly fresh. The only object that kept its position in all the years I was growing up was the girondole mirror over the fireplace. With its convex glass it bent the whole room into itself, an unvarying eye that never passed judgment on what it saw.

Mother and Archie did a great deal more than move the furniture around. They frequently redecorated—and not just the living room, but the kitchen, bathroom, and the never-used recreation room downstairs. They didn't lack for accessories with which to change a room's character. Copper for the kitchen? Colorful cups, saucers, and dishes for the plate racks Archie had made? Oval picture frames? These were all to be found under the eaves.

After Pa died, we discovered that the house he had built for us was about to be sold for unpaid taxes. He had been too proud to let on, not even when Mother found him sitting on the edge of the coal bin weeping, or even after he had gotten himself blind drunk on beer at a local bar and she had to go fetch him. Dad cashed in an insurance policy to pay off the taxes, leaving us poorer still.

I realize now that Mother and Archie allowed themselves to be swept along by events over which they believed they had no control and that it was the house that kept them afloat. Without the house to challenge them and keep them busy, they might have drowned in reality, and they were proud when friends raved about their latest changes.

Mother and Archie were both gifted. Mother could sew and my uncle could too. They ran up curtains and draperies on the Singer; they recovered pillows; they produced swags. Archie taught himself how to upholster, smashing his thumb more than once as he fumbled with hammer and tiny tacks. He boldly retied springs, not always getting them right as a muffled twang under the backside proved on more than one embarrassing occasion.

Mother and Archie were great painters and paperhangers as well. They picked up color schemes from the Chinese carpet, which offered them a full range of hues. Their boldest experiment was their most successful: They found a dark green in the grape leaves that wreathed one of the rug's moon gates and used it for the woodwork and the ceiling. For paper that time they chose a bold floral pattern, bouquets of full-blown pink and red roses against a white background.

Occasionally, Mother's and Archie's frustrations with each other reached explosive proportions when a project they had undertaken was not going well. Wallpapering could be particularly vexing. Mother would be holding the slack, limp end of the moist paper and my uncle, balanced on a stepladder, would be maneuvering the leading edge up to the ceiling when something would happen—a tear would develop, or a section would cling to the wall prematurely in an awkward twist. Poison would fill the air, but not for long. The sight of the new paper, several panels of it smoothed down in place over the old, tired paper, served as the perfect antidote.

How they loved the decorating magazines. They would thumb through them looking for ideas, pointing out rooms to each other. Once, inspired by an article about decoupage, they did as the pages instructed and pasted the covers of the issues they could not bring themselves to discard on the panes of the door between living room and hall. I can see that door to this day, each cover serving as a window into someone else's world.

I admired the energy that drove Mother and Archie on. So many of my warmest memories are of them together, pouring themselves into their schemes. They were not happy people; they had been damaged by life and lived it tenuously. But they were never happier, nor more in charge, than

when embarked on change. How wonderful it was to come home from school and find the living room sparkling fresh after they had redecorated it, all the furniture polished and the windows as bright as air, and it would stay fresh for a long time afterward. In autumn, the crisscrossed dotted-swiss curtains would go up, washed and stretched and redolent of sunshine. The room would take on a coziness, especially by lamplight. I wanted to sit there and read. With the first cold days, the fire would be started in the coal furnace. The steam radiators would hiss and clank, and soon there would be the smell of hot metal and the roasting paint Archie had inadvertently splashed on them—not a bad odor at all.

This passion for change carried Mother and Archie forward. But the reality they tried so hard to stay ahead of slowly crept up on them. If my mother had hoped that my father would come home to live, he never did, except for periods of unemployment. Mother began to let their bedroom go, gradually piling it with boxes of oddments and stacks of old magazines ("I want them for ideas," she would say when my father, there between jobs, told her to throw them out). She was barricading herself in, I think, building a wall against the world. Her messy bedroom became the last of our secrets.

At one point Archie got a job, as a window dresser for a big Fifth Avenue furniture store. Often after being paid he would arrive home bearing a gift for Mother—a pair of earrings, a bracelet, the kind of chunky jewelry Joan Crawford wore in the movies. Archie's employment ended, for reasons he would never explain, and Mother went out and worked as a typist. The house held its own for a while. After Mother died, Archie attempted to keep it up, but his efforts were about as long-lasting and effectual as fluffing up a pillow. When he died, the house seemed to close in on itself, abandoned, the garden rank, the trees leaning.

My father, retired, carried on by himself in the rooms he set aside as his own, but the house was too sodden with memories and tinged with death for me to want to visit him there often, and so we met in my home, brightened by the presence of my two vibrant daughters.

I love the house I live in today. My wife and I have many of the possessions that I grew up with and I am delighted they are ours, but I own more of the past than that: I have strengths that came from what I experienced as a boy. I learned patience and respect and compassion, and in the face of adversity, I became an optimist. Not surprisingly, I like rearranging our furniture. I realize, as Mother and Archie surely did, that rearranging the furniture means starting over.

E U D O R A   S E Y F E R

Behind the Parlor Door

t was a summer day in 1930 when my grandmother came to live with us. I remember waiting with my doll Genevieve on the front porch steps of our old Victorian house in suburban Chicago. My father had left the day before to drive to Wisconsin after Grandma. Her furniture had already been shipped.

It wasn't hard to figure out that my mother was not one bit pleased about Grandma's arrival. All week her irritation had been growing as she moved her treadle Singer sewing machine and Priscilla sewing cabinet from the back parlor, gradually turning it into a bedroom for Grandma. She stacked and crowded her own blue willow dishes in the tall kitchen cupboards to make room for Grandma's Haviland china, complaining to my father about his mother's arrival and her possessions.

"I know, I know," my father said. "I'm sure she's just as unhappy about this as you are. But there's nothing else to do."

The Depression was gaining momentum and Aunt Dell, who had been supporting Grandma with her teacher's salary, had suddenly started receiving IOUs instead of paychecks. It was the fate of many schoolteachers in those years. My father's salary as an economist for the U.S. Department of Agriculture's Chicago office was more secure in those insecure days.

Sitting on the porch steps that afternoon, I was wishing my mother would come out and wait with me—or that I had a sister or brother to sit beside me—but my mother was not the type to stage a welcome she didn't feel, and I was an only child. So I clutched Genevieve and together we kept the watch.

Finally, my father's black Buick with its running board and box-trunk mounted on the back pulled into the driveway. My father opened the door for Grandma, helped her out of the front seat, and supported her as she began to move slowly toward the porch. She walked with a side-to-side sway, obviously hurting with each step. I stood on the porch, heart pounding, suddenly shy.

Grandma was a heavy, big-boned woman. Her face was pleasant with smile-wrinkles fanning out from the corners of her pale-blue eyes, but she was plain, and because she believed lipstick and rouge were sinful, she did nothing to enhance her appearance. Her thin gray hair was pulled back into a tight little bun. She wore a shapeless dark print dress with a lace collar which she could detach and use on other dresses. Her wardrobe consisted of several of these print dresses which she made herself, all from the same pattern. The skirts reached almost to the tops of the black oxfords that she ordered from the Sears Roebuck catalog, a new pair each spring; it was a seasonal rite.

Compared to my mother and her friends, with their bobbed hair, knee-length dresses from Marshall Field's, and high-heeled pumps, Grandma looked odd and old-fashioned—like a picture in a book of Mother Goose rhymes.

But the day of her arrival marked the beginning of a unique four-year alliance between Grandma and me. We loved each other with an unspoken devotion: I was her only grandchild and she was my only living grandparent. To cement our special relationship, we shared the name Eudora, although my name was hyphenated with Elizabeth, the name of my other grandmother.

In the evenings while my mother and father sat in the front parlor listening to the long-legged radio, I would knock on the big sliding double door between Grandma's room and the dining room. "Come in," she always said, happiness in her voice—and I would slide the door open just enough to squeeze myself into her cozy but separate world, then close it behind me.

The room was large, and Grandma's massive four-poster bed with its dark blue-and-white coverlet dominated it. In one corner stood a slant-top desk where Grandma kept her ink bottle, dip pens, and stationery. Grandma wrote letters daily—to faraway cousins and friends—and she was rewarded with an equal number of incoming letters which the mailman delivered to our mailbox twice a day and I, in turn, delivered to Grandma.

Against the south wall between two windows was her large walnut dresser and in the sunny west window was the comfortable caned rocker where Grandma rocked the days away. Because it was so hard for her to walk and climb stairs, Grandma never went to the second floor. She spent her time in her room and the dining room, with an occasional morning in the kitchen where she made her special fried doughnuts.

My mother attempted to adjust to Grandma's presence. A former teacher of education, Mother had spent years in midwestern teachers' colleges. She was spunky and independent and high-spirited, accustomed to being in charge. When she finally agreed to marry my father at age thirty-eight after a ten-year courtship, her idea of a wife's duties had not included tending an ailing mother-in-law.

Although Grandma joined us in the dining room for all our meals, she and my mother found little to talk about.

"Our book club is going to study Jane Austen at the next meeting," Mother said.

"Cousin Emma wrote that little Charlie has scarlet fever," Grandma said.

"Madame Schumann-Heink is going to sing at the Sunday Evening Club. How lucky we are!" my mother said.

"This apple cake is delicious," Grandma said.

As soon as our meals ended, I would help my mother carry the dishes to the kitchen and Grandma would hobble back into her room. Sometimes, after dinner my father would follow Grandma and they would visit for a little while in her room, but he'd soon emerge, slide the door closed behind him, and retreat to the front parlor with *The Chicago Daily News*.

I never heard Grandma complain about her isolation. Instead, she centered her attention on the backyard as though it was the most fascinating place in all the world:

"Eudora-Elizabeth, come smell the lilacs through the open window."

"Look! The cherry tree's in bloom."

"The maple leaves are turning the backyard to gold."

But for me, Grandma's room itself was far more fascinating than anything outside the window, because it held her many treasures. There was the little blue copper-luster cream pitcher with white Grecian designs molded in relief. It rested in its place of honor on Grandma's walnut whatnot shelf. "You can hold it if you're very careful," Grandma said. "My mother brought this with her from Pennsylvania when she traveled west to Wisconsin. She was just a young bride when she set out to homestead." I would cradle the little blue pitcher and think of its long hazardous journey. "It's a miracle that it's still in one piece," Grandma sighed.

Another prized possession was her button string. She lifted it carefully from its little cotton drawstring bag and together we examined each button. "This button is from the dress I wore on my sixteenth birthday—such a pretty dress, with little tucks all across the front. I spilled lemonade on it that day." Grandma laughed, remembering. "And this little jet black one is from my mother's silk Sunday dress. The brass one is from my father's Union Army uniform." Each button had a story, and to me each story was momentous.

I was most fascinated with the picture on the wall above Grandma's bed. Entitled *The Little Hero*, it showed a pretty little girl wearing a dainty pink dress, carrying in one hand a sword and in the other a rifle. Behind her, the portrait of a Civil War soldier hung over the mantel.

"Tell me the story," I would beg, and over and over Grandma would recount it: "I was just a little girl like you when my father and my two big brothers went off to fight in the Civil War. They looked so brave and handsome in their uniforms, but it was hard for us at home, especially for Ma. She was left with four little children and a farm to tend. She worked so hard. And she worried about her menfolk.

"One day, a package came for me from out East and when I opened it, this picture was inside. My brother Eddie sent it to me. 'For my dear little sister,' he had written. It was the most beautiful picture I ever saw and I was the happiest little girl in all the world. Every day I looked at it and prayed that my father and brothers would come home safely.

"When they finally came home, Eddie was on crutches. He lost a leg in the war and I cried and cried when I saw him. But he taught me songs like "Tenting Tonight on the Old Camp Grounds," told me stories about the places he'd seen, and showed me that there are things more important than a leg."

I was horrified. "Oh, Grandma! What's more important than a leg?" Grandma grew serious. "Enjoying all you've got instead of grieving over what is gone forever."

After we examined each of her treasures, Grandma always added: "Someday, this will be yours." It was thrilling to think that I would eventually own these things that my grandma loved.

In 1934, Grandma began to change. Sometimes, when I slid through the door into her room in the evenings, she would be lying on her bed in the darkness. Other times, as I neared the door, I'd hear her softly singing to herself, "We're tenting tonight on the old camp grounds," and I wouldn't bother her.

Something awful was happening to Grandma. She was growing thin and frail. The doctor came, only to announce, "There's nothing we can do for her."

The day after school was out in June, Aunt Dell came to stay with Grandma. My mother and I took the train to Wisconsin to visit relatives— an early-morning train into Chicago, where we transferred to another train to Savanna, Illinois, then another to Wisconsin. It was my first long trip, an adventure to remember. I liked the porters helping me climb up the steep steps onto the train, the scary feeling of walking from car to car on the way to and from the dining car, the little stainless-steel basins where I washed my hands (again and again). I opened up the window to hear the train whistle and feel the flying cinders prick my face.

Uncle George, my mother's brother, met us at the station. My mother said, "I don't know how long we'll be staying with you. We won't go home until it's over." We stayed in Wisconsin all through June and until after the Fourth of July. When we finally went back, everything was different.

My father had moved Mother's treadle Singer sewing machine and Priscilla's sewing cabinet back to the sunny west window in the parlor; Grandma's rocking chair was in an upstairs bedroom. The big four-poster bed had been carried to the attic, and Aunt Dell had packed all of Grandma's treasures and her Haviland dishes in big wooden barrels which were stored in the cellar.

I knew I'd never see Grandma again.

When I was a senior in college, my father died and my mother returned to teaching. She retired reluctantly when she was seventy-one and moved to a little house near mine where she could be independent. "Don't worry about me," she laughed. "I'll never move in with you. I'd be as miserable as you'd be." And we both knew what she was thinking.

She died suddenly on the afternoon of her eighty-eighth birthday at a small party I was giving for her. That morning she had shoveled snow from her front sidewalk. She couldn't have planned it more to her liking.

As I had been promised, I inherited my grandmother's treasures. *The Little Hero* hangs in its lovely old walnut frame in our living room, the button string remains in its little drawstring bag in a dresser drawer, and the blue copper-luster pitcher rests high on a shelf. Now and then I lift it down and show it to one of my granddaughters. "This came all the way from Pennsylvania with my great-grandmother, your great-great-grandmother," I say. "It's a miracle that it's still in one piece."

And in our pine cupboard, Grandmother's Haviland china, pure white and fragile as eggshells, rests side by side with the choicest pieces of my mother's beloved blue willow. When I look at those dishes, as I often do, I remember both my grandmother and my mother—women who wasted no time "grieving over what is gone forever."

Transients

CATHERINE CALVERT

My Mother's Gifts

y mother made twenty-eight moves in her married life and I shared twelve of them. As army brats, my sister and I depended on her gift for making a home however dispiriting the circumstances. In cottage, barracks, or garage apartment; in city, suburb, or small town: across America and in Germany—whatever our house, my mother would create a center for the family for a year or two. And then she would do it all over again.

Her strengths were her personality and character, of course, but some of her weapons were material, literally. By my mother's standards—there were many and they were high—we were not at home until every window was properly dressed. The green army trunks that held her curtain collection were among the first things she laid hands on as the movers left the driveway, unfolding what looked to us like potentially great dress-ups and to her like the makings of home.

She would bring out voluminous billows of white silk—stitched up

when she was a bride from the postwar largesse of surplus parachute silk—
fine and filmy as soap bubbles, with the same iridescent sheen. She would
pick up the curtains with a cheerful farm print and I would find in them my
first memories, when I was transfixed by the chicks and the cows on the
curtains and matching pillows she had sewn to do something clever with an
army cot in temporary quarters. (In army terms, "temporary" meant a few
months and your home on a two-year tour of duty was "permanent quarters.")

My mother was endlessly inventive about finding bolts of material
inexpensively and creating picturesque effects with rickrack and fancy stitchery. She had to be. When you travel from a redbrick Georgian Colonial in
Virginia to a flat ranchette on a Kansas post to a Philadelphia row house, the
last thing they will have in common is the size and shape of the windows.
My mother's greatest challenge came in Germany, when our apartment consisted of six maids' rooms, a living room, and a kitchen. We, excited at the
thought of not one but two rooms apiece, cheered. She looked at the windows
and groaned. But brilliant forager that she was, she made a trip to the PX
and found something new to all of us—colored and candy-striped bed sheets
that when lined and hung beneath a valance brought new life to government-
issue furniture in shades of off-brown.

If my mother suffered any pangs of dislocation while she was making
our nest, I didn't know about it, but I remember how hard those early days
in a new place were for me. One particular hot July afternoon—in the row
house in Philadelphia, where my father, an officer in the Quartermaster
Corps, had been posted to a new army depot—is as vivid in my mind as if
it were yesterday. My sister and I had retreated to the basement, belly-flopped
on the cool tiles with our comic books, seeking solace down where the boxes
were piled head high. Those boxes contained our lives, or at least most of
what is important when you are eight (me) and six (my sister) and you are
swimming against that undertow so familiar to children who move nearly
every year.

In the first few weeks in a new place we would lurch around diso-
riented, craving—well, playmates certainly—but even more certainly that
sense of home we had just relinquished and had to build anew. It was all
very well for adults to talk about new opportunities and adventures, but for
two little girls, unmoored again, novelty had little to recommend it. We
always got used to our houses eventually and settled into the corners with
cozy familiarity. We learned where the sunbeams played on a cold winter's

day, which hydrangea bush or grape arbor made the best Indian tepee, where to hide with a book and apple out of reach of parental voices delivering chores. But we could never stay.

In Philadelphia, we were in an alien land again, and from upstairs on that heat-drenched day came a hum as constant as the sound of the cicadas. When I climbed all the stairs and went into the small sewing room, I saw a familiar scene: my mother at work, driving her little Singer sewing machine in great long miles of stitchery while a panel of drapery fanned out at her feet. She was almost always even-tempered, but she was so intent on her work that she was cross with interruptions, especially of the Can-we-have-some-Kool-Aid? kind. She corrected the *can* to *may* and sent us out.

After the curtain trunks, the next boxes and crates my mother reached for contained the other kind of homemaking material that she would deploy in new quarters—family treasures. Whether we lived with our own belongings or government furniture (which is to ordinary furniture what K rations are to food), whether we were moving thousands of miles or just a few hundred, my mother traveled with certain talismans that were our symbols of home. Most came from her own mother and grandmother and linked us with our lineage as surely as any of the family tales.

There was always a place for great-grandmother's converted oil lamp with brass cupids on the base and a glass shade covered with roses, and my great-great-grandmother's sampler—promised to me because I was the next Catherine in the line. We brought along the hooked rugs made of my mother's outgrown clothes when she was a little girl, and they prompted stories of what had happened when she had worn, for example, that coat of blue. The quilts that came from both her grandmothers she would spread open for us, and name the pattern, and remind us that while Grandmother Dally made very decent quilts, Grandmother Stewart's were particularly fine.

When my mother was finished arranging our houses, they didn't look like most other people's, I thought when I was small, and I liked ours better. Except for a Korean scroll, we didn't, like so many army families, travel with dozens of souvenirs of previous duty stations. Not for us the Japanese tea set or the span of ivory elephants. When I would visit a friend whose proud parents had swept away their past and lived in the spare simplicity of what was then known as Swedish modern, I wondered how a family could live, rattling and rootless in such a barren expanse.

I was comforted by traces of other lives that preceded mine when I felt lonely. I would polish silver and wonder about the other Catherine whose initials were engraved there. I would pull open a drawer in great-great-grandfather's tall 1840 chest of drawers and find daguerreotypes labeled Wheeling—pre–Civil War faces captured nearly a hundred and fifty years before. My ancestors. Even in Germany, far from my parents' families, which had remained rooted in West Virginia and Kentucky for two hundred years, they comforted me.

As surely as my mother would send along her silver wrapped in burgundy felt and her cut-glass salad bowl cushioned with tissue paper, she carried with her rituals of family life that were as much a part of home as the furnishings: things that were done, things that were not done, holiday celebrations and daily necessities. There were the usual rules about elbows and posture and prayer. And expectations that had the weight of law: books were important and so was ladylike behavior; moderation in all things (vocal tone, consumption of sweets) was a virtue; and the family was the center of the universe.

A ritual was enacted each evening when, by 6:30, we were in our places, the candles lit, the napkins in our laps, the water jug on the table— even if it was the first night in new quarters and we were having scrambled eggs and sharing spoons. That, in an ever-changing world, is no small matter to a child.

At holiday times like Thanksgiving, my mother made dinner a full-dress celebration. What my sister and I loved about Thanksgiving was re-union. Christmas was almost too exciting, a blur of toys and candy. Thanksgiving meant easy time spent with grandparents, who would travel almost any distance to be with us, or, if we were too far away, with friends whose army careers had matched our own, who held the weight of family in their hearts. Often my mother would add someone to the table who was lonely at holiday time. Along with every American family, we rejoiced in tradition: cranberry juice with a bit of sherbet in it, antique glass dishes that flashed rainbows and held spiced crab apples, slightly walleyed pilgrim and turkey candles, half-melted in their packing crate. There was Thanksgiving bounty that had nothing to do with food in the stories of times past and the pleasures of the present gathering.

Perhaps it is not surprising that when I grew up I settled down, clinging to one city where I live surrounded by bits of the past. I know that I cling to the familiar as an antidote to the dislocations of that nomadic childhood. My parents have settled down, too; their curtains this time were made to order and not by my mother. For a while, I fought change in my parents' house as I do in my own. When my mother began to give me things—table linens, plates—I would refuse them; I wanted her house, finally, to be the same from year to year. But these days, I accept her gifts, knowing something more important is being passed along, and that the passage from mother to daughter has its own rhythm.

Both of us, several times a year, may mention a nostalgia for the time when we would bundle our lives into boxes and try some place new. Perhaps that is why when my Scottish husband begins to talk of a move to Europe, I look at my own two little girls (the ages we were in the Philadelphia row house) and my heart simultaneously soars and sinks. They know the world outside their windows; they love the life they live. I worry and wonder if I have the strength and the wisdom and the grace—the real gifts my mother shared with us—to build a home in the wilderness that change brings.

A Packet of
Snapshots

Y ou'll understand when you're older."
As children, we accept that implicit promise of an explanation—in some vague time to come—of all that we don't understand about our parents' lives. Only when we are older do we realize that there are things we may never understand, about their lives or our own, and that the best we can hope for are clues. So it is with the mysterious moves of my childhood.

I can still hear my mother on moving day. "Ye gods, how I'd love to live in a hotel!" she is saying, using her best drama-school diction, arms outstretched, eyes rolled heavenward in deliberate avoidance of wooden crates leaking excelsior, barrels stuffed with crumpled newspaper, and odd bits of furniture standing exactly where the movers left them.

In her bridal year she *had* lived in a New York hotel.

"Your father thought I was looking for an apartment, but I was actually going to auditions," she once confided to my brother and me. Either the auditions or her method of contraception failed, because instead of a career in the theater, my mother had launched herself willy-nilly on a career of motherhood and ever-larger suburban houses, mostly rented by my father and moved into, sight unseen, by the rest of us.

Minor in geographical scope—Midwest to East Coast—our moves were major in number: seven by the time I was eight. Some were Depression-related: Moving was better than unemployment. Others, I now realize, were symptoms of a certain restlessness in my father that he gradually outgrew and that might have been related to his service as an infantry officer in France during World War I—a time when he fought in the trenches and was gassed.

Hotels were by then out of the question; even my mother saw that. But she used to speak longingly of the brief time we had spent in a three-room apartment on the North Side of Chicago. "It was only an efficiency apartment, but I loved it," she would say. "Efficiency apartment" was one of those Depression-era terms intended to make people feel good about being hard up. If they couldn't afford space, at least they could have everything within easy reach. Later, I wondered how efficient it could have been for my mother to have all of us—the dog, the cat, my father, my brother, and me—within easy reach. I decided that what must have appealed to her was the hotellike aspect of those living arrangements.

My brother and I also loved that apartment, not for its efficiency but because it sat smack on Lake Michigan, with a patch of beach on which we spent every day of the summer of 1931. We liked the apartment less in September, when we went off to a school where we sat two to a desk meant for one, and where we thought the teachers were mean. We knew about the Depression—we'd heard of it from our parents and on the radio, we'd seen the word in the newspapers—but I don't think we had any idea that our teachers in that crowded school weren't being paid, that they weren't mean so much as they were overworked.

We resigned ourselves to the defects of the Swift School, thinking we wouldn't be there long anyway. We seldom went back in September to the school we had left in June, and as the list of schools lengthened we liked to recite in reverse order the names of all those we had so far attended: Nichols, Larimer, Lockwood. Tuscan, Nassau, Swift, Border Star, Bristol, Pierre Laclede. The list got me up to fifth grade and my brother up to sixth.

Our teachers in those schools, who presumably read our transcripts, must have anticipated learning gaps, instability, even school phobia; now, looking back at our nomadic childhood, I wonder how we survived. How did my brother and I (our younger brother, who came along later, had a more conventional time of it) manage to do well in each new school, make friends in each new town, invent new games to occupy ourselves each time we sped along a highway into new territory?

There are many possible answers—we had each other, we had our books, we loved seeing new places—but the real answer was my mother, my gently bred, high-spirited mother. Neither dependent nor submissive, she didn't hesitate to tell my father how fortunate he was to have found her, because few women would have put up with constant uprooting. Yet I see now that hard as those moves were, they were also, for her, a stimulus and a challenge. Having put the theater behind her and hotel living into some fantasized future, she proceeded to dramatize our lives, turning each move into a new and exciting production, with parts for all of us.

She was an expert at networking long before the concept had a name. Two hours on the telephone in a new house and she would have created a whole new social life—found out about Scout troops, the local women's club, Episcopal churches High and Low, theater groups if any, and amateur choral societies (she also sang). The social life usually included my brothers and me since, unlike many children I have known (my own, for example), we liked to play with the children of our parents' friends. Intensely sociable, my mother kept in touch by mail with people in every town we had ever lived in.

The fact that I have vivid, if not strictly chronological, memories of almost every house I attribute partly to the flurry of excited anticipation my mother stirred up over each move, and partly to her way of telling my brother and me of things that happened and things we did in one or another of our houses. We never tired of hearing her stories; they became an oral history that kept our own recollections alive.

At 5955 Côte Brilliante in St. Louis, the second house I lived in but the first one that I remember clearly, there was a small backyard where my mother used to let me sit while she practiced on the upright piano in the dining room. The yard opened onto an alley, and as I sat listening to my mother's music I watched the passing show: peddlers hawking fruit and vegetables; the milkman making deliveries in his wagon, bottles clinking, horse's hooves clattering on the paving bricks; blocks of ice being hauled in huge tongs up the back steps and into the kitchen (that was the last house in which we had an icebox rather than a refrigerator).

Next, we moved across the city line to a house in Webster Groves that had an apple orchard in back and a sleeping porch upstairs. My brother and I closed our eyes there to leafy darkness, lit by the sudden spark of a firefly, and opened them to the pale green of summer mornings in the first fresh heat of the day.

In Maplewood, New Jersey, where we spent most of one year, we received on Christmas a beautifully wrapped box of fancy-looking bottles with a card signed by the family next door. The family was duly invited over to share in the contents of one of the bottles. I don't remember much about that, but I do remember my father's astonished comment when he opened the box: "Good Lord," he said, "and all this time I've been driving to Newark in the dead of night!"

The comment, meaningless to me at age seven, made sense later, when my mother had added it to her repertoire of what happened when and where. It seems that we lived in Maplewood during Prohibition. The trips to Newark were made to restock the wine and liquor cabinet and would not have been necessary if we had known that our next-door neighbor was either a bootlegger or a man with very good connections.

In my adult life, people have often asked me why we moved so much, and assume that my father was in the military, but in fact, he was an attorney. Since most attorneys stay put, there must have been reasons why my father didn't, even if I have never been sure what they were. "Transfer" was my mother's word for our moves, but I know that at least once—on our first move from St. Louis to Kansas City—my father left one firm for what seemed like a glorious opportunity at another. In a fit of optimism, and in the face of my mother's repeated statements that she never wanted to own a house, *never*, he bought one in the Country Club district, resodded the lawn, joined the golf club, and settled in for a long stay. Ten months later, his new firm went into bankruptcy and we hit the road for New Jersey, leaving behind us an unrented house.

My mother was not above evoking the Kansas City experience as an object lesson in the perils of home ownership. From that time on we rented, and my mother managed to come as close to hotel living as possible on a moderate income in a suburban house. There was always someone who cooked and cleaned, and someone else who filled in on the regular person's days off. At some point in the morning, my mother would talk to the maid, telephone the grocer, and then, as nearly as I recall, put food out of her mind.

Her system with regard to interior decoration was similar. When we moved into a new house, my father put up curtains, paced the floors for carpet measurements, bought new furniture if it was needed. My mother graciously accepted his choices, and it's hard to say whether it was because she liked them or because you don't check into a hotel and change the furniture.

I'm sure I often wished for a mother closer to the conventional model, someone who could bake cookies and teach me to knit. But I muddled through cookbooks on my own, and I found one of those stores that give knitting lessons if you buy their yarn. With my mother I did other things. I remember her taking me and my brother to an outdoor performance of *As You Like It* at the Century of Progress Exposition in Chicago in 1933, and I remember a birthday party a year or so later when she took me and my five best friends to hear *Madame Butterfly*. If the art she exposed us to was a bit beyond us, we soon caught up, and in that way, too, she gave us a world that could travel with us.

Eventually, my mother did move into a hotel, but it was a hotel staffed by nurses and orderlies, with doctors on call. Many of the residents were on special diets, and many, including my mother, were in wheelchairs. My mother didn't like that hotel, although, characteristically, she organized a social circle for herself there. Some members of the circle could converse with her, others could not; it hardly mattered, as long as they could listen.

Long before that time, my parents had moved into the New York City apartment where my father spent the last eighteen years of his life. My mother lived there for twenty-three more years after my father's death. When my mother gave up her apartment, I went through the accumulation of decades of living that she'd left behind her, and found in a closet several boxes of photographs. Most were snapshots taken by my father. There were pictures of my older brother with his new sled, of my younger brother in his cowboy boots, of me in my confirmation dress, of all of us with our pets— and in the midst of all these was a little packet wrapped in tissue paper and tied with ribbon. Inside were pictures of houses, labeled on the back with the address. There were no sentimental inscriptions on any of them. There didn't have to be; the packet spoke for itself. Or rather, my mother spoke. I could hear her voice saying words she had never said out loud, but that I realized I had sensed throughout our lives: "If you know you will have to leave a house, you might as well pretend it's a hotel."

The voice said something else to me but I didn't know what, until a day when I was in Chicago on business and found myself on Michigan Avenue with some time to spare. I asked directions from a woman standing next to me and climbed onto a Number 151 bus. It must have taken at least forty-five minutes for the bus to lumber through the fashionable Near North Side, with its beautiful, classic buildings, and into the unfashionable Far North Side, which was an architectural jumble.

In order not to overshoot my destination, I got out a couple of blocks too soon and walked northward. Suddenly, my breath caught in my throat and my feet stopped moving. I felt as if I had stepped into a time warp. There, bordered by well-tended plots of grass and shrubs and dwarfed by the glassy high rises around it, was a neat, five-story redbrick apartment building. In front of it was the beach, next to it was the courtyard where I used to play with my friend Virginia, and beyond it was the lake, charcoal blue in the gathering dusk. As I stood there I felt a profound longing to call to my mother, "Look, they've saved it—your little efficiency apartment is still there!"

I couldn't do that, but I could look for those other houses in the photographs my mother had so carefully preserved. In Webster Groves, once I was on the right block I immediately recognized our house, now in the midst of much newer dwellings. The orchard was gone, but it still looked like the rather elegant farmhouse it originally was. The woman who lived there took me on a tour, and what I wanted most to see—the sleeping porch—was just as it had been. As I left, the woman's granddaughter asked me shyly if it was true that the house was haunted. I said I had never heard anyone say so, but my unspoken answer was yes, it is haunted, for me.

So far, I have found six of our fourteen houses, and every one is still standing—proof either that miracles happen or that my father had a good eye for real estate. But on the day when I reach an address and there is no house, or a different house, I will simply tell myself, as my mother must have told herself, that what you lose can live in your mind forever.

Going Back

War and Peace in a Very Small Place

or years, the image of the village in western Ukraine where I was born tantalized me. Only a few yellowed photographs had survived World War II and the five postwar years we spent in Bavarian refugee camps before we were allowed to come to America. As I was growing up my mother would tell stories that I suspected were embroidered—about a cherry orchard, an oxbow in the river where the fish were so bountiful they could be caught by hand, a pair of chestnut Arabian horses that were the envy of the entire parish. Telling the stories would bring tears to her eyes, but sometimes her voice would grow hard with anger at the inhuman regime that destroyed her family and the happy, civilized life they had led in Zariche. The village was part of Poland until the outbreak of World War II, was occupied by the Russians for a time, then by the Germans, and after the war was claimed by what was then the Soviet Union.

I had only a few fragmented memories because I was a toddler when

255

we left. My most vivid image of my birthplace was of a flock of geese that ruled the yard and terrified me.

No one in my family had been back for forty-seven years; foreigners were not welcome when our village was part of the Soviet Union. The opportunity to return came in 1991, when I was invited to Kiev, the capital of Ukraine, to teach a three-month course in Western journalism at Kiev State University. From the moment I accepted the invitation, I knew I would visit Zariche. My husband and student sons were not free to come, but my seventy-four-year-old mother and her older sister, Katya, both widowed, were eager to accompany me for part of my stay.

Although I had left too young to have emotional attachments, I wanted to discover and touch the past. I wanted to see the family's rambling three-hundred-year-old wooden house with its stables and barn. And I was fascinated by the figure of my grandfather. Well educated and liberal, he had been an outspoken opponent of both Nazism and Bolshevism and had helped Jews get false papers to escape the Germans. He died under mysterious circumstances when we were still in a refugee camp. Frightening rumors reached us, never to be denied or confirmed. Was he really murdered because of his politics? Was my grandmother really allowed to starve to death afterward? How can a family absorb such mysteries?

So one of my goals was to learn the true dates and circumstances of their deaths. Another was to have family members visit and mourn at their graves. It was only right that we do so because they had died alone, without even one of their five children present. Their eldest son had been arrested, imprisoned, and executed by the Russians in the tumult of the war. Their three daughters were able to escape to freedom with their husbands and infant children as the war drew to a close (another early memory of mine is being strafed as we lay prone on the ground next to the train carrying us west—a practice considered safer than remaining on the train). And they lost their surviving son to communism. He became a party member, moved away, and disowned his heritage. Our visit to Zariche was a pilgrimage and an atonement for leaving my grandparents, even though they had made the choice to stay on.

We entered Zariche on a foggy, rainy September afternoon. During the hour-and-a-half drive from our hotel in Lviv, the capital of western Ukraine, we hardly spoke, ignoring the driver, who tried to point out the sights. Anticipation mingled with dread. I think we all tried to suppress our expectations, but every so often my mother or Katya would start to say, "Do you remember . . . ?" and describe a happy event from her girlhood.

I had a vague image of an enchanting old house among the cherry trees.

But even our most modest hopes were soon shattered. The village was so small and shabby that we actually drove past it. When we turned around and came back, Katya and my mother were not sure this was Zariche. Rain had turned the unpaved road that leads to the village into a morass of black mud. Small cottages on either side of the road were partially hidden by untidy wooden fences. Some of the houses were no better than shanties with crudely patched roofs and cardboard replacing broken windowpanes. Except for a flock of noisy ducks and geese, the main street was empty.

Seeing the honking geese, I somehow knew this was the place. When we came to the church, Katya and my mother recognized it. Their voices rising in excitement, they told the driver how to get to the old homestead. After the car stopped, my mother and my aunt rolled down the windows and peered out into the fog. The family homestead was gone. In its place stood two sturdy one-story brick houses. The orchard had been uprooted to make a field, which lay fallow. The oxbow was overgrown with weeds and littered with rusting cans and household garbage.

Minutes ticked by as we sat in the car saying nothing. Then Katya began searching her purse, found a handkerchief, and blew her nose. Finally, I ventured forth alone and made my way to the brick houses. Mud covered my sneakers and splattered my jeans. Rivulets of rainwater were running into my eyes, and my hair was plastered to my face as I struggled uphill through the mud. I thought of knocking on the door, but what could I say to people who lived on land that once was ours? I was on the verge of tears. Why had we come?

Nearby, someone cleared his throat. Driving a rickety old horse cart was a small man, crinkled by hard work and hard times, his shoulders hunched against the rain.

"Your family is from around here?" he asked. I nodded and gave my grandfather's name.

The man's face lit up. "I knew him," he said.

"What happened to the house?"

"Burned down."

"Who lives here now?"

"Two families."

I had other, more important questions but I could tell he would say nothing more. He watched me walk away. By the time we got back to the village church, word had spread that *Amerikantsi* were visiting. Several women came out of the houses. One of them, Vira, recognized my mother, who had taught in the village school before the war. Vira volunteered to meet us at the cemetery at the far end of the village, where my grandparents were buried. First, she would find the priest and tell him we were here.

The cemetery was a desolate, forgotten place. Weeds grew knee high. Metal crosses lay toppled every which way. Katya, who was wearing open-toe shoes, stepped into a puddle and almost fell. She began to weep. My mother's face had turned white. She clutched at her purse and was whispering to herself. We began to search.

Finally, I found the double grave. A rough concrete cross stood over it. My mother and my aunt had sent money for the memorial a few years into Mikhail Gorbachev's perestroika, but we did not know until this moment that anything had been erected. A metal plaque bearing my grandparents' names was attached. It did not give the dates of their deaths.

We placed the flowers we had brought at the foot of the cross and prayed. Our tears mingled with the raindrops. My mother and Katya began to pull at the weeds. Katya suggested planting flowers. My mother objected. She said a bush would look tidier and require less weeding. Katya said flowers were prettier. They were arguing and crying. I tugged vainly at the wooden forms still attached to the crude concrete apron around the graves.

Vira had arrived and was taking credit for the cross. She seemed proud of the work done. I asked her when my grandparents had died. She said no one was left in the village who could remember. I did not believe her. I saw Katya slip her money as we left the cemetery.

When we arrived at the church, the priest was waiting. Father Ivan was a young man recently graduated from one of the newly reopened seminaries. He unlocked the church with obvious pride and invited us inside, out of the rain. For thirty-five years, the church had stood locked and unused. Its exterior walls were pockmarked with bullet holes, and the bell had been melted down during World War II for ammunition. The German-Russian front had halted for two days in the vicinity of Zariche and half of the village had been destroyed by artillery.

The church, though damaged, was spared. In the past two years, it had been repaired. The nave was newly whitewashed, the wooden filigree gilded, and the icons of the saints restored. Several of the largest icons were draped with linens embroidered in blue and white thread. When the priest turned on the lights, everything sparkled. Father Ivan said that on Saturday, four days hence, they would be celebrating the feast of the village's patron saint and dedicating a new bell that had just been cast. Would we return and be the parish's guests?

We promised to try. Returning to Lviv, we discussed what we should do. My mother and my aunt wept. Too many years, too much grief weighed us down.

I decided to go back for the village festival and my mother agreed to accompany me. My aunt, crushed by the desolation she had seen, declined. Saturday turned out to be sunny and warm. In the sunlight, the mud began to dry; large puddles glistened like mirrors. The village looked less forlorn. Down by the church, the post office and general store had been decorated with colorful bunting, flowers, and greenery. Adults had on their Sunday best. Little boys wore embroidered shirts with tight stand-up collars. The long braids of little girls were caught up in enormous organza bows in colors of the rainbow. Dozens of candles illuminated the church altar, and the sweet smell of incense drifted through the air.

After church services attended by about a hundred and fifty villagers, probably two thirds of the population, we were surrounded by people who hugged us, plied us with questions, and invited us to their homes. We were no longer strangers.

Although they were not sure we would be back, two families had gotten together to prepare a welcoming feast. When we entered the three-room cottage where the feast was being held, we found the table already set, as is the local custom, with *zakuska*, the first course of cold dishes. There were salads of cabbage, carrots, and beets, an aspic of pork studded with garlic cloves, a platter of sliced sausage, and a platter of sliced yellow cheese. Stuffed hard-boiled eggs were decorated with tomatoes sprinkled with chives and dill. Two bottles of vodka stood in the center of the table, together with a towering bottle of Crimean champagne.

We were given seats of honor on either side of the priest, who sat at the head of the table. The women, wiping their hands on their starched white aprons, came out of the kitchen. There were nine of us around the table. After Father Ivan blessed the food, serious eating began. Baskets of sliced rye and white bread were passed. Instead of butter, paper-thin slices of *salo*, a peppery fatback, accompanied the bread. A welcoming toast was raised, then another one, and a third. Conversation began to flow.

The *zakuska* was followed by hot chicken bouillon called *rosil*, then by platters of fried chicken and meat-stuffed rolls of cabbage called little doves. We drank the champagne, which Father Ivan had brought, with the dessert, which consisted of two enormous tortes and a sweet roll layered with dried fruits and jam.

A groaning table is the traditional sign of hospitality in this part of the world, but remembering the empty stores in the city, I was amazed by the bounty, even though two families had pooled their resources. As if reading my thoughts, our host turned to us and said, "The land is not poor. The problem lies with the government."

America fascinated our hosts as their lives fascinated us. Information was exchanged, questions were asked. Did we serve meals such as this? Was vodka available in America? Were we all rich? There was much to tell in just one afternoon.

As the party broke up, I privately asked the grandfather, who had been both imprisoned and exiled for his political views, about my grandparents. He said he did not remember when or how they died. "It's so long ago," he said, and looked away. I did not believe him. But he was more forthcoming about the homestead. "After the house burned, the land lay unused for years," he said. "Then a man returned from Siberia and wanted to settle here." He built one of the houses. The second one was built by another man who survived Siberia. "They are good people," he added, looking me straight in the eye. It was a long, wise, eloquent look. It said: Let the past rest and accept what you have achieved by returning this day.

The afternoon was fading. It was time for us to go. Everyone came out of the houses to say good-bye. New conversations started. It was dusk when we finally left the village. A procession followed our car as our driver, trying to bypass the worst of the puddles, wove slowly down the street. I asked him to drive past the cemetery and pause by the hillock upon which loomed the dark outlines of the two brick houses. There was sadness in my heart, but also a sense of closure.

I had been able to reconnect, to come as a stranger and leave as a friend. I had names and addresses in my notebook, lists of requests I would fulfill once I returned home. Some families needed medicines that were not available there. Father Ivan said a new set of vestments would be nice.

This time, we talked and laughed on the way to the hotel in Lviv.

I often relive our visit, and I know now that people of goodwill matter more than possessions or embroidered memories, more than forcing out old truths. Because good and kind people invited us in, my mother and I were able to touch the past and be healed. Katya, too heartbroken to return, did not have the means to put the past to rest. My mother and I were very lucky.

Passage to Kerala

onkeys lay spread-eagled in muddy wayside pools and ravens took refuge under drooping jacarandas. It was a sweltering summer's day in southern Kerala. We were speeding along a narrow coastal road, the black Fiat rattling with every bump. On one side was the aquamarine glare of the Arabian Sea, on the other the dense green foliage of the coastal palms. Hot air rushed at my face through the open window of the car. I was groggy from jet lag, my bones ached to lie down, yet I couldn't stop my heart from rising like a balloon. I was going home.

Home for me is usually a memory, and I go back to India every year to reinforce it. The long journey takes me from New York to London to Madras, then by a small plane to Kerala airport, where Ranga picks us up for the two-hour drive. Ranga had been a bright-eyed young man when he drove me to nursery school. Now in his fifties, he still maintains and drives the two ancient Fiats of Vaikom House.

261

When the car was surrounded by a herd of elephants crossing the road, Ranga stopped. I turned around in delight but my husband and the girls were fast asleep. One of the elephants thumped the road with dung as she crossed. My smile widened. Welcome to Kerala.

We were heading for my grandfather's house. He is a criminal lawyer, and the volatile tempers and simmering passions of Vaikom village mean good business for him. Legend has it that a man in a drunken brawl yelled that he had my grandfather on his side before sinking a knife into another man's throat. The entire village calls him Swami, which means lord; my grandmother is referred to in a less grandiose fashion as Akka, which means elder sister.

My grandparents are an unusual couple. Swami is a strict, stern disciplinarian who has followed a rigorous routine all his life. He rarely smiles, and speaks only when necessary. Akka is garrulous, with the cheerful fatalism of someone who has given up trying to control her world. She is always fussing over people, feeding them, taking in strays. Her sisters-in-law cluck their tongues disapprovingly and say that Akka runs Vaikom House like a railway station.

My paternal great-great-grandfather bought Vaikom House from a British army colonel in 1857. A handsome two-story bungalow with whitewashed walls and sloping red-tiled roofs, it has housed our family ever since. Unlike other castes in Kerala, we Brahmins are patriarchal, so Swami's four sons and their families live in Vaikom House and his two daughters live with their in-laws elsewhere. Vaikom House is perfect for a child lost in the anonymity of a large family, with many balconies, eaves, and dormers that can become a secret refuge.

Family members fall into roles, but they are not rigid. My father alternates between teaching English literature at the local college and managing the family farmlands. He is also the purveyor of dreams, the person to whom the children turn to talk about changing the world. Everyone goes to my mother to vent their sorrows and fears. And all defer to Swami.

Relationships blur in a joint family. I called my aunts and uncles Big Mother or Little Mother, and Big Father or Little Father. They used to hug me and scold me like a parent. Cousins were like sisters and brothers, and as we grew older, this closeness extended to their children. In fact, my charges on this trip were Maya and Surya, children of my cousin Deepa and her husband, busy physicians in New York; they will join us here a few days later, when my brother and all the cousins will be back and Vaikom House will revert to its former bustle and glory.

"Wake up! We're here!" I shook the girls as Ranga carried the large suitcases inside. A warm body enveloped me from behind. "Ma!" I cried, hugging her, quickly examining the delicate features for signs of aging or ill health. Dressed in her usual pink cotton starched sari, my mother looked cool and fresh. My nieces with their short hair, frayed jeans, and hanging T-shirts greeted their Indian cousins, who were radiant in long silk skirts and colorful blouses.

Akka and Swami stood at the threshold, holding the *arati* oil lamps as they always did when we returned. Akka circled the lamp around us in a traditional welcome. Even since last year, Akka had lost weight and Swami's tall frame was bent. Would I see them next year?

As the others went in I paused on the threshold. The swing, the unruly garden, the hole in the veranda railing, everything was the same. The huge hall was bare, its red-tiled floor burnished by generations of bare feet. I took a deep breath, reveling in the smell of magnolias and mango. It was so good to be home.

The house stands on two acres. Akka lets the garden go its own way, so it is a forest. Fragrant jasmine creepers twine around jackfruit trees, pine grass grows under papayas. Crows caw, monkeys chatter as they swing from tree to tree, and at night the croak of the tree frog puts us to sleep.

There was a feast waiting for us: puffy rice dumplings called *iddlis* with coconut chutney; crepelike *dosas* with spicy *sambar* gravy; two kinds of sweets; three kinds of curries; yogurt, pickles, and *pappadum* lentil wafers. Banana leaves lined the floor of the hall. We sat down in batches—the children and men first, then the women, and finally the servants. Later when we were opening gifts upstairs, Sita, my youngest niece, snuggled next to me. Everyone says Sita resembles me. She has a gentleness of manner that comes from not having to struggle for anything. I recognize that trait but do not possess it anymore. I grew up believing that everything is predestined and that you must have good karma to achieve success; the burden of achievement is off your shoulders. But in America, people talk about taking charge of your life, and ten years of competition there have sharpened my edges.

My husband and I live in Connecticut in an old, temperamental barn that vaguely resembles Vaikom House. Within that cavernous space, I try to re-create the sanctum I remember. When I return from India, I bring bits of Kerala with me. Brass elephants, bronze Buddhas, and lacquer boxes crowd my mantelpiece; colorful saris fill my closet.

Over the years, the oak beams that crisscross our ceiling have absorbed the fragrances of my cooking: cumin for digestion, fennel for cooling the body, fenugreek for lustrous hair, cardamom as an aphrodisiac. I brought spices with me when I came to New England as a college freshman, and on my marriage day, the women in the family doused me with turmeric water.

Mine was an arranged marriage. Swami began making enquiries about suitable alliances when I was in college, and the search grew more intense when I went on to graduate school. Swami heard about my husband's family from a friend, and with a letter of introduction sent my horoscope, which had been charted at birth.

Apparently, the horoscopes matched, because my future father-in-law wrote back asking for a meeting. When I was on vacation in India, my clan gathered to inspect my possible husband-to-be and his parents at tea. The visitors were smothered with hospitality: platters of sweets, snacks, fruits, nuts. Everyone made small talk and stared covertly. My future husband suggested that we take a walk. The room grew silent as the elders pondered the propriety of this suggestion. After all, Swami and Akka hadn't even seen each other before they got married, and although my parents had met, they had not spoken.

We walked out before anyone said a word. It turned out we had a lot in common. Both of us had studied in the United States, and we compared notes about Indian restaurants, college life, cheap airline tickets. He had to return to the States immediately while I stayed behind to finish my long holiday, but he called me every day for two months; he still has the $1,200 telephone bills that prove it. One day, he asked me to marry him.

"Why don't you come and ask me that in person?" I replied flippantly.

Much to my surprise, he did. Two weeks later, on a Madras beach, he proposed again. Of course, I accepted, and then the elders took over the wedding preparations.

I don't think either of us was in love when we got married, although I liked his self-confidence, his unbridled laugh, his quick mind, and the fact that he didn't hesitate to fly eighteen thousand miles to propose. He certainly had potential. But now it is a source of unending amusement to Akka that her self-centered, independent granddaughter begins every other sentence with "Ram says" and "Ram thinks" and "Guess what Ram did today." Somewhere along the way we fell in love, and I tell my American girl friends, "I may have taken a different route, but I got there."

•   •   •   •   •   •   •   •

Growing up in Vaikom House was exciting. With over a dozen children and a dozen adults in the house, something was always happening. Children fell sick and recovered; couples fought and reconciled; babies were born, usually in the middle of the night in Akka's bedroom with the help of a midwife. Cousins got engaged or married, and all the ceremonies were conducted in the house. Relatives visited for a few days, or stayed for a few months. People from far and near came to seek Swami's legal advice and Akka's reassurances.

During my childhood, there was an ayah to look after the children, two servants to clean the house, a cook, a gardener, a driver, and my grandfather's two law clerks. The ayah, a thin, wrinkled woman with a permanent frown, was our main contact with the rest of the household. She would wake us up at 5:30 and sleepily we would troop downstairs, where Swami would be waiting for us. We would follow him to the Noorni river that linked every backyard in the village.

As Swami stood at the edge of the river and washed himself in a dignified manner with small buckets of water, the fourteen of us would go neck-deep, clothes and all, into the fiercely cold river. Together, we would sing the Sanskrit hymns and chants that Swami had taught us. Swami believed that every Brahmin child ought to know these verses codified in the Vedas. It was his opinion that singing in deep water at dawn would strengthen our voices, and much as we hated it, we were powerless to refuse. As the sun's rays warmed our heads, our voices would lose the hoarseness of sleep and we would finish the chants in beautiful harmony. We would wait quietly until Swami returned to the house, then all our pent-up energy would explode as we wrestled in the fast-flowing river.

After school, the fourteen children converged on the veranda swing, a wooden plank the size of a bed suspended from the ceiling on four long chains, to play an endless game of Train that took us to distant lands. The swing was also where Swami dictated his case notes after breakfast. Akka took her afternoon nap there, servants gossiped, clients waited to see Swami, husbands and wives exchanged confidences.

• • • • • • • •

The annual *shraadam* usually takes place halfway through our vacation. It is an elaborate, daylong ceremony when the clan gathers to honor our ancestors. The staff is given a day off and the family women gather in the kitchen at dawn to prepare the feast that will feed twelve Brahmin priests, two cows, our entire family, and all the crows in the neighborhood. Crows are supposed to carry the souls of our forefathers, so the more we feed the better.

There are strict rules: Dairy can't mix with grains; everything has to be fresh and prepared according to an age-old menu. The young ones rush between storeroom and stove carrying grains, shredded coconut, vegetables, water, spices. My cousins and I do the preparatory work, and our mothers help Akka preside over the stove in harried harmony.

The men get the brick fire pit ready in the hall with stacks of dung, twigs, and wood shavings. At 7:30 the priests arrive. They light the fire and begin chanting. Swami, whose knowledge of Sanskrit verse is as good as any priest's, joins them with gusto.

Four hours later, we are summoned from the kitchen. By then, the cooking is done. All of us squeeze into a circle around the dancing fire. As the smoke rises and brings tears to our eyes the priests invoke eight generations of our ancestors by name: Shoba Laxmi, Swami's mother, after whom I have been named; Swami's father, the Sanskrit scholar and healer who could cure illnesses with a touch; their parents, grandparents, and great-grandparents.

"Carry this ghee, O Agni, Lord of Fire, to the ancestors of this family! Bless the procreation of this lineage! Shower them with health, wealth, and happiness!" the priests chant as one by one we pour the sacred clarified butter into the fire.

I watch Maya tenderly as she steps forward to pour the ghee. With her scrubbed face and long Indian skirt she looks pure and innocent. This *shraadam* is for her, to connect our children with India.

My youngest cousin Sheela is in danger of disconnecting, it is thought in Vaikom House. She has just been admitted to a graduate program in the American South. All the elders argue against sending Sheela abroad. Sheela's mother is convinced that Sheela will get assaulted or will run off with a white man.

266

"You sent Mani to London!" Sheela accuses her mother.

"That's different. He's a man."

Sheela stares at me pointedly. I look away.

I am American enough to believe that Sheela and Mani ought to be treated the same way, yet I know that a daughter is different from a son. I understand Aunt Gowri's justifiable fear that Sheela might run off with a white man and never come back. But Sheela got her way. Aunt Gowri said a mother's will is no match for a daughter's tears. Deepa and I have promised that we will watch over Sheela in America.

Every Indian I know in the States dreams of returning to the homeland. We talk about it at parties, make plans to buy tracts of land together and return in a certain number of years. But there is always a reason to stay— to finish graduate school, get a promotion, save some more money—and the years go by. I often think of Vaikom House when I work in my Connecticut garden at twilight. American twilights are quieter than they are in Kerala. There are no parrots chattering as they fly back to their nests, no monkeys grabbing fallen coconuts and fleeing from an angry gardener. The stillness of an American twilight provokes weighty thoughts about my fast-approaching thirtieth birthday: *What am I doing here? Where am I going?*

I pull another weed out of the ground and begin to fall back into the fatalism that is inherent in every Indian. I can hear Akka saying, "Everything is predestined and there's nothing you can do about it." But Ram and I will decide for ourselves where we belong.

Stories From the Hamam

very March for as far back as
I can remember, the *martenichkas* arrived from Bulgaria. In late February,
my sister and I began to wait for the postman and the square envelopes that
he slipped through the brass mail slot of our front door on South Forge
Street in Akron.

Among the letters that scattered our entryway the *martenichkas* were
easy to spot, in part because they bulged and in part because of the colorful
stamps that covered a full quarter of the envelopes. Most of all we recognized
the handwriting—elaborate Z's, backward R's and N's, bisected O's—that
flouted everything Miss Krause taught us at Spicer Elementary School. My
mother explained that with the exception of Aunt Anka, my godmother,
none of my aunts wrote in English, and that their Cyrillic alphabet was unlike
ours.

My mother translated *martenichka* as "little March," and said they welcomed spring. Inside each envelope were a card, a silk handkerchief, and the little *martenichka* itself, a bundle of silk threads, one red, one white, bound into figures of a boy and a girl. Gathered into three-inch lengths no thicker than my earlobe, each was folded in half and then divided and tied with contrasting thread to form a head, arms, legs, hands, and feet. Eyes and mouths were stitched in X's, and if we were lucky the boy might wear a hat and the girl an apron. Joined by a few twisted threads, the figures were looped in dance like the sour cherries my sister and I dangled over our ears in late spring.

The *martenichkas* were among the few tangible links to my mother's home, which she left in 1935 when she married my Dubuque-born father, then a decoder at the American Legation in Sofia. When my mother left Bulgaria, she had no way of knowing that twenty-five years, a world war, and a cold war would separate her from her mother and five sisters.

Prewar Sofia had been elegant, my mother said: the cosmopolitan capital of a kingdom, a city of roses, of gold-domed churches, and streets paved with golden bricks. The Subeva sisters, rich and beautiful, had grown up beside parks and strolled arm in arm along boulevards. They breathed the freshest air and drank the sweetest water from Vitosha, a mountain that overlooked the city.

Akron compared badly. In the forties and fifties, it was still a rubber town. Smoke and soot blackened the air. When my sister and I came in from playing, my mother lamented our "filthy dirty" state, then plunged us into the claw-foot tub. There, like a professional body scrubber, a *teljakinja*, she rubbed the skin on our backs, arms, and legs with a rough silk washcloth used in Turkish baths and told us stories of Sofia's *hamam*.

The *hamam* was where women met to soak and scrub and, when the time came, to find a bride for their sons. My mother was chosen twice. She refused the first suitor, who threatened suicide. She was considering the second, the son of the Spanish counsel, when he was killed by a train in Varna, a resort on the Black Sea. The handsome Spaniard had been the first to give my mother powder and perfume and she loved him with the ardor of an eighteen-year-old. When news of Guillermo's death reached Sofia, my mother made up her mind to join a convent, but the priest shook his head and said that with such eyes she could never be a nun.

There were other stories. One concerned the death of my mother's brother, who died six years before she left Sofia. When I was very young, I knew only that he had died. Later, I understood that a streetcar had struck him. I was twelve when my mother told me Ivanco might have stepped in front of the streetcar. In the end, I knew that he had committed suicide because he had fallen in love with a gypsy he could never marry.

Aunt Anka's story, like Ivanco's, developed as I grew older. What consumed me about my aunt's not having married I cannot say; perhaps it was simply that she was my godmother. Aunt Anka had been the most sought-after sister. Men were wary of the too-beautiful Luisa but felt comfortable with Anka. She was pretty and clever, a linguist.

My mother first explained Aunt Anka's spinsterhood by saying my godmother feared men wanted to marry her for her money. When I was nine, my mother revealed that Aunt Anka had loved an Italian named Roberto, a businessman who lived in Bulgaria until he emigrated to Australia. I accepted Roberto's exit as an explanation until, at sixteen, it occurred to me that Aunt Anka should have escaped with him. Impossible, my mother said. While bathing in the *hamam*, my grandmother had learned Roberto's secret: His brothers were crosseyed. She warned her daughter about giving birth to imperfect children, and Aunt Anka, who could also have married any man in the British Legation, put away her embroidered wedding nightgown.

My mother's wedding pictures proved that my grandmother was acquainted with perfection. Not one of her daughters was cursed with what my mother called pork-chop cheeks. The sepia portraits showed women of faultless beauty: arched eyebrows, almond-shaped teeth, piano fingers. I studied these photographs trying to match the curious names—Anka, Slafka, Betka, Nikolinka—to the pretty faces. All remained as foreign as the smiling bride in whom I could not find my mother, the woman the photographer had elevated to the center of the picture, her train of Irish silk swirled around the box on which she stood.

In Akron, my mother worked hard. She canned peaches and sour cherries, pickled green tomatoes, and made soap from grease and lye. She scrubbed clothes on a washboard, starched and ironed, baked bread and made yogurt.

My mother sang arias, "Un bel di" and "Mi chiamano Mimi," in high clear notes and insisted on her American name Martha, not Marta. She made her own cigarettes, spreading tobacco onto rectangles of paper, rolling them up like Bulgarian cheese pastries, licking the seams, sealing them tight. My mother listened to the radio for news of Bulgaria, played jacks with my sister and me in our kitchen on a stretch of mustard-colored linoleum, and taught us to say, "*As te obitscham*," I love you.

Love was important, but marrying well was too. Aunts Betka and Luisa had managed this; their husbands were not handsome but were educated and well-to-do. When my father proposed marriage, the priest was summoned to inquire of the Iowa clergy just what sort of family the Duffys were. The reassuring answer, written in Latin and postmarked Dubuque, arrived in time to plan a June wedding.

After the war, such a query would have seemed superfluous. The Communists came to power on September 9, 1944, and changed everything. They seized the important things: freedom, husbands. Aunt Betka and Aunt Luisa's husbands left for work one morning after breakfast and were never seen again. Such things happened. Men jumped or were pushed from windows, and widows, even if they knew, dared not speak. Instead, they wore black bands on their arms, silence on their lips. One guessed what was in their hearts.

Even Aunt Anka disappeared. My grandmother and aunts were beside themselves, calling on the British Legation where Aunt Anka worked, and knocking on every door in Sofia. A week later, my aunt returned. For months, she hardly ate and stared into nothingness, telling no one what had happened—not even after forty years when Aunt Slafka, her closest sister, asked for the last time.

The Communists confiscated our family villas in Bojana, and in the city, crowded in their apartments, my aunts were forced to make room for strangers—perhaps spies—authorized by the government to move in. My aunts were unable to speak in front of their children, fearful they might be quoted at school or play. Hardship and confinement magnified differences, even between sisters, and as the years passed, Aunts Anka and Luisa, who unwillingly shared a bedroom, spoke less and less to each other.

The one thing the Communists hadn't ruined were the *martenichkas*. The cards were still hand-painted, mostly in the colors of the Bulgarian flag—white, green, and red. A *shop*, or peasant, still appeared on most.

In 1965, my husband and I left our teaching jobs at the University of Missouri and he joined the engineering faculty at Robert College in Istanbul, 250 kilometers east of the Bulgarian border. That I would one day travel to Sofia by such a circuitous route had never occurred to me, and yet in 1966, in the dead of winter and of night, we arrived with our infant son at the Turkish-Bulgarian border on the Orient Express. The Bulgarian militia men were shouting in the corridors, banging on doors to sleeping compartments, shining flashlights in our eyes to see if we matched our passports.

Twelve hours later, as the train pulled into the station, I saw my smiling aunts waving bouquets from the platform. The sepia bridesmaids of 1935 had stepped from the wedding portraits now wearing heavy tweed coats. In middle and late-middle age they were round, pretty, and full of life. My aunts greeted me with cries of *sladko, sladko*—sweet, sweet—as though I were a child and lovingly pinched my cheeks between index and middle fingers.

During that first visit, I studied my aunts, looking at them to find something of myself, for what bound us together all these years, and discovered a closeness far stronger than our dark hair, Mediterranean skin, and small hands and feet. The better I knew them, the more I admired them: resourceful, joyful, and brave.

On the surface, the Sofia of 1966 was not unlike the Sofia of my mother's stories. Near the city center, the palace was still gold-ocher trimmed in white, modest compared with the opulence of Istanbul's Topkapi Sarayi. A block away, the Russian Orthodox church, lacquered green and rust and as exquisite as one of Fabergé's eggs, crowned a small hill. In the quarter where my mother grew up, the same iron-gray, three-story buildings overlooked the park where she had played, and beside it yellow streetcars jerked their way along the tracks under bare limbs of horse chestnut trees.

In the streets, no one smiled. Bulgarians walked with their heads bowed, carrying string bags they hoped to fill with whatever might be available—cabbage, light bulbs, shoestrings, even turnip seeds. Outside the baby-food store women formed lines, each behind a baby carriage waiting for a day's worth of freshly mashed carrots and potatoes.

In Aunt Betka's apartment, I saw something of the life my mother had described. That Aunt Betka married before the war was evident in her walnut furniture, a table that seated twelve, Rosenthal china, Czechoslovakian crystal. Standing at windows framed with heavy mahogany and looking at a golden square and domed church, one could almost forget how Aunt Betka's husband disappeared and that three families and a stranger were living in five rooms, sharing a bath, kitchen, and 1937 Frigidaire.

The rule was two people per room. This meant that Aunt Slafka and Uncle Todor, who married after the war and lived in what remained of his father's four-story medical clinic, had two rooms—one for their daughters, one for themselves. They shared a dark, cold kitchen and two-burner hot plate with Uncle Todor's parents and married brother. Otherwise, they lived,

ate, and slept in a sunless room with beds pushed to the wall doubling as
sofas. Mornings, Aunt Slafka emptied ashes, stoked the coal stove, and swept
with a short-handled broom, but in the late evening, we gathered at a drop-
leaf table, ate winter *turshija*, pickled cauliflower, carrots, and green tomatoes,
and toasted the future with *slivova rakia*, fiery plum brandy.

To sponge-bathe, we heated water, but to get really clean, Aunt Anka
took me to the *hamam*. Amused by my reaction to public bathing, my aunts
joked, saying I had nothing to hide; I would see women of all kinds—tall,
short, fat, thin, and women like Yasemin, a Lebanese beauty whose sole
imperfection was a slight extension of her coccyx that gossips called a tail.

Hamam etiquette demanded one see without looking. This applied
to all women, not only Yasemin. Once, my grandmother had overheard Aunt
Anka whisper, "*Le-lej, goljamo dupe,*" what big buttocks. At home, she taught
her daughter to see silently, rubbing Aunt Anka's mouth with a hot red
pepper.

The *hamam* itself was a massive space, in structure the marriage of
mosque and church, open, with wide arches, white tiles. Under the great
central dome was a circular pool of warm mineral water in which naked
women gossiped, softening skin, opening pores. After a leisurely soak, they
made their way to benches interspersed with marble fountains from which
hot and cold water poured. There, some washed with soap and rough cloths,
dousing themselves with water scooped up in copper bowls. Others for a few
stotinki hired a *teljakinja* to rub their bodies until the outer skin rolled off in
dark threads, leaving a smooth, pink layer underneath.

That afternoon in the warmth of the *hamam*, our nakedness half
hidden by steam, our words disguised by running water, I might have asked
my godmother why she hadn't married, what she had feared. But by then I
realized my insisting on an answer would hurt Aunt Anka more than her
mother's red peppers had.

In Australia, my grandmother's predictions came true. Roberto's
wife had given birth to cross-eyed children. Ten years after my godmother
and I bathed in the *hamam*, Roberto wrote to say his daughter would undergo
corrective eye surgery in Zurich, and being so close he would visit Sofia. His
wife had died; he wanted to see my godmother.

Think of how this might have ended: Aunt Anka might have married
Roberto; she might have found him unappealing after thirty years; they might
have at least shared a glass of wine. But it was the still-beautiful Luisa who

drank the wine. Rather than reveal what the years had done to her, Aunt Anka sent her sister, to whom she hardly spoke, with money to entertain the only man she ever loved.

Aunt Nini, the youngest, died too soon and Aunt Betka died of old age, her husband's pearls around her neck. Aunt Anka, who at thirty feared imperfection and at sixty was too battered by life to take a second chance, died alone.

Love takes courage, the kind my mother had—to leave home for a distant continent with a man whose family no one knew. And now that she is alone and winter nights are long, my dauntless mother, who took America in her stride, leaves Akron and returns to Sofia to wait for spring. I imagine her with aunts Slafka and Luisa remembering, retelling stories, and like the *teljakinja*, exposing layers only to find another more enticing underneath.

The *hamam* has closed for renovation, and with the Communists out of power, other changes are afoot. The family villas have been returned and are rented to the French and Belgian embassies. "*Le-lej*," my mother said when she called to tell me the good news about my aunts, "they are richer than I am." And then she added, "Who will give them back the last forty years?"

Spring greetings continue to arrive. The cards are no longer hand-painted, the handkerchiefs no longer silk; only the *martenichkas* remain the same.

Aunt Slafka has visited us in Ohio, and my cousins come and go with increasing frequency, bringing me things I crave: sweet paprika, rose oil. They appear with camcorders and walk from room to room saying in Bulgarian, "This is Julia's living room, this is her kitchen, her cat, her VCR." When I ask about the past and the old family stories, they shrug their shoulders; they prefer to look to the future.

Without the Mango

Tree

We are standing, my eldest sister and I, outside the front door of our old house. At the invitation of the current owners, we have come back to admire the restoration they have performed. All the vulgarities of the interim owners have been thrown out, they have assured us—the marble flooring, the wet bar, the modern this and up-to-date that. They have even given the house a name it never had: MARRIOTT HOUSE is etched in glass over the front door. The house is back to what it was, they have said. Come and see. Anytime.

But how could they know, these new owners, the way it was? The house we grew up in, that our father grew up in before us, would make no sense to restoration-minded people. My grandmother's boudoir, for instance, the cavernous corner room in which my parents later kept their theater costumes—two vast chests and three wardrobes stuffed with ostrich-feather capes, buckled boots, buttoned boots, bustles, togas, old telephones, hats upon hats, beards, wigs, and stage jewelry—is it a boudoir again now, with its prospect of the sea, its balding pink carpet and flowered wallpaper?

And what about all those pantries? The cake pantry, the flower pantry, the silver pantry, and the crockery pantry? Cupboard after cupboard filled with two complete services for seventy-two, shelves deep enough for huge silver salvers, meat covers, platters, glasses by the dozens and dozens?

My parents were theater people, entertainers both in and out of the home. My mother ran an acting school and produced plays. My father ran his father's business and acted in his spare time. Most of the local actors supported themselves in other ways, and so rehearsals took place at night and on weekends. When they were not on the stage, my parents were in the broadcasting studios. Because television was not introduced into South Africa until 1976, radio drama was still very popular when I was growing up in the fifties and sixties.

Our house was made for parties. With its vast hall, its huge dining room, living room, breakfast room, library, and the deep veranda that faced out over Durban and the bay, it could accommodate hundreds, and very often did.

Some of the furniture and most of the drapery my parents inherited with the house. The rest they bought at auctions in the first full flush of ownership. Once everything was in place, however, they lost interest. What money they had, they put into edibles and wearables. If the roof needed tiling, if a spring poked out of one of our mattresses, they found a way of making do—patching the bare spot, turning over the mattress. Most of the crockery was simple stuff in stock patterns, chipped and crazed; the glass was not crystal; the silver was largely English plate, dulling through from use. The place was always in need of some paint, the brocades and linens were faded and worn, the down pulverizing, the curtains disintegrating in the sun. Deep gouges had been scratched into the doors by dogs wanting to come in or go out. The dogs, in fact, were everywhere—on the furniture and under it, in our beds, roaring down to the front door as the guests arrived laughing and shouting in voices trained to carry.

"Daahling!"

"Nigel! You were *simply* marvelous!"

The after-theater parties started well after midnight and ran sometimes till dawn. Up the back stairs to the old nursery, where I slept, came the noises and smells of the kitchen. The cook shouting orders, the squabs out of the oven, gravied rice and mushrooms, glazed carrots and homemade breads carried down the long dark corridor, past the pantries, from the kitchen to the dining room. And then Cedric, a producer who had no children of his own, would come upstairs to fetch me, the baby, and carry me down into the lights and the crowd.

·   ·   ·   ·   ·   ·   ·   ·

The owner opens the door and smiles at my eldest sister, then at me. At the age of nineteen, this sister married and moved around the corner into an even bigger house, on more land. When my father ran out of money and had to put our house up for sale, he offered it to her but she didn't want it. To me, it was obvious that she didn't want to be the one to carry on. She is the least theatrical person I know. Our middle sister, who lives half a mile away and is big on dramatic flair, won't even come back to look. "I've seen it once," she says. "That was quite enough."

I follow my eldest sister into the hall, watching how she takes care not to look around too curiously. Perhaps she just isn't curious. She has spent her life wishing she were as far away as possible, while I, who have lived in America for twenty-five years, cannot seem to stop coming back. I have already seen the house twice since we sold it.

The owner is carrying on about the wrought-iron balustrade they have restored on the staircase, the brass stair rods that they had had to order from overseas. In a way, I pity this new owner. She has our silence to contend with, the judgment it seems to bring down on her head. My sister is quiet by nature, comfortable with silence. I am not. In fact, I have a horror of it. I tend to jabber on in order to put people at their ease. Now, however, I am deprived of speech. With all its neat arrangements and coordinated colors, its photo-ready angles and gleaming surfaces, the place is even less itself than it was under the interim owners.

When I saw it last, it had the marble floors, huge porcelain dogs, gilded cornucopias, fountains. In a way, I found these grotesqueries comforting. Lost and gone forever, they seemed to say, *sic transit*, mourn at your peril. This time, it is not even vulgar. It has become commonplace.

I see our floors again, sanded smooth and finished to a gloss. The banister, too, has been stripped and oiled. The brass switch plates are back, and the pebbled glass doors to the breakfast room, even the scrolled door handles. Things shine, flawless, and they match. Up the stairs is a set of botanical prints identically framed and matted in a soft moss green, the same color as the runner on the stairs. And then there is a neat flower arrangement, still girded by its moss-green florist's bow, on a small table where our vast Cape Dutch chest had stood.

We, too, had flowers in that spot, every week a billowing profusion of whatever my mother found in the garden—huge fronds and ferns and colored leaves, or an arrangement of green hydrangeas, or agapanthus, anthuriums, dahlias, cannas, and always the odd caterpillar or locust or praying mantis waiting to jump out. The whole mélange was reflected in the enormous mirror that hung behind the chest.

Without that chest, that mirror, and the other, smaller Chinese chest next to the front door, where the telephone sat, without the dogs roiling around on the Persian rugs, and someone on the phone covering the mouthpiece and shouting, *"Shut up!"* the hall indeed makes better sense. I see the distances as they must have been intended by the architect: the clear path from the front door to the living room, from the bottom of the stairs to the cloakroom door.

"Shall we have tea on the veranda before we look around?" asks the owner, leading us through the living room—perfectly coordinated in peach and cream, with two seating areas, wall-to-wall carpeting, balloon shades, more florist flowers—to a wicker ensemble outside, the tea tray laid out on a table in the middle.

By now, I can see that my sister is alarmed by my quietness. She has begun to engage the owner in chat—the last meeting of the gourmet club, the private school situation. Down below us, where the cricket lawn used to be, is a swimming pool and pool house. As a child, I had nagged for a pool down there, any pool. I'd even dig it myself, I had said. But they had just laughed. As the youngest, much younger than my sisters, I seemed only to entertain them with my suggestions and requests. "What's wrong with the sea?" they asked. "Who wants to swim in a pool when you can swim in the sea?"

Me. I did. I wanted a place where we could all swim together, just us, no strangers. I wanted my parents home for dinner, like other parents. I also wanted us to go on a holiday in a caravan trailer, not to the mountain resort we went to every year over Christmas and New Year, where children had to eat in a separate dining room. The whole idea of a caravan holiday seemed wonderfully cozy to me, fictional almost. The family all in one place, sharing things, even dinner, and everyone with little tasks to do, and no one out of earshot.

But I knew it was hopeless. We weren't that sort of family. And my mother was handicapped for caravan living. She couldn't cook. Nor, I presume, could she wash clothes, or iron, or clean. Only in her bedroom had I ever seen her out of stockings and high heels. And anyway, we were always fighting—my mother with my father, them with us, us with each other. Had the house not been built of stone, with large grounds around it, the ructions and the insults would have carried across town. As it was, my friend, the girl next door, once asked me—after a particularly loud fight for domination of the bathroom—whether I'd ever been strapped for swearing. Strapped? Such a thing was unheard of in our house. Physical violence was not our way. We practiced insult and slander instead.

Only when we were apart did peace reign. My mother in her study, timing scripts. My father listening to himself on the radio in the living room. Upstairs, my middle sister hogging the boudoir phone while the eldest was hiding in the sewing room, watching for her fiancé to arrive so that she could leave through the side door unnoticed. And me, flying around the garden with the dogs. Or creeping under the house, exploring the dark, tortuous corridors and the chambers of the crawl space there, inhabited by rats. Or climbing to the top of the mango tree to survey the world as I knew it.

•　•　•　•　•　•　•　•

Tea is over and the owner suggests a tour. We follow her through an enclosed veranda, where the pantries had been, to her gourmet kitchen, from which we can see the tennis court they had blasted into the hill behind the house. Then there's the gaming room in the old garage for billiards and cards, and the wine cellar built under the house, well stocked and temperature-controlled. There is a gym down there too, with Exercycles and weights and pulleys. The owner tells us, smiling happily, that as a boy her husband had often walked past our house and vowed that it would one day be his. And then, when he'd made the money, *voilà*, he bought it! And now that they have spent so much on the restoration, they are holding off on other things, like the garden.

Coming back into the house, I realize, suddenly, that there is hardly any garden left, and none of the trees—palms, mango, avocado. As we follow the owner up the stairs, I run my hand along the banister to feel the contours, the upward twists at the corners. The scratches have been sanded out. So have the long grooves carved by generations of zippers and buttons sliding down, bump, to the bottom, late for supper.

"Do you have children?" I ask. Are they allowed to climb things not meant for climbing, I want to know. To slide? To swing? Yes, there are children, a girl and a boy. The girl is in the old nursery, my room. It is now a Girl's Room, in pink and yellow with stuffed animals, and frilly pillows, pillows, pillows. The Boy's Room is wood-paneled and blue. Each has its own bathroom. No fighting, I presume. Or cursing. Or swearing.

Standing at the door to my parents' old room, I steal a smile at my sister as the owner demonstrates the vast master bed. For some reason, it is raised onto a platform like a throne. Beside the padded bedstead is a panel of buttons. They control the whole house, she tells us—lights, TV, music, intercoms, bells to the kitchen, burglar alarm. Through that door is the master bathroom, redone with each successive owner. There are potted palms this time, and a skylight, several sinks, the inevitable bidet. And then here, through the door to my father's dressing room, is another room, and then the old boudoir transformed, it seems, into a smoking room, with dark, masculine colors, and a sound system built into one wall.

I slide out onto the upstairs veranda and they follow. Isn't the view wonderful, we ask each other. Until this moment, however, I have never thought of this as a "view"—the ships waiting to come into the harbor, yachts tacking into the wind, the bluff blue-gray and the city white in the afternoon sun. I have stood here as a girl of thirteen or fourteen, staring out and wondering about my life. How would I free myself from this place at the bottom of the world, from these people whom I loved and hated? Where could I go? And when, when, when?

I consider my own daughter's childhood in San Francisco, and I realize, with a pang, that she wasn't allowed much climbing either. Nor shoes on the furniture. Nor rank swearing. Perhaps, I think, I practiced these constraints to teach her manners she wouldn't learn elsewhere in America. Perhaps it was because the house we lived in wasn't dramatic enough to accept gouges and nicks. Or perhaps it was because the house was of normal size. No one was ever out of earshot. Even the neighbors were slap up against us on either side.

But really, I understand suddenly, turning to go in, to leave at last— my sister consulting her watch, the owner's smile losing its starch—really, it was my own ambivalence, something in myself that had me contradicting and repeating the world I had grown up in. On the one hand mending slipcovers and curtains when they showed signs of wear, keeping the dogs off the furniture. Yet, on the other, constructing lavish birthday parties for my daughter, and dress-up clothes—sequined robes and bridal veils, fur muffs, jeweled tiaras, satin cloaks, velvet doublets. And taking trips, without her sometimes, waving good-bye, her small face up against the window, so left behind, so very familiar.

When we reach the gate, I stop to look back. There are the study windows just the way they were—the leaded glass restored, the varnished teak. I myself had knelt at those windows, watching my parents make their way along the path to the garage, night after night, off to rehearsal.

"Come on, old girl," my sister says. "Let's go." The new owner has appeared at the windows. She is drawing the curtains against the sun. It can be relentless at this time of day, savage without the mango tree to take the brunt of heat and light.

Sneaking Home

t he house is very old," the young woman told me emphasizing *very*. "Almost two hundred years."

"Really," I said, trying to sound sincere. I knew exactly how old it was. It was 125 when Charlie and I bought it, and 149 when he died and I sold it, not to this young woman, but to her predecessor. That was 13 years ago. Not too far off.

"It's big enough for a family, but it would work for a couple, or even one person," she said, looking at me speculatively. "We added a bedroom and bath on the ground floor. You could close off the upstairs except when you had guests, or your children visiting, or something like that."

"It's not for me. I'm looking at it for my daughter. She lives in Oregon and she's planning on moving back to New York. She's always liked this part of Westchester."

I'm such a phony. I just had to see the place while it was on the market. If I told the truth, she might not show it to me.

I remembered how we fell in love with the house, each of us for a different reason. When Charlie walked through the woods the day we found it, he walked tall. I could tell he saw himself as a man of property, owning three and a half country acres instead of just a backyard. I had read magazine articles about young couples buying old farmhouses and fixing them up and making them charming. What we probably should have had was a nice new development house where everything worked, where there were young neighbors with children, but at the time we thought that was just too ordinary. We thought we were special, and needed a special house.

This young woman, so proud of her handiwork, reminded me of myself years ago, taking pride in renovating an antique. She told me on the phone about the new horse barn and the work they had done on the house. Now she pointed out the details.

"The kitchen has been completely redone, as you can see. European cabinets. Ceramic floors. Center island."

"New walls too?"

"We paneled over the old ones."

Ah, then they wouldn't have seen the heart with Charlie's and my initials, "BB loves CB," that I painted on the wall just before we put Sheetrock over it to cover the cracks. I remember putting the date on the heart for some future owner to find. I wrote " '57."

"You'd better put 1957," Charlie had said. "They might think it was 1857." We thought we were pretty funny.

I looked at the kitchen enviously. Oh, what money can do. When we moved in, the floor had two different kinds of linoleum, green in the center and marbleized black around the edges. It hadn't been done for style. The couple we bought it from explained that the linoleum had been put in just after World War II, when there were shortages of everything. They hadn't been able to find enough of one pattern for the whole floor because the room was so big. The kitchen was badly laid out, too, and cooking dinner was like going on a five-mile hike.

Now it was efficient and beautiful. Copper pans hung from iron racks and French doors led to a little patio in back. When we lived there a tacked-on, makeshift half bath had occupied the patio's spot, with our washer and dryer in it. The old bathroom door wouldn't stay closed, so we put a spring on it and had to leap out of the way when we left the room to keep from getting hit. The bathroom was hot in the summer, so we dug up a maple sapling in the woods and planted it next to the window to keep the room cool. My mother-in-law told us we were planting it too close to the house. She would have been right if the bathroom had not been removed, but now the tree, grown to a foot in diameter, stood at the edge of the patio and shaded it like a canopy.

"The house has its own well," the young woman said. "It's quite deep. Of course, we have city water now. The well is just a reserve. If there's a drought, you can use the well water."

I remembered the well, and how I wondered what I was getting into when the broker showed us the pump house, and what a friend said when we moved in: "You mean you go down three hundred and eighty feet and all you get is water?"

The trouble was, we didn't get that much water. I remembered the time the faucets ran dry during a dinner party and how in desperation I took the glasses off the table after the main course and used the water to make coffee. I remembered another time when the electricity went off during an ice storm and the pump wouldn't work, so I melted ice cubes for water for the baby's formula.

We walked into what was once a lovely dining room. I had put French doors on the west side of this room and a small patio outside. The sun used to stream in through those doors across the old pine floors. No more. Instead of French doors to a patio, there was a single door opening to a new bedroom. The dining room had been turned into a huge bathroom, with a claw-footed tub sitting in the middle, an old hatrack with a basin in it, and old toilet with a high water tank and a chain hanging down from it. Very funky. The young woman waited for me to admire her new-old bathroom. I mumbled something. I thought it was a desecration.

We went into what had been the living room. Now it was a dining room. Not a bad idea, with the table drawn up cozily in front of the fireplace. But there was no west window because the new living room had been built on that side. I thought of how pretty the old living room was on sunny afternoons, and how just before Christmas one year we looked out and saw a deer run across the lawn, and how my four-year-old daughter asked, "Will it come back at Christmas?" believing it was a reindeer. The new living room had just a small window on the west instead of a big one, and the only furniture in the room was a pool table.

We went upstairs. Nothing there had changed. Even the red-and-white-striped wallpaper that I had hung in the children's bathroom twenty years earlier was still there.

"The tile is quite old," she said. "I think it's Italian." Indeed. I had put it in myself. Not a bad job, either.

She led me outside and I followed as if I didn't know where we were going.

"There's a two-car garage. I imagine it was a barn, years ago, when this was a farm."

No. It had been a one-car garage, not very old, attached to a decrepit toolshed. We needed a second garage for an ancient car a friend had given us for Charlie to drive to the station and couldn't afford a carpenter, so we enlarged the shed, bought some secondhand garage doors, cut them to size, and hung them, more or less successfully. All we had to do then was to extend the roof.

I was about thirty at the time and I thought I could do anything. We bought tar paper and shingles and I announced that Charlie had done enough work and I was going to shingle the roof all by myself. The new section of roof, which I was going to cover, was eight feet long and each side of the peak was about six feet high. What I didn't know was that you put on a row of shingles, and then you overlap the next row about four inches higher, so all you gain in each row is four inches. I sat on that roof for days in the heat of summer, hammering hundreds of nails and refusing Charlie's help until I got it done.

We tore up the wood floor of the shed. The dirt under it hadn't been rained on in maybe fifty years. It was so powdery we choked, and in it we saw skeletons of mice. On Father's Day, I gave Charlie a single piece of gravel with a note saying the rest would be delivered the next day, and the following weekend we threw in a whole cubic yard of gravel, shovel by shovel, for a garage floor. When Charlie drove the old car into the new garage for the first time, the two kids and I stood on the lawn and blew whistles and banged on a drum to celebrate. And now this young woman was telling me it was a converted barn. Ha.

We walked up behind the house past the rock outcropping. It was bare now, but it used to be dotted with daffodils in the spring and half covered by marigolds in the summer. I talked so much about my rock garden in the old days, my first days of gardening and not always successful, that Charlie suggested I abbreviate the phrase and just call it the R.G. My children told me later they thought a rock garden was a basic part of every home, like a living room, because I had mentioned it so often.

"You'd probably want to take out this grape arbor," the young woman said. "It doesn't amount to much."

But I had created it. It was just a low square of vines in the middle of a sloping lawn when we moved there. There was no place to sit outdoors—we hadn't built the patio yet. I decided to level the ground under the grapes, and Charlie agreed to put in taller posts and train the grapes over the top. Every day, I dug up enough dirt to fill my children's little red wagon, and hauled it away. In the summers, after it was finished we used to sit under the arbor and have drinks before dinner, looking out at the pond across the road and feeling European.

The grapes had been good too, but they had led to a huge chore. Charlie said wistfully one day, "It's too bad you don't know how to make jelly." That was a challenge. I consulted my cookbook, picked and picked, and after that made forty or fifty jars every summer.

I got tired of it. The grapes ripened in September and the family helped to pick them, but nobody wanted to help me pull off the stems and sort the grapes. In the hottest days of the year, I boiled pot after pot of grapes and had red juice dripping for days from a muslin bag that looked like an unspeakable internal organ, and then boiled pot after pot of juice and pot after pot of jars. The big kitchen was filled with steam and exasperation. I quit for a couple of years till one evening when Charlie and the kids spoke longingly of how good the jelly had tasted. I had a job by then and was going to be busy the next day, so we put the two cars in the driveway with their lights beamed on the grape arbor and picked until midnight, and I made jelly again.

"Let me show you the grounds," the young woman said. "We've had all the trees cleared. We have a horse. That's the barn and tack room I told you about."

We walked up to the top of the lawn. Everything had changed. The land had originally been part of a farm and had been abandoned and allowed to go wild. When we moved there, it was overgrown with locust trees that grew like weeds to about twenty-five feet and then died and became shrouded in honeysuckle.

The honeysuckle had grown relentlessly; it was impossible to keep back. Once I borrowed two goats from a friend, hoping they would eat the honeysuckle, but they preferred my rock garden. The honeysuckle made the woods mysterious and otherworldly. Once my son, at the age of ten, told me he had dreamed of going out to the woods and finding that under the vines were the four secondhand cars we had had in his lifetime, which he had cried over when they were sold.

Now the dead trees and vines were gone and I saw the shape of the land for the first time. There were three levels of fields, with stone walls rising from one to the next. Only the large maples and oaks had been saved, and they stood out over the tall grass.

I strolled up the path where I had walked with my husband and children, where, in fact, I had carried my baby daughter in my arms.

"There's a big flat rock here, and that's how you know you're at the end of the property," she said.

I felt sorry for her. Didn't she know that was Picnic Rock? Didn't she go back there in the summer for cookouts, and feel as if she were miles from home in a wilderness? Didn't she walk home in the dark with her husband, giggling and stumbling, with flickering flashlights, holding little children by the hand, feeling like a settler coming to the clearing when she reached the lawn and saw the lights in the kitchen?

That's when I had one of my flights of fancy, the kind that had brought me to the house long ago. The house and land were in good shape now, and I had more money to spend than when I was young. I could buy it and move back. I could hire occasional help. I'd be back where my memories were.

I looked at the young woman. She was probably like me; she had probably taken on more than she could manage. I asked where she was planning to move to.

"Oh, we want to be farther out in the country," she said. "There's room here for only one horse. We want more."

Oh. She was dreaming of bigger things. I knew about dreams. And I knew about yesterday's dreams: good to remember, not to relive. I snapped out of it. Back to my pretty, modern house, with a garden that is just the right size, perfect for a woman alone, perfect for this time of life.

"Thank you for showing it to me," I said. "I don't think it's quite what my daughter is looking for after all."

Contributors' Notes

Rick Bass, a native of Texas, is the author of *Winter: Notes from Montana, The Watch, Platte River*, and other books. A short story collection, *In the Loyal Mountains*, was published recently, and a nonfiction book about grizzly bears is due soon.

Helen Park Bigelow lives with her husband in Palo Alto, California, and publishes personal essays in San Francisco newspapers. She is at work on a novel.

Betsy Brown of Ossining, New York, was a reporter for thirty years in San Francisco, Honolulu, and New York, the last ten of those as a free-lance columnist for the Sunday edition of *The New York Times*. She has also written for *Newsweek* and several women's magazines.

Dale Mackenzie Brown, who lives in Alexandria, Virginia, is an editor of long standing at Time-Life Books. He has written several books, including one about the Alaskan wilderness and another about the painter Diego Velázquez.

Eric Brown heads a corporate training firm, Communication Associates, where writing is among the subjects taught. He lives with his family in Memphis, Tennessee.

Catherine Calvert lives in Europe with her husband and daughters after a New York magazine career editing and writing at *Mademoiselle, Town & Country*, and *Victoria*. She is now free-lance.

Jacquelin C. Devlin, a former journalist and newspaper editor, is putting the finishing touches on a novel set in the Far East. She lives in Madison, Connecticut, and Cambridge, Massachusetts.

Brian Doyle edits *Portland,* the quarterly magazine of the University of Portland, Oregon. His writing has appeared in *The American Scholar, Commonweal,* and *Reader's Digest,* among other magazines. He lives with his wife and three young children in a Portland suburb.

Kitty Burns Florey's sixth novel, *Vigil for a Stranger,* was published in 1995 by Broken Moon Press. She lives in New York City.

Lynn Freed, born and brought up in South Africa, now lives in Sonoma, California. In addition to many articles, she has published three novels—the last two, *Home Ground* and *The Bungalow,* take place in South Africa.

Joseph Giovannini, an architect, author, and critic, was formerly with *The New York Times.* He lives in Manhattan with his wife, writer Christine Pittel, and their young daughter.

Elaine Greene, Features Editor of *House Beautiful,* is the editor of the "Thoughts of Home" column and this book. She has worked for the past three decades at shelter magazines and is also the editor of *Mark Hampton on Decorating* (Random House, 1989).

Elaine Greenspan's most recent book, *A Teacher's Survival Guide,* was published in 1994. A retired high school English teacher, she is working on a young adult novel. She and her husband raised their three children in Albuquerque and remain there.

Ann Pringle Harris, an adjunct professor of English at the Fashion Institute of Technology in New York, has published numerous essays, some of which have been anthologized in collections by American women. Her travel articles appear frequently in *The New York Times.*

Helen Henslee is the author of the novel *Pretty Redwing.* She lives in the New York area with her husband, writer E. L. Doctorow.

John Hough, Jr., lives with his wife in West Tisbury and writes a column for *The Martha's Vineyard Times*. He has published six books including three novels, the most recent being *The Conduct of the Game* (Harcourt Brace Jovanovich, 1986).

Susan Kamil lives in New York City and is Editorial Director of The Dial Press.

Claudia Limbert, who married and had four children before she began college, is Associate Professor of English and Women's Studies at Penn State's Shenango campus.

Marybeth Weston Lobdell, a native of Texas, lives with her husband in Armonk, New York. She was Garden Editor at *House & Garden* from 1971 through 1981 and is on the executive board of the National Wildflower Research Center. She has written a play about Comanches.

William Bryant Logan is Writer-in-Residence at the Cathedral of St. John the Divine and a free-lance garden writer. His book *Dirt: The Ecstatic Skin of the Earth* has just been published by Riverhead, a division of Putnam. He lives and gardens on City Island, New York.

Amanda Lovell, Associate Editor at *Mademoiselle*, is working on a book about antique Christmas tree ornaments. She lives in Pound Ridge, New York, with her husband and younger son.

Helena Mann-Melnitchenko, a teacher for almost twenty years, now concentrates on writing. In addition to her travel articles she works steadily on a novel set in the New Jersey Pine Barrens. She and her husband have a house near the ocean in southern California.

Jean Kinkead Martine wrote short stories for all the leading women's magazines during the fifties and sixties. Thereafter she wrote advertising copy for the small agency she and her husband ran until their recent retirement.

Frances Mayes published *Ex Voto*, a book of poetry, in 1995, and in 1996 *In the Country of the Sun,* her nonfiction book about living in Italy, will come out. She is the chair of the creative writing department at San Francisco State University.

Daniel Menaker spent twenty years as a fiction editor at *The New Yorker* and is now Senior Literary Editor at Random House. The author of two books of short stories, he has a new novel, *The Treatment*, which will be published by Knopf. He is married to the journalist Katherine Bouton.

Mary E. Mihaly was a senior editor at *Cleveland Magazine* from 1988 through 1993 and is now a free-lance writer. She has a travel column in *Industry Week* magazine.

Spencer Harris Morfit is an advertising and public relations consultant from Boxborough, Massachusetts. In addition to memoir writing, she has been publishing articles on psychotherapy.

Shoba Narayan received her master's degree in journalism at Columbia University in May 1995 and is working on a book about Indian arranged marriages. She and her husband live in Stamford, Connecticut.

Sue Nirenberg, a lifelong Manhattanite, spent eleven years on the staff of *House Beautiful*. She is a free-lance writer of magazine articles and books, mostly on beauty, health, and fitness.

Joyce Orrell lives in a small community outside Seguin, Texas. She writes short stories and has two books in the works: one on her mother and family called *Pink Talk*, and an untitled Texas-Oklahoma romance.

Mimi Read of New Orleans generally writes about design, architecture, travel, and food for a variety of national magazines. She has also been a newspaperwoman.

Jill Schary Robinson's first best-selling book was *Bed/Time/Story* (1974). She lives in London with her husband, Stuart Shaw, a management consultant, and has finished a new novel, *Star Country*, to be published by Ballantine in the spring of 1996.

Witold Rybczynski is an architect and the author of *Home* and the best-seller *The Most Beautiful House in the World*. His most recent book is *City Life*.

He and his wife live in Philadelphia, where he holds a chair in urbanism at the University of Pennsylvania.

Ania Savage is a free-lance journalist, lecturer, and university instructor living with her husband in the Denver area. She has participated in numerous cultural exchange programs in her native Ukraine since 1991 and has just finished a book, *Echoes of War*, which enlarges upon her essay in this collection.

Jay Scriba, a lifelong journalist, was a columnist and feature writer at the *Milwaukee Journal* for more than two decades. Now retired, he and his wife divide their time between the Indiana family farm and a summer place in Marquette, Michigan.

Eudora Seyfer, who lives with her husband in Cedar Rapids, Iowa, writes frequently about antiques and self-help for seniors. She is the co-author of two books, the latest of which is *How to Be Happily Retired*.

K. E. Smith, a free-lance writer and editor, is an adjunct instructor in German language and literature at Miami University in Oxford, Ohio, where she lives with her husband and two daughters.

Antonia Stearns, a free-lance writer, lives in Framingham, Massachusetts, with her husband, a retired Foreign Service officer and author. His last posting was ambassador to Greece.

Diann Sutherlin writes for magazines and is the author of three nonfiction books including *The Arkansas Handbook*. She, her husband, writer Craig Smith, and their three children make their home in Little Rock.

Kim Waller, a frequent contributor to *House Beautiful*'s design pages, was a teacher and poet before becoming a magazine writer and Features Editor for *Town & Country* and *Victoria*. She and her husband shuttle between Manhattan, Connecticut, and Maine.

Julia Duffy Ward and her husband live in Oxford, Ohio, where she teaches creative writing and English as a second language. Her travel essays appear occasionally in *The New York Times* Sunday travel section.